MAN (DOWN) THE TUBE

A Tale of Hard Graft

and Shenanigans on the London Underground

By
Andrew Melville

Cover picture: "C" stock train at Earls Court on a District service
to Edgware Road.
(Photographer: Jim Edgar)
*This picture of a scruffy, graffitied train in a gloomy station epitomises LUL
at the time I worked as train crew. It was an all-too-common a sight in the
early 80s. The train interiors were often as bad. It hardly encouraged
custom and gave an image of a badly-managed system. It's not a very
happy scene and should have been avoided.*

PREFACE

The London Underground fascinates (and often frustrates) many people, whether they are regular users or not. And the Underground is rarely out of the news for long, with its seemingly continual round of "difficulties" with staff and trade unionists.

Over the years, books have been written on its history and others on the underlying politics of recent years. Some staff have written of their experiences. But, as far as I know, none has been written from the point of view of those managers who seek to run the railway, day by day. This has been written to try and address that gap.

I am writing from a personal point of view, but I have incorporated the experiences of a number of my colleagues. For obvious reasons, and since many of the people involved are still in the organisation, I have tried to keep anonymity. Also, some details have been left vague for the same reason, although the incidents are true.

To try and avoid confusion, I have generally used the term LUL (London Underground Ltd) throughout, although the official name of the underground changed from time to time.

My thanks to all those in LUL who have contributed to this tale in different ways; and to Jim, Paul, Norman, Mike, two Brians and others who have viewed parts of the MS, and/or made valuable corrections, comments and suggestions

This tale is dedicated to the devoted staff of LUL (London Underground Ltd), which daily tries to keep the railway running. They are the real heroes of this story!

And to my wife and family, who spent many holidays, week-ends and nights "home alone" whilst I tried to do my bit!

INDEX

1 – BEGINNINGS – THE "WAY IN"

I joined London Underground in the mid-1970s, when I was looking for a reasonably well-paid job for about 18 months that only needed short-term training. In a Job Centre, I saw an advert for guards on London Underground. With my interest in railways and transport generally, I thought it would be a good idea and so applied. I ended up staying for over 25 years.

Having completed my training, I became a guard and then a train driver, then working my way into management. During my career, I worked on at least a part of virtually every line, save the Waterloo & City and East London Lines. These jobs were full of interest, although, of course, many days passed when there were few things of great moment to report. With the vagaries of working with the public, on a railway system that was suffering from under-investment and subject to the extremes of the British climate, I don't think the job was ever boring.

The following gives something of my view of the way LUL was run, from the varying perspectives I had over the years. Whilst I must take responsibility for what I have written, I am not alone in my views, as may be judged from the contributions I have received from past and present staff.

2 – STAFFING STRUCTURE AND FUNCTIONS

For those of you who are not familiar with the workings of the London Underground, here is an outline of how it worked in those days. I have had to simplify this for the sake of avoiding tedium. Those 'in the know' can skip this chapter, if they like.

Basic grades of staff

In the 70s, the theoretical line of promotion for staff in the Railway Operating Dept[1] was as follows:-

> Platform staff (variously Porter/Railman/Railperson – now Customer Service Assistant)
> ↓
> Station Foreman)(both later Supervisors of two grades)
> Station Inspector)
> ↓
> Station Master (later, Station Manager)
> ↓
> Group Manager

Those who wished to proceed to the train grades could apply after a spell as platform staff.

However, there was a phase that some staff went through before the above. LUL accepted a number of early school leavers in a form of apprenticeship. These had to be given some continued education in the 'three Rs' whilst they pursued their industrial training

At times, some recruits could be taken directly into the Station Guard (*see* below) and Station Foreman grades, if considered of suitable standard. This was like having a 'bye' in the first round of a tournament.

---

[1] You can still see vestiges of this in the letters ROD on the doors in some stations

At each stage, there was a thorough training programme, both in classrooms and 'on the job', with examinations and appraisals, only staff reaching the required standard being passed for the higher grade. The classroom training was largely undertaken by front-line staff who worked as Instructors for about two years, whereafter most hoped to move into a management position.

Train Staff

Staff who wished to work on the trains applied to become a Station Guard. As such, they were nominally still platform staff but were used to cover casual vacancies for full-time guards. When a vacancy occurred, they became full-time guards. Guards were trained as emergency drivers. They could drive a train on their own in rare circumstances, such as if the driver became unable to drive, so as to avoid blocking the line, especially blocking trains in tunnels.

After about two years, guards could apply to become drivers (Motormen). If they passed the course, they became Guard/Motormen, which meant they remained working as guards but could be used to cover casual vacancies on the driver's roster. When a full-time vacancy occurred, they would fill a permanent driver vacancy.

Signal Operating Staff (Signalman and other titles)

In the early days of railways, these people used to stand by the line, authorising trains to pass, just like traffic policemen on roads. Indeed, they were called policemen for many years - hence the old 'main line' railway use of the nick-name 'bobby' for a signalman. (The modern railway police have a very different job.) Subsequently, signalmen used to work in a building called a box or cabin, usually elevated, so they could see over the trains and survey their area of command.

The underground had fitted into the later pattern from the start. There were even some signal cabins in unenviable positions in the tunnels.

Two things changed this.

One was the introduction of automatic signalling, operated by trains through the medium of track circuits. Simply put, a track circuit is a low voltage current fed into one rail of the track on which the wheels run[2]. Since the train axles are made of metal, as the train stands on the track the current is passed from one rail to the other rail as a 'short circuit' and thus to other electrical equipment. In its simplest form, this was used to indicate to the signalman the presence of a train in a certain place[3]. The equipment later became more sophisticated and operated the signals, changing them from green to red as a train passed and then back to green when it was a safe distance away.

The second thing was that improved control equipment could mean that the signalman could be further away from his 'patch'. Combined with the automatic signalling, he could oversee a wider area and was more able to control the operation of trains. LUL signalmen were then placed in Regulating Rooms, with illuminated diagrams showing where trains were. Locally, special equipment (called 'Programme Machines'[4]) controlled movements when all was running well, the signalman intervening when trains were out of order or the service disrupted. The signalmen became more involved with the regulation of the service on a minute to minute basis and the name Regulator (often shortened to 'Reggy', with a hard 'g'-sound) was applied for some time instead of signalman for those signalmen in Regulating Rooms.

Subsequently, another name-change made them Signal Operators and the rooms were called Control Rooms. Following further

---

[2] The 'running rails', called such to distinguish them from the 3rd and 4th 'current rails', which carry the high voltage current to drive electric trains

[3] *"Red for Danger"* by LTC Rolt, (first published in 1955 by John Lane and subsequently by Pan Books) is a very readable account of railway accidents over the years, with consequent changes to railway procedures. It gives details of this development.

[4] The early ones – still used in places – had a roll of plastic, like a pianola or mechanical organ roll, with patterns of holes in it, operating electric circuits as it moved along over time.

changes in structures, many have had a further change of rôle and title.

Centralisation of signalling was by no means complete during my time on the railway and so the above system applied in varying degrees on different lines and locations.

As on the mainline railways, there used to sometimes be friction between train staff and the signalling staff.

Other grades and sections

There were also Travelling Ticket Inspectors, a grade that later became called Revenue Protection. The staff who worked in the Booking Offices was, at that time, quite separate, although they and train staff could transfer to supervisory and management grades later in their careers.

One must not overlook the staff who worked on the signalling and allied equipment (what is often known as the Signals and Telegraph (S&T) Department). At that time, they were known as Automatic Equipment Technicians (AETs). (I say more about these in Chapter 6.) Then there were those who worked on the track, known as the Permanent Way (often shortened to 'Pee-way') Department.

There were others, but they do not form such a large part of this account.

Then we come to the grades that had more of an overseeing role on the railway.

Area and Traffic Managers

Area Managers (AMs) used to be known as Divisional Inspectors – with their black macs[5]. Many staff still called them DIs ('Dee-

---

[5] The term 'Black Macs' is generally used to refer to the old-style supervisors and managers on the railway, who often wore such coats. *See* Appendix.

eyes'), although they now had a dark ink-blue uniform, with 'scrambled eggs' (gold insignia) on their caps.

The AM's job was very much a case of literally running a railway, but with less of the routine jobs and more of the 'icing'. An AM was one of a small group - an *élite* - who oversaw a line, each of which was one of a pair.

At the time I joined LUL, there were four Divisions on the railway[6]:

- Metropolitan ('Met') and Jubilee
- District (often called DR, from District Railway, as it once was) and Piccadilly ('Pic') – so this Division was often referred to as the 'D&P'
- Northern & Victoria ('Vic')
- Central & Bakerloo

The first two especially were sensible couplings, as the pairs of lines ran alongside each other and shared stations and infrastructure in many places. In most cases the second line was quite different from the first. You will see that, in two instances, a 'surface stock' line was joined with a 'tube' Line[7]. The Northern, with conventional crews, was paired with the automated Victoria Line. Only the Central and Bakerloo were, at that time, very similar in stock, age of tunnel infrastructure and other aspects, although the Central was much longer, of course, including the post-war extensions. These differences made for much variety in the job.

The AMs were each allocated to a Division. Thus, they needed to be able to deal with the both lines in their group, although mainly involved with one. As an example, a group of AMs was

---

[6] You will see that the Circle Line is not included in this list. This is because the Circle is actually a service, not a line like the others. It was at that time jointly operated by the Metropolitan and District Lines. Similarly, the Hammersmith & City Line ('H&C', sometimes called the 'Hot and Cold') and East London Line were also operated by the Met, at that time.

[7] Surface stock lines are those with the bigger size of trains, roughly the size of Main Line railway vehicles, whilst tube lines are the small size ones that run in tunnels like big pipes. Popularly, however, the whole Underground system is called "The Tube".

responsible for the Northern Line from Borough to Edgware, including all stations in between, minus those stations that had platforms for the Northern Line, but were allocated to another line, but plus the platforms on other lines at some other stations. Thus, for instance, all of King's Cross St Pancras (Underground station) was considered a Met station, despite having Piccadilly and Northern Line platforms, whilst all of Tottenham Court Rd was regarded as a Northern Line station, despite having Central Line platforms; Moorgate was a Met station, but with Northern and British Rail platforms.

AMs were responsible for trains and stations, including the booking offices, plus signal boxes, depots and the track. Bailiwicks included some disused stations like Lords, St Mary's, City Road and Bull & Bush/North End.

Northern AMs would take care of the Victoria line, where appropriate, and *vice versa*. As the Northern AMs were stationed at Stockwell and Euston (as well as Golders Green) and the Vic Line ones at Highbury, you can appreciate that, if there was an incident on the Victoria Line, a Northern line AM was often the nearest. Also, a Central/Bakerloo AM at Oxford Circus might attend a Vic Line incident there, whilst a Northern/Vic man might go to any incident at King's Cross, Victoria or Euston Square, if he was nearby. AMs sometimes had to liaise with managers on other lines. And, as only the Met/Jubilee and District/Pic AMs worked overnight, they could end up handling a problem on any line in the middle of the night. But, with the varying backgrounds, the AM grade had a considerable pool of experience.

The AMs had two basic areas to cover.

Firstly, there were the routine jobs like station inspections and accountability for overseeing promotions and training of staff on the line. During the peak hours especially, they would visit different key areas to monitor what was happening and generally manage by what is now termed 'walk-about'. This gave them an additional opportunity to see and be seen, including to speak and be spoken to. Interaction with staff of all grades was vital.

The second aspect was what could be called 'fire-fighting' or incident management. If an incident occurred, the AM would be advised and he would often proceed to the site, dependent on how necessary he thought that was.

Incident management - the 'blood and guts' bits - were the best part of the job for many of the AMs, including me. The great thing about the AM job was that one usually got warning of an incident and thus got time to THINK before actually taking serious steps. But, sometimes, one had to make an instantaneous decision. One of my colleagues took a look at a piece of track once and told the Controller to suspend the service immediately. This was a drastic decision to make, as it caused considerable disruption, and he admitted later that he was glad when an engineer arrived and confirmed he was absolutely right to do so.

And for all of these aspects of the AM's job, there was the accompanying office work and report-writing.

In the course of my pre-management career, I came across AMs of various kinds. By and large, they were alright; although there were some exceptions. An AM could come from almost any grade – trains, stations (including the Booking Office, which was a separate grade in those days), signal box or an office environment. Some of those AMs who weren't from a trains' background found the job rather a culture change (to say the least) from the environment they were used to. Generally speaking, I thought a train-crew background was desirable; but, having said that, some of the best AMs I later worked with had never been train drivers.

The AMs were liable to a bit of baiting by train crew, especially if they were not too aware of train equipment. I suppose any respect I felt for an AM was largely dependent on their ability to do the job.

A question often asked in management circles was what were the limits of an AM's authority. No one ever defined them. They were the on-shift representatives of LUL's highest management. There was virtually nowhere on the railway an AM could not go. At some times of the day or night, an AM could be the most senior manager of LUL actually on duty on the railway (although there were more senior managers available at home 'on call'). In effect, they were told to do whatever was needed to sort out a problem, provided they could account for their actions afterward. Divert the Bakerloo Line to Upminster? – yes, if the AM thought necessary; but explain why in the report.[8] This gave a considerable responsibility and feeling of actually influencing affairs. Many staff respected AMs for that, but respect still had to be earned by their competence and attitude to staff.

To me - and to many others - the job of an Underground Area Manager was one of the most enjoyable occupations possible.

The Traffic Manager (TM) was a promoted senior AM, who moved to the Line HQ and used to oversee the AMs. They normally stayed at the Line HQ and checked reports, did some admin and oversaw events if there was a serious incident or disruption to the service for any reason. If a disciplinary matter was serious enough, a member of staff might be sent to see the Traffic Manager. They were in authority over the AMs, but, in my later experience, it was very unusual for them to make an issue of their seniority. It was certainly not expected that an AM needed to be told what to do. The TM would not normally interfere with what we did, even though we were officially accountable to him. If he thought we had goofed he would say so and, if he could see an incident brewing or if he wanted us to do something, he would ask. Of course, asking was understood as an order, but neither side would be so crass as to express it that way. There was a mutual respect and so friction rarely happened where I worked. No self-respecting AM would want not to be involved in a problem on his patch whilst he was on shift. In any case, when a TM was not on duty, one of the AMs would cover the TM post, so it was almost a case of *primes inter pares* ('first among equals').

Controllers

In theory, there was a Controller for each line on shift, each called, not surprisingly, the Line Controller. In fact, since the lines were

---

[8] I exaggerate, of course.

paired for much of their existence (*see* above in the section "Area and Traffic Managers"), there were times such as overnight, holidays and weekends when one Line Controller would oversee two lines.

When I started work on the Underground, the Line Controller was a god-like figure, who was never seen, being up in his room somewhere, yet master of all he surveyed. He was often referred to by older staff as "the Old Man".

I remember being with a new guard one day, when I was driving on the Hammersmith and City line. We had some kind of incident on the way to Hammersmith. The Guard had come up to my cab and I'd contacted the Controller using the standard formula:
>   "WHO (I was),
>   WHERE (we were) and
>   WHAT (had happened)."

He was amused. "Why did you tell him all that, when he can see where we are?" I explained that, once we left Praed Street Junction near Paddington, he would probably not know where we were until we almost reached Hammersmith, as there were no (open) signal boxes in between. He was staggered to learn this, having the popular image of a man watching a diagram with winking lights.

You see, "all he surveyed" was not always very much in reality. In those days, many Controllers could actually see nothing but the room they were in, plus some telephones and files. There were only a few Controllers who had illuminated diagrams to show them the position of trains. They largely relied on staff all over the place telling them of any incidents/disruptions. True, they would 'phone around from time to time, but essentially they worked on the assumption that all was in order unless told otherwise. And that was a fair assumption. Everybody on the railway had a job to do and much of it was laid down in print. Normally, everybody was expected to do his or her bit; they did and it worked. The 'Golden Rule' was that, if ANYTHING went wrong, one told the Controller immediately. The Controller came into his own when things got away from the laid-down plan.

Some signalmen would 'phone the Controller every quarter hour or so in the rush hours with the following sort of message: "34 is 2 [minutes late], 76 is 2, 32 is cancelled, 33 is out of turn with 26, 35 is 3" – indicating the disagreement with the timetable.

Like many other jobs, that of a Controller was not for all and I don't think it would have been my cup of tea. An AM told me he had once been a Controller, but realised he must stop, when he sensed his hand shaking every time he put it on the control room door at the start of the shift. Yet he was very good at the management job. 'Horses for courses' is the maxim.

The first time I saw a Controller at work, he'd just received a call to say the driver of a train at a terminus was unable to remove his key from the control panel of his train. The Controller made about 10 'phone calls, to make alternative arrangements, pending the train's remaining there until a technician arrived. About 7 minutes later, he got a call from the local Station Manager (SM), who was an old hand and had been a driver for many years. He had had the same problem before and managed to release the key. The train was now ready to go and the Controller had to make another round of calls to undo what he had done, stop the technician *en route* and get the train back running again.

One or two Controllers were bullies; some were excellent. I think most were good or very good at their job. One evening, whilst I was driving around the south side of the Circle line, a driver reported a suicide under his train somewhere at the east end of the District. I listened to the Controller, reassuring and advising the driver. At the same time, the Controller had his own job to do and the repercussions of an incident like that for the service throughout the line (and thus for the Controller) are usually far greater than the actual 'at-site' incident. It was a good example of how a Controller should be.

Good Controllers (which, in the view of staff, were those who were competent and who treated staff with respect) were regarded highly. Probably the best I knew was the one who resigned in disgust, after a false harassment case against him and 20 others rumbled on for over two years (*see* chapter 9, "Sex and Race Issues").

At the time of which I am writing, the Area Managers and Controllers worked well together. The Area Manager was higher in grade, but there was essential symbiosis and mutual respect, as each needed the other in their job and acknowledged their differing abilities. Generally, there was no need to 'pull rank', although it had to happen occasionally.

Above the Line Controllers was the Headquarters' Controller. He was stationed at 55 Broadway, again, in those days, with just an office, telephones and files. But the HQ Controllers were amongst the *crème de la crème* of LUL operating staff. I think they had all once been Line Controllers. They knew virtually everything there was to know and one rarely contacted them without getting information, help or excellent advice, should one need it. But they were normally only involved with serious incidents and items that either the Line Controller could not handle or where the Line Controller was fully involved in the incident. At such times, the HQ man could deal with contacts with the fire brigade and other emergency services at arm's length from the hurly-burly. They also kept a record of serious incidents that were on-going and liaised with senior 'on call' managers, where appropriate. One essential thing they did was to arrange catering for staff involved in an ongoing incident that might last some hours.

Over the last few years, a new 'hi-tech' centre has been provided at 55 Broadway to oversee serious incidents.

Station Managers (originally Station Masters) (SMs)

Most of the SMs were competent. Some were very good. A few were … .

The name Station Manager used to apply to those in charge of a station or sometimes more than one. Those who oversaw the train staff at their depots had previously been known as Yard Masters. By my time, the two groups were known by the same term. Some of the relief SMs worked in both capacities and, at some of the smaller depots, where they were attached to a Station, the SM covered both the station and the train staff accountabilities. This caused a bit of a problem for some of the SMs, who didn't have a 'trains' background. One afternoon, a train failed to couple up outside an SM's office. There was some hilarity amongst the crews, who initially stood and watched. After a while, the SM called me aside. "Do you know what the matter is?" he whispered. It was obvious, but he had no idea and he was clearly afraid to make his ignorance too noticeable. I felt sorry for the guy – but, then, he should have known.

The SM's training course at that time was almost entirely to do with the admin skills – especially the paperwork – there being virtually nothing on the 'soft skills' of managing people. The lack of that ability showed in some of the SMs.

The SM had a 'pig-in-the-middle' sort of job. He had to run the railway, minute by minute, and account for problems to the Area Manager and above. But he needed to work well with the crews under him. The way things normally worked was that, if staff sought to work with the SM and not always work 'by the book', he would try and let them have time off when things were working well. To put it kindly, the job was not suited to all who held the position. They had to keep the crews 'sweet' - as much of the day could go well or otherwise dependant on the cooperation of the crews - and 'give and take' on both sides could help things along. But if the SM gave too much and found himself short of a crew, he could put his own job under scrutiny. Some crews only wanted to take. But others knew the rules. I remember one driver saying he'd do anything for a particular SM - even work a couple of hours extra for no payment - because he knew the SM was fair-minded and would remember the favour and return it. Indeed, I found staff could often get more from many SMs than they gave back.

I like to think I had a good *rapport* with the SMs with whom I worked. In any case, I was rarely badly treated by any. One Saturday night I was the night-shift spare driver[9]. At about

---

[9] *See* below and Appendix.

midnight, the SM said I'd better get a move on if I was to catch the last train home. I pointed out that, although the service started later on Sunday mornings, I could still do half-an-hour's work if needed. "Look" he said, "'op it. What I tell anybody if there's a problem is my business." It was his way of thanking me for the times I had put off my meal break or did some other thing to help him out when he had no one else to do a job.

One SM I knew could be awkward. If one was spare, it was normally accepted that, near the end of the shift, there was little one could do. If all the staff on shift were booked on duty, the spare crew could ask to go (say) an hour early. This SM knew where I lived and on what trains I could get home, as he lived in the same direction. If I asked to go just before my train went, he would often say "no". That was his prerogative, so I said nothing and waited. But, later, just after my train had gone and I had another 25 minutes to wait for the next, he would wander in to the mess room and ask "are you still here?"

At times of service disruption, things could get quite 'hairy' for the SMs. I recall an evening when, due to some problem or other, my guard and I from Baker Street worked our train well beyond where we should have been relieved, albeit we gradually got later and later. Eventually, we put the train in a siding at Rickmansworth, about 15 minutes after we were supposed to have started the second part of our duty at Baker Street. I think the SM was thankful we had not given up earlier. He told us that we had best have our meal relief. After about half an hour, he said to wait another half an hour and, if he had not called on us, to go home, as it was just not worth going up to Baker Street any more.

At times when the service was disrupted, one could be given *ad hoc* instructions by supervisory staff along the way. This could be interesting.

It needs to be explained that a railway, by its very nature, needs 'slack' built into its organisation, because, if it stands still, it cannot fulfil its purpose. This slack includes spare crews. They sit in the mess room, doing nothing, reading or watching the television. A layman would think they are a waste of money. But things happen out of the blue on a railway and spare staff is an insurance policy. If someone fails to turn up for work or a train breaks down or a driver becomes sick or needs to urgently go to a toilet or a 101 other things, the railway can be disrupted. The SM's job included utilizing those staff efficiently to cover any needs there may be.

Whilst most staff got to work on time, some were repeatedly late. One morning, there were two late arrivals. Bill arrived late and made a cup of tea. The SM looked alarmed. "Aren't you going to get your train out of the depot?" he asked. "Haven't you sent the spare man down?" asked Bill. "No. I sent him down for X (who had failed to arrive earlier); you're so reliable I didn't think you'd be late." We wangled around it somehow, but it shows how being reliable can be a disadvantage, because, if Bill's train had been late, his lateness would have been recorded, not the other driver, penalising the more reliable man. Although all lateness should have been recorded, many SMs did not always do so, if they could cover it with a spare.

One of the SMs owned some holiday homes on the East Coast. When a public 'phone was installed in the staff area of his depot, he included this number in his publicity, so as never to miss a possible booking. He was an amiable chap, but, if he had a quiet time, he would wander into the train-crew mess room for a (somewhat one-sided) chat. After one such session, a driver observed with a grin: "never thought there would come a day when the spare man would beg for a job to get out of the depot".

Part of the SMs job at one depot was to go to the next station down the line in the evening to collect the takings from the car park ticket machine. That station had a pub opposite and it was understood that there might be a slight delay in his returning when he undertook this ritual. One or two regular SMs would also disappear for a time to a nearby hostelry. We knew where they were and could get them if needed. This was normal in those days and no harm resulted. On one occasion, the Controller telephoned and asked for a shunting move that I could well undertake on my own. I said I would do it, but he insisted on speaking to the SM. I wondered if he knew where he was and wanted to interrupt his refreshment break!

On another occasion, when I was still a guard, I had gone to the siding to get an afternoon train ready for service. I had passed my driver's exam by then and so, as it was getting late and the driver had not arrived, I did his preparation as well. I had worked out a way of doing the 'brake-test'[10] on my own by then, although the Trades Unions were still insisting on two people to do it. A couple of minutes before departure, I 'phoned the SM to ask where the driver was. After an expletive, he explained he had overlooked the lateness. I told him I would sneak the train into the platform on my own and he could remedy the error there, with no one being the wiser. He thanked me profusely. He had only recently been promoted from driver and did not want to blot his copybook. Had there been a delay, HE would have been accountable, as it was his oversight. It was no problem for me, but that's what I mean by give and take. As it happened, there was still no driver available, so I was 'promoted' to driver on the spot and a spare guard allocated to take my original place.

The SM's job needed a cool head. One rookie SM had to be taken from his desk after a few days, when he started cancelling trains two hours in advance, as he thought he would not have staff to run them. Poor man, I think he was on the edge of a breakdown. One day, another SM was bemoaning the fact that he had no driver for a train. "Have you got a driver?" I asked. "No," he replied. He seemed upset when it was pointed out that he had no alternative but to cancel the train. He used to take it all personally.

Frankly, I don't think the SM's job would have suited me. It needed a particular sort of person – one who could keep five plates spinning at once.

---

[10] This is a compulsory test of a train, before it enters service. The crew has to confer during the test.

3- HEALTH ISSUES

This is an important matter in the safety-critical environment of the railway.

Basic Fitness

As with any safety-critical occupation, there needed to be health standards for those working on the railway. All prospective employees had to pass a medical examination and staff could be sent for check-ups during their career if there were doubts on their fitness – for example, after an accident or serious illness.

Essentially, general physical fitness, good sight and hearing are required.

The requirement for good sight is obvious, but it included the need for proof that the employee was not colour-blind. Road traffic lights have their aspects in a regular order from top to bottom, so one can tell what colour is illuminated by its position. This is not possible to deduce on a railway signal, especially in the dark. Prospective members of staff had to read numbers from one of those books with kaleidoscopic dots, to see if they were colour-blind or not.

I read once of drivers who could not read the traffic notices with their small print, without glasses, but they had to hide in a corner, lest they be seen wearing them. One of the first relaxations was to allow drivers to wear what were still called 'spectacles', but they had to be in accordance with an approved design. The medical record was endorsed that the person must wear glasses when on duty. Staff had to take their own glasses to the official optician and they would make a duplicate set to the approved design. This had a small mark on it and the Station Master was supposed to check when staff booked on for duty. The wearer's own glasses had to be kept available in case the LUL glasses broke or whatever during a spell of duty. Later, the special design of glasses requirement was dropped.

One day, an Area Manager got into the cab with an older driver. The bell rang as he was speaking, but the train did not move. He pointed out to the driver that the bell had rung and off they went. But something made the manager suspicious. He noticed that, when the train stopped at the station, the driver looked at the bell (it was an old train, where the bell was visible). He waited until he saw the hammer move and hit the bell before starting the train. The man was sent for a medical and found to be quite deaf. Even when I joined, a guard I knew told of one driver at whom one had to shout or he would not hear. Mind you, the guard to driver telephones on some of the trains were not the easiest means of clear communication.

I had one driver on my staff who wore a hearing aid.

A driver was rejected from working on one line because (allegedly) he could not climb up into the cab. However, I suspect that this was an excuse. To put it simply, he was not a very capable man and was shunted (excuse pun) from line to line, because no-one seemed willing to challenge his suitability. Whenever it was put to him that he was not capable of doing the job (which was the truth), he claimed racial discrimination. The reason for the reluctance of some managers to challenge his ability is now apparent. The last I heard was that he had been referred back to his last depot for 'further training'. The whole thing had become a farce. (I deal with this vexed subject later, under 'Sex and Race Issues'.)

Toward the end of my career in crew management, I was asked if I thought someone with a false foot could be a driver. I assume LUL was trying to take care so as not to offend the disabilities' legislation then coming into effect. My response was that no-one should be debarred from a job just because of a disability. The criterion must be that they can do the job safely - meaning for their own and other's safety. If their disability prevented that, then they should not do the job. If the person with (say) a false leg or foot could do the job, then there should be no hindrance to them. In fact, I understand the man in question decided not to pursue his career with LUL and I don't know what the current position on prosthetic limbs is.

A recent issue is recreational or other drug-taking. Cannabis remains in the blood for about 30 days, so it is impossible for someone to smoke cannabis whilst off-duty, such as they might take alcohol, and return to duty with no trace, unless they have more than a month off work. Yet the drug may not actually affect their performance of their duty. But, if they are tested positive, there was an automatic termination of employment (unless there was some very exceptional 'excuse'). A bus manager told us one day of the difficulties they were having, as apparently suitable staff were turned down at the medical examination stage for slight traces of drugs. I assume LUL faces the same problems now. We actually had a driver, who had been troublesome. One day, he passed a signal at danger. He was tested for drugs and alcohol (as was becoming normal) and he was found to be positive, so he was sacked for that, rather than any other reason.

In earlier days, a fair degree of stamina was required. On buses, it was considered that driving was not a job for the ladies – at least until power steering and improved gear-change was brought in. It is for that reason that one found lady tram drivers, but not bus drivers until well after the last war. Mind you, I am aware that ladies have done very strenuous work in many areas, especially in war-time and in other cultures.

On the Underground, one piece of equipment that needed to be man- (or woman-) handled was the emergency coupler. This was quite heavy and it had to be taken from its stowage space in the train to the end where it was needed - no mean feat and usually requiring two people. Also, it sometimes needed some degree of strength to re-set the tripcock[11] if it was activated. One often needed to get out of the train and on to the track to do it. I recall one guard complaining that his young lady driver had to call on him to re-set the tripcock more than once, because she was of slight build and could not do it. These were practical issues, although, with modern equipment, most of these were overcome and brute force was less necessary.

---

[11] See Appendix

When more and more women came into train crew duties, we were increasingly faced with the situation of dealing with 'ladies' problems'. In particular, some women had a poor attendance record, stating gynaecological matters were the cause and they were unable to do better. They would then refuse to discuss the subject with their manager, partly from embarrassment, often because he was male and partly with the excuse that he was not a doctor. In some cases, cultural differences caused this to escalate. One of our lady doctors was very supportive and said that we should send any problem members of staff to her. She was convinced that modern medical practice should be able to cater for most of these problems and enable female staff to attend work regularly. Of course, if they could not, one has to ask if LUL was unreasonable in saying that a staff member's failure to keep to their contract consistently was not LUL's fault and therefore the member of staff should be sacked.

The only criterion should really be suitability for the job - gender and health not being issues in themselves. Mind you, suitability should include a good mental attitude – sometimes not found in staff. Indeed, a factor in risk analysis is having staff with the right attitude reducing an organisation's proneness to incidents. But that's another matter.

As one would expect, some staff became unfit as they got older.

Pride would keep some staff - especially train drivers - from admitting health issues, but at the time I joined there was protection for them. They could be moved to another job at a loss of 10 shillings (50p) per week. This used to be a lot of money, but the value lessened as the salaries rose, since the 10/- difference remained the same. Drivers would often take alternative work on a station, where there was usually overtime to be had. They could thus soon make up the 10/-, if it was critical, and many were glad to get away from train driving.

Stress

Frankly, I believe that there is a lot of hot air expressed on this subject, whilst legitimate concerns are overlooked. The Trade

Unions(TUs) have not done their members service by their attitudes in this respect.

Train driving is not, in itself, very stressful. It is like many jobs: some people might find its demands stressful and they should not take it on. It is true that there are potential stress issues and they need to be analysed. I've known train drivers that have alleged they can't drive a train because of a 'near miss' whilst at work – and then drive many miles home in their car. Likewise, one who said he had to stop work in the middle of his shift because a laser pen had been shone in his eye and he knew not how much harm it had done his eyesight. Yet he immediately drove 50 miles home and took a few days off 'sick' to boot.

But there are legitimate stress areas.

Shift working is not a healthy life-style. That is medically-accepted. It is especially so where, as on the railway, shifts can change almost daily. I found it played havoc with my personal plumbing! I never settled to night shifts and only managed because it was usually safe to have a few minutes shut-eye at some point, which normally revived me. I also found it difficult to sleep in the daytime. Having said that, some people seemed to manage the shift pattern much better than others.

LUL had some consultants make an investigation into shift work and came up with some fairly predictable conclusions. They included such suggestions as grouping late and early shifts as much as possible. Another recommendation was that a person should not work shifts that gradually became earlier throughout a short period (*eg,* starting successive days of the week at 07.00, then 06.00, then 05.00). A friend who worked 6 months of nights and 6 months of days found that preferable to changing more frequently, as she settled into a routine.

Other stress issues are, of course, the effects of shift working on family life. Having to work Bank Holidays and weekends habitually can cause tension at home. Also, getting up at 3 or 4 in the morning, especially with a fretting baby having reduced one's sleep, is stressful. It is true that a train driver's pay is now good for the work (other railway shift staff have less pay), but the demands are still there to affect performance during the periods on duty.

I particularly remember one colleague, who was challenged by his wife that he had worked every Christmas for their children's young lives; also, a new recruit, who dropped out at the end of the first week's training, as he said he didn't want a commitment which would mean missing those communal times off. A wife constantly complaining that she and the children "hadn't been to mother's for X weeks" (for example) can wear the other partner down. On the other hand, some staff, if they had family members living near-by, would take their own family to relatives, if they were working on Sundays.

If a driver has problems, his manager can sometimes 'fiddle' his shifts to help for a short time. But that often goes against staff Trade Union agreements.

One way to try and reduce these pressures of shift work is to bring in fixed shifts, where the people work more or less the same hours and days each week. LUL has been experimenting with this system and recently introduced it at one depot. Another method, which I favoured, is to have a syndicate/Mafia system. Essentially, this works as follows. Each member of staff in the syndicate receives their duties from their manager. They then put them all in a pool and each receives instead a job that they prefer, according to the time of day they wish to work and/or the day off they wish to have. This has the psychological advantage of being 'managed' by the staff, giving them some sense of control over their work-times. I have seen it professionally assessed that staff work better if they work the hours they prefer – and, anyway, it seems common sense. But there will be limits. You may recall a high-profile case were a young mother successfully challenged LU for (allegedly) forcing her to leave their employ because they had not done enough to change her shifts to meet her needs. But what if many other staff with young families want the 'easy' shifts? Is it fair to those who have to do the 'difficult' ones?

Other groups, who officially worked 8-hour shifts, came to an arrangement amongst themselves, to work fewer 12-hour shifts. In some jobs, I felt this to be preferable, as the cumulative traveling time to and from work (which can be considerable) was reduced and, thus, overall, the wear and tear on the staff was less.

I certainly favour staff involvement at that level. I would have liked to have seen this with the allocation of holidays, too. Each year, staff are allocated different periods off in rotation. But this means staff with school-aged children will sometimes get periods allocated outside school holidays. Whilst children can be taken out of school in term-time, it is not advisable. Staff can try and change their holiday period, but there are often too many 'chasing' the same dates. This, too, can be stressful. I suspect that some reduction in the train service at times when many regular travellers are on holiday would be possible, thus allowing more staff to take leave then.

But shift working conditions actually suit some people better.

One driver I knew, who was a very intelligent man and very keen on sci-fi, gave me his reasons for being a train driver, which was below his mental capacity. He pointed out that it paid well, gave him reasonable amounts of time off work, was not mentally demanding and allowed him to pursue his interests. I'm not saying he was typical, but he was not alone in holding that view, which is a valid one.

A colleague, whom I knew was more than capable of promotion (probably to a 9 - 5 job), stated that there were two reasons why he did not seek it. One was that he was lazy (which was not true) and the other was that, with shifts, he could arrange his hours to do other things in which he was involved (which was true).

Another man, who had been displaced from his shift-work job to a 9 - 5 post, was to be interviewed about a further change. The person interviewing him was concerned as to his reaction at learning he was to return to shift work. In fact he was over the moon, as he could get back to his (mid-week) fishing. Many men preferred to have time off mid-week, to avoid week-ends.

A personal 'plus' of the hours was seeing my children more when they were young, either in the morning or at night, and able to take them to or from school frequently (most '9-to-5-ers' can't do that), with the week-end work a 'minus'.

It is especially difficult if one's circle of friends have never worked shifts or week-ends. I remember discussing this with a man who lived in St Helens (Lancs) some years ago, who said that the social life he knew was based on the fact that most of the men worked shifts in the local factories and was timed accordingly.

The effects of a person under a train (PUT) incident[12] vary and I speak a little of that in the chapter on that subject.

The introduction of OPO highlighted another area. It may be imagined that, with a two-person crew, the driver had nothing to do whilst the train was standing at a station, whilst the guard had nothing to do whilst the train was between stations. This is an over-simplification. In particular, with OPO, as a train leaves a station, the Train Operator has to
- continue to watch the signal/s (it/they should have been also checked before moving off, but a signal can revert to danger in emergency),
- watch the in-cab or end-of-platform monitor/mirror to see if any incident is occurring on the platform,
- check and watch the 'door closed' indicator and
- see if the track ahead is clear.

It is actually impossible to do all these adequately. Yet, if he misses any of these and an incident occurs, the driver could be considered negligent.

To try and overcome these matters, some mirrors/exterior CCTV monitors have had a repeater of the signal indication fitted in the housing; in-cab signal indications would be needed to make an equivalent on those lines with in-cab CCTV. Also, some signals have had a co-acting signal added, so that the driver can see the aspect better whilst operating the doors. But the need is far greater

---

[12] See also the later chapter on this subject.

than these changes. The effects of possibly causing a person to be 'dragged' by the train if caught by it can be worrying. A re-assessment of the driver's workload, an ergonomic study and probably a radical re-arrangement of the driver's cab and other equipment is needed.

On the other hand, when investigating allegations of 'workplace stress', often leading to time off work, I frequently found that the domestic environment was the root cause and that then spread into the work environment. Staff then said the latter caused the former, whilst the reverse was the case. I suppose they thought that if it was workplace-originated stress they would have some case against LUL.

The pastoral role of the manager then came into play and I certainly liked this aspect. Sometimes, one felt one helped; other times it all seemed hopeless, the situation was so awkward. I was amazed at the situations some people got into, beyond what might be considered the normal strains of living.

One guard came to me with a tale that sounded like a story-line from *"East Enders"*[13]. His attendance, which had been good, had become bad. The story he told was essentially as follows. About the time he came to work for us, he had formed a relationship with a girl, who had previously had an attachment to a man now in prison for murder. (I suppose, in past generations, she would have been called a 'gangster's moll' – and I say that with no disrespect intended.) Anyway, in the sub-culture to which he belonged, he sent to and got permission from the gentleman in prison that he could take up the relationship with this lady. The guard now lived with her and there was a child in the home. But, recently, the convicted murderer had sent a message that he withdrew his approval. The guard was concerned that some threats had been made to him and he was afraid that the intimidation would escalate. Also, his work took him through an area where gang members operated and he felt vulnerable. He had been taking time off work because his partner was afraid to be at home alone. He felt the only solution for him and his partner (since they did not

---

[13] A British TV soap-opera, purporting to show life in the East End of London.

wish to end their relationship) was to 'do a runner' to somewhere in the north of England and start again. He asked if there was a way he could leave his present job urgently without a bad record. Although the story sounded far-fetched, I felt it held together and I believed the basics of it, at least. I examined his record and found a loop-hole, whereby he could leave work very quickly, whilst I could write a letter of recommendation that was true and verifiable, yet left out details that would not be 'helpful'. He left LUL with his letter, much relieved, and I heard no more.

Another young fellow came to me. He had gone to his country of origin about a year before, returned with a very young bride, who could speak no English, and they now had a baby. He wanted his wife to be a "modern Asian girl" (his words), yet she hardly stepped out of the house, still spoke no English and (I suspect) was suffering from post-natal depression. There was thus friction at home. I did not find it easy to advise him positively without adversely criticising. I pointed out that his wife had come from the familiarity of her village home to a big city in a strange country, with a language and culture she could not understand, living with a man she probably didn't know well before she married and now felt all alone with a tiny baby and little support in her new state of motherhood. He seemed to think that, if he could just be transferred to a work-place nearer his home, all would be well. I did what I could, but there was a waiting list for transfer, with a number of others thinking they too should be 'special cases'. I don't think he really understood anything I told him and I feared that he and his family had an uneasy time ahead.

Another guard had married a woman who had formerly been the partner of a man who ended up in a psychiatric prison. However, the *ex*-partner had now been released and had threatened to kill the woman. She was literally in fear of her life. All this, of course, impinged on his health, attendance and work generally.

These were some of the more extreme cases, but situations like them were by no means rare.

Time off

Allied to the fore-going is the question of time away from work.

People who have never worked shifts often make comments that it is convenient, as you can get two day's work done in a day. This, of course, fails to take into account that shift workers sometimes have to be up at three in the morning or get home at 1 or 2 in the morning. Few 9-to-5-ers would do two day jobs in a day. Having said that, some 9-to-5-ers do other jobs in the evenings and it is true that shift work can allow you to do some 'moonlighting'. Many of us did so, to help finances, when we had a young family to bring up.

An alternative was to have a wife who worked at times that alternated with the LUL shifts. Many staff had this domestic arrangement, necessitating working regular early or late shifts – hence the shift swapping I referred to earlier. A driver I knew had to give his wife his shift details a month or so in advance, so she could coordinate her shifts. I'm not saying this is in any way ideal and I know of one guard, who used to meet his wife on a station platform and exchange their children, as each was on their way to and from work. Another guard used to bring his son to work sometimes and he would sit for hours in the train, near his father.

Many staff managed to fit in two jobs OK. It was officially forbidden to have a second job without official permission from LUL, but, as few ever got permission, most did the work and kept it quiet. For some reason, staff with PSV[14] licences were allowed to drive buses on their LUL rest days. Since the official reason for not allowing a second job was that staff might not be fit for the railway job, I found the exception for bus driving quite odd.

Of course, there were many occasions when staff would be unfit for duty for varying lengths of time. And, unfortunately, there were staff who used the facility of sick-leave for their own ends. One or two staff tried the trick of going sick for a day or more,

---

[14] Public Service Vehicle – *eg,* a coach or bus

whilst doing another job, thus getting paid twice for the same day. This could lead to interesting situations.

One day an Area Manager stopped his car at traffic lights and was run into by a following lorry. When he went back to exchange insurance details (and, possibly, a few well-chosen words) with the lorry driver, he found one of his guards driving the vehicle. I think a Disciplinary Board (DB)[15] was the follow-up to that event.

On a pleasant afternoon, two drivers were having an after-lunch chat at one of their houses. One of the drivers (a regular guy) said he needed to get ready for a late shift. The other said he had done a day's work already and said he thought he'd take the evening off 'sick'.
"You like your car, don't you?" the regular guy asked.
"Yes," replied the other.
"Then you wouldn't like a brick through your windscreen, would you?" asked the first.
"Why?" was the response.
"Because I'm the spare[16] driver this evening and I don't fancy doing your job" was the rejoinder.
So they both went to work.

One summer's evening, my wife and I were invited to a barbecue. I therefore put in for the last two hours of my afternoon shift off (at loss of pay), so we could be there in good time. There should have been no problem, but, when I got back, I was told that someone had not come to work, so the person who was going to do me a favour had to do that job instead. We got to the barbecue late – only to find the absent driver there with his wife. Sheepishly, he admitted he'd taken the evening off 'sick'.

Managing sickness in many industries is a difficult area of management and this was certainly so in LUL. As is often the case, a few spoilt things for the many.

---

[15] *See* Chapter 11
[16] *See* Appendix

This, of course, leads on to the vexed question of sick leave/absenteeism. There will always be an argument about which is which.

Absenteeism is not new. Just after the war, numerous Sunday trains were cancelled on the railways. Sunday work was overtime and many staff would not work overtime because of the sharp rise in income tax. But, by the time I started, most staff would come to work on Sunday, because of the extra money. Frankly, I never liked taking time off and, when I first started with LUL, taking time off meant losing money. But I admit that, on one occasion, I felt very ill, but just could not afford to miss the 16 hours' Sunday money and struggled in, taking the next few days off (by then I was entitled to sick pay for weekdays.).

Most workers know if they are really sick or not and there will always be those who make a greater attempt to attend work when they are not feeling 100%. In a safety-critical job like running a railway, one cannot get away with not being fully alert as one can, say, in an office environment. Also, feeling ill can be exacerbated if getting up at 3 in the morning.

I recall going to work one day when I felt unwell. Having driven the first trip and back, I realised I was not concentrating and was likely to over-run a red signal or something. When I got to the end of the line, I asked the SM to arrange for a relief when I reached the nearest depot, as I didn't feel fit. "No," he replied, "you get off now. I'll get someone to take your train immediately." I said I thought I could get the short distance to the depot. He asked if I'd looked at a mirror. When I did, I saw my face was a greyish green colour. I looked as bad as I felt.

I have mentioned elsewhere the pressures of family life and the difficulties of attending regular, weekly events if one is working alternate early/late shifts. If staff could not change a rest day, the options were to take 'special leave' (not guaranteed) which involved losing pay, or 'going sick', which was paid for most staff. Little competition, one would have thought. This was compounded by the LUL counselling unit advising staff with 'problems' to 'go sick' whilst sorting them out.

But there was also the Lateness and Absence procedure to think of. I will try and explain this in simple terms.

If staff were late or absent, they got a mark or point. After so many points, they received a Warning notice. If poor attendance continued, they proceeded up the 'ladder' of Warnings (Level 1, Level 2, Level 3) and eventually appeared before a Disciplinary Board. Each successive level of warning was issued by an ascending level of manager. At each stage, items could be challenged if disputed and staff had the opportunity to ask for discretion for deletion to be given over any item. The Warning was then signed to accept the validity of the remaining items.

At least twice to my knowledge, LUL revised the system. Each time, an amnesty was given and many staff, who should have lost their jobs, got yet another chance. The system became so ineffective that it was seen as a bit of a joke by many staff. I remember one poor attendee going to a DB. His colleagues said that he would probably get his final, final, final, final, final warning this time. He did. Many of the staff thought he should have been sacked long before.

Over the years, the TUs tried to get more and more absence discounted for some reason or other, diluting the system still further. The managers were still supposed to have discretion about deleting an item, if they thought there was good reason. This caused a problem, because one man's discretion is another man's unfairness. If I examine A's record and decide to allow him an item, using my discretion, and then do not do so for B, I can be seen as unfair. TU reps often claimed a manager "had not used his discretion". What they meant was, of course, that the manager had not deleted the item. Discretion, to them, only meant discounting an item, not saying it should stand.

A manager on one line, whom I knew, had a concept he called the 'cup of compassion'. It goes like this: Over the years of a member of staff's career, he builds up 'credit' by being a good employee, attending work regularly and doing a good job. If he is then sick or does something wrong, it is reasonable to use more

34

from the cup of compassion he has filled up. An employee that is often absent and/or is making repeated errors has a very empty cup when a manager considers what action to take. I think that's a fair way of looking at things.

Another problem was getting tabs on all this.

Let me pose a scenario. You are a manager of an office, with, say 20 staff. Everybody in your office is normally there from 9 until 5. On Monday, A doesn't come to work and doesn't 'phone to say why. On Tuesday, A arrives on time. How do you tackle it? Most would say: chose a convenient moment and speak with A and then take appropriate action.

Now imagine you are an LUL Centurion manager. You were supposed to have no more than 100 staff (hence the term 'Centurion'), but now it could be twice that or more. A is supposed to come to work at 05.30 on Monday, but doesn't and sends no message. So a spare driver does the work or the train is cancelled. On Tuesday, A arrives at 05.30. His train leaves at 05.40. The 10 minutes are to book on, read any notices and walk to the train. You must interview him before he starts work. Impossible without causing a delay to the service. So, either the train is cancelled or the spare driver takes it again. You interview him for 20 minutes. His train has now left for a 2-hour trip way down the line, so he sits in the mess-room unproductively for 90+ minutes. Even if he follows his train down the line, it is all a waste of time. And, if his absence record is such that an official warning must be given, he must not be interviewed about that at the same time as the first interview. The unions insist on two separate interviews. Also, if the driver wants a TU rep present, it could mean that another spare driver must be used for the TU rep's train or that may have to be cancelled. This could involve four people being tied up for two hours each. If you think I have made this a complicated story, ask any LUL train manager and he will say it's actually simplified. True, the Centurion manager has managers on shift to assist him, but they also have other duties and often he needs to see his staff personally. It's fraught with difficulties that managers with a stationary staff do not have.

Of course, as I've just shown, going sick meant others had to do one's work. For the first few days, a spare driver had to do it, but if you were going to be off for more than a week, longer-term cover would be arranged, if available. Otherwise the train/s one was due to work would have to be cancelled. Whichever way you looked at it, absence meant the company, other staff and the public suffered. An employer is not a charity and must be allowed to rid themselves of staff who cannot – or will not – work.

When staff had a serious, long-term illness, their termination of service on medical grounds needed consideration. An alternative was redeployment within the company in work for which they were suited or could be re-trained for an alternative job. But you can appreciate that, in a labour-intensive situation like train-driving, the options for an alternative job (which often had to be classed as 'non-safety-critical', because of the employee's disability) were limited. And, even if there was a job, the employee was sometimes just not suited.

This was a time-consuming process, but was necessary. Sadly, many staff used the system as a 'skive'. Some GPs would wittingly or unwittingly assist. The GP would often claim patient confidentiality when asked if the person was fit for work. Yet, if the manager tried to make a decision, the staff and their TU reps would say the manager was not a doctor.

Sometimes a GPs said a member of staff could come to work but the staff then told their manager how they couldn't face their regular job but could do 'light duties' (which usually meant sitting about all day, as there was really little if any such work). This frequently happened and put the manager in a difficult position. On occasions, I used a ploy that seemed quite effective. I wrote to the GP to say that the patient's duties involved climbing in and out of trains, walking on track with 630 volts of current in the rails and possibly helping elderly passengers to climb out of a train and walk along the track in tunnels in an emergency. Could the GP confirm that he thought this work was OK for the patient in his/her current state of health? That usually got a response. It may seem harsh, but a driver or guard needed to be able to tackle these eventualities without warning, at any time. And I was responsible for knowing they could do it without endangering themselves or others.

Whilst these arguments rumbled on and the manager tried to get the information he needed, the staff member remained off work and the 'performance' of the depot suffered. The manager's own position was also suffering as absence at his depot reflected on him. For a manager to have a high level of absence at his depot was deemed as showing him to be a bad manager. Yet he had to work to a system agreed by people who rarely had to use it and had never experienced managing highly mobile staff. Usually, after a lot of time and effort was spent on investigation and the staff members realised their time was up, they would come back to work, whereupon the manager would be involved in another *tranche* of absences and he had to start more investigations. Small wonder that a few managers sought to bend the rules (possibly with the best of motives) to get rid of staff, bringing more disrepute to the company, but also reflecting badly on managers who sought to treat their staff fairly.

I'll give some examples.

A manager once had eight staff on long-term sickness. We were reasonably sure that most of these involved exaggeration of their cases. At this time, the one member of staff we could have easily disposed of on medical grounds was one who had been a good employee for years. The manager concerned managed to pull some strings and get the good employee a job using his expertise in a non-safety-critical environment. If only life were more often that easy. Frequently, managers knew they were being taken for a ride by staff, but were virtually powerless to stop it.

One of my staff was off sick with a knee injury, due to an alleged assault. Even though it was a simple operation that would return the driver to work in a couple of days, there was a long waiting list for the treatment on the National Health. I could have it done privately at a fraction of the cost of the sick pay we were paying in a week, but could not do so without a tax problem, because private medical treatment was considered by the Inland Revenue a 'benefit in kind'. Even though LUL would only be paying for treatment on 'selfish' business grounds, the driver was liable for tax on the cost of the op. Naturally, the driver preferred to stay off sick and wait for the National Health treatment.

A crazy comparison was with staff who had a drink-related problem. LUL spent small fortunes on putting these staff through counselling and rehabilitation programmes, many of which were unsuccessful. Of course, these re-hab programmes meant the patient was off work for lengthy periods. The payments for the treatment never seemed to raise the tax problem I mentioned above. I asked one of our senior employment managers why there was this discrepancy. He could not or would not give an answer, but mumbled something about an "arrangement" with the Inland Revenue.

One member of my staff was off sick, claiming to have been assaulted on duty. For some reason, I telephoned her previous employer. Although he said he dare not put it in writing, he said that she had twice been sick whilst in his employ, claiming to have been assaulted (once sexually), but he was fairly sure the claims were false.

Like many big companies, LUL had an investigations team. They checked up on passengers travelling fraudulently and conducted routine tests of Booking Clerks and ticket collectors, to see if accountancy formalities were followed. They also kept watch on staff claiming to be sick, where there were serious doubts as to the genuineness. They had video and still cameras to record what they saw. The investigation team was not well supported by LUL. I was once asked to hire a car for them, as their only van was tied up on another job. Had LUL put more funding into the investigation team, almost certainly the results would have been worthwhile, not only as a result of those actually caught in the act but the effect on those thinking they would get away with the same thing *("pour encourager les autres.")*.

But, even when one witnessed an incident, all was not plain sailing. One member of staff was found helping another staff member clearing out his house, whilst undertaking some re-building. He was seen and filmed carrying stuff out, whilst off sick. Yet his manager was not allowed to press the claim, as the man maintained that he had "just called around and helped carry out a couple of things as a favour". On another occasion, managers found a driver clearing out his house whilst away from work. He got away with that because his sickness certification from the doctor expired the day before he was seen, so at that moment he was technically only absent, not actually working whilst claiming sick pay. Yet it was obvious from the state of the house that the work had being going on for days if not weeks, whilst he had been receiving sick-pay. But this was another instance of a technicality undermining a case.

I have to say that some managers (including me) had an approach to discipline on attendance issues which was somewhat firmer than was becoming popular in higher management. Essentially, my starting point was that we had a contract with the member of staff. They agreed to do a given amount of work and LUL agreed to pay them a given sum of money. If a member of staff did not fulfil their side of the contract, why should we? Of course, it was not as simple as that and, if there were good reasons why the person could not attend work, in an enlightened society one could hopefully arrive at a reasonable solution. But, if they could not or would not fulfil their contract, surely the employer was not unreasonable saying that "enough is enough" – or, rather, "not enough is not enough"? But LUL's contract with the employee had virtually become: "if you attend work, we will pay you; if you don't attend work, we'll pay you anyway." In such a situation, is it surprising if a significant number of staff sought to exploit it to their advantage? And is it fair to the majority who attended work regularly, even when they did not feel 100%? They ended up doing more work for no more pay.

One manager called a very poor attendee into his office one day. He started by congratulating him on attending work regularly for 2 months. He said that he would make a deal with him. If he could keep it up for another 4 months, he (the manager) would give the poor attendee an extra week's leave ('on the house'). He knew I had overheard and, after the employee had gone, he said "You probably think I'm mad, Andrew, but I'll never have to make good on that promise; he'll never make the four months. And, even if he does, I'll be no worse off, as he'd normally have had a week off in that time, anyway". He saw me less than a week later and told me the man had, as predicted, failed to stay the course, having had a day off only shortly after that meeting. Yet, amazingly, few of these people lost their jobs, surviving the system that had become lax in the extreme.

After the agreement for paternity leave was implemented, one manager was presented with two requests by the same driver within two months – one for a baby by his wife and one for a baby by his mistress. It seemed that the paternity leave agreement meant that he was entitled to leave for both.

A member of staff asked for repeated time off for family deaths. His manager, reasonably, asked for death certificates. The TU rep said this was unfair; the manager should take the word of staff, without corroboration. On another occasion, a colleague asked for some supporting document for another request for time off. The member of staff said privately that he didn't object, but that his TU rep said he mustn't provide it, on principle. So someone went to the Public Records Office and obtained the document. The manager gave the envelope to the member of staff, asked him to give it back and then put on his report that the member of staff had given him the certificate (which he had).

Another of my staff kept going sick, saying he was under stress, then returning after a couple of months, saying he was OK, then going sick again after a week or so. I sent him to see one of our doctors in the LUL medical service. He was a New Zealander. At that time, the doctors were helpful. After he had interviewed the man, he telephoned me to report back.
 "Hi, Andrew," he said in his New Zealand drawl, "I've just seen your man."
"What do you think?" I asked.
"Well, to use highly technical medical terminology, he's what we in the profession call stark, staring bonkers," was the reply.
Mind you, his official report was somewhat differently worded.

After he left, we had a number of doctors, who were nowhere near as helpful. At one time, I used to be able to have case conferences with the LUL medics. We would discuss where we were with the patient, what the options were and so on. But that was stopped. The new generation of doctors kept quoting 'patient confidentiality', as if they were GPs. But the people they saw were not their clients – LUL was. They were there, essentially, to give LUL advice on whether or not the staff was fit for duty. If not, would they ever be; and, if so, when? It was for the manager to decide what to do, based on their report.

Sending people to the LU Counselling service became even worse. Often, the Counsellors would not say anything except that the person could not possibly work, with no prognosis or time-scale. Staff would go to see them after a 'person under train' incident or other traumatic situation, the latter often domestic. The Counsellors admitted that it took at least four sessions to form an opinion as to whether the person was genuine or 'trying it on' (it happened). With the time taken to set up the sessions and then report back, this meant that a member of staff could be relieved from work for six weeks or more, whilst it was established if they were fit.

A management colleague was in the cab with the driver after a person under train incident when the relieving driver arrived. The first thing the relieving driver said to the incident driver was "What-ho, mate, six weeks off then?" He hadn't seen the manager. Mind you, such was the climate by then, he would probably have said it even if he had known the manager was there.

Such events made the manager's life difficult, especially as he wished to concentrate on those who were genuinely ill. A manager had a driver who had terminal cancer and he sought to keep his pay at the full rate and his job open for as long as possible, until there was no hope of his return. Sadly, the driver died very soon after, but the manager's actions ensured that the man died whilst (technically) still a train driver and so his family got an appropriate benefit from LUL, which they would otherwise have lost if he'd been retired medically earlier.

These are just examples of issues that came up daily. Many were much simpler, but others were equally or more complex.

It was frustrating to find one was forced to grant concessions to staff, who often had no intention of taking any steps that would mitigate their 'problem.' I think that is probably a by-product of the current philosophy of "it's not my fault" and so "someone else must sort it out for me." Besides all that, the amount of management time spent on such cases was frequently inordinate and, compared with the outcome, very wasteful. As a general rule, one spent 90+% of one's time on less than 10% of one's staff. In consequence, the good staff got too little attention.

In a recent edition of a Trade Union magazine, it was reported that, LUL management claimed that the average number of days *per annum* off taken by workers in the UK was 7, whereas the figure for LUL staff was 17. Noticeably, the report made no effort to rebuff that claim. It merely went on to suggest the LUL's attendance policy needed softening.

It is interesting to note that, whilst writing this, two large UK organizations have had their staff attendance problems in the national news. Also, their attempts to curb it with 'attendance bonuses' seem noteworthy, as middle managers repeatedly asked for this to be tried on LUL and were repeatedly vetoed at Director level.

Against all this, one must point out that the majority of the staff came to work regularly, did their job, caused no problems and went home again, asking no more than their pay. But they had to bear the brunt of the extra work whilst their colleagues were absent – for which they received nothing extra. Hardly fair.

4 - INCIDENTS

Weather

Bad weather brought its own fun and games on the railway.

Now would be a good time to talk about a special service that LUL operated when it was snowy, icy or low temperatures were expected. Water is a good conductor of electricity, but ice and snow are not. I think this is because the molecules that actually conduct the electricity are fluid in water, rather than stable, as they are in ice and snow.

A proportion of the trains were fitted with tanks that could hold de-icing fluid – a thicker version of the stuff motorists put on their car windows. During the day, when suitable weather conditions applied, these would spread the liquid on the current rails, to try and stop icing occurring. The movement of trains during the day helped to stop the build-up of snow. Of course, on lines where there was a less frequent service, such as to Amersham and Chesham (it was half-hourly or less back then) a build-up could occur between trains. But trains normally did not run at night, so special precautions were taken. After the last passenger train, trains without passengers were run on all sections of line not in tunnels. These laid the fluid I have just mentioned and were known simply as de-icing trains. One train made a trip just after the last passenger run and then a further trip was made before the first passenger train in the morning. To allow trains to run, the traction current had to remain on, whereas it was normally switched off to allow for maintenance. Sometimes the trains ran with no fluid in the tanks, but at least it helped to keep the line clear. One morning, on a clearance trip up-hill from Harrow to Rickmansworth, accompanied with continual flashes of arcing from the train, I nearly stalled, as the train could not pick up enough power to keep momentum. I just made it.

Additionally, various kinds of heaters sought to keep points from icing up and the signalmen used to change the points periodically during the night to try and keep them free of snow and ice.

One very cold night, when still a guard, I was (ahem) riding with the driver on an empty train, coming down hill from Amersham. We were following the last passenger train fairly closely and the driver was coasting along at a reasonable speed for the conditions. We passed thorough Chorleywood, where was a yellow signal. The driver gently applied the brakes and dead silence ensued. The train just kept going, with no reduction in speed. I suspect that the train in front had melted the frost on the rails and it had re-frozen to a thin sheet of ice, with no friction. We headed on toward the red signal ahead. There was nothing we could do. As we passed under the shelter of the M25 viaduct, the first sense of retardation was felt and we began to slow. The signal cleared as we sailed past. We continued down hill even slower!

Sometimes, if this sort of thing happened, the best way was to release the brakes and apply them again – a bit like ABS today. But often the wheels locked and there followed a horrible "clomp, clomp, clomp, clomp" sound as the wheels had got flat surfaces on them.

One winter's afternoon, when I was a guard, my train left Baker Street at 14.30 and headed north. It began to snow heavily and, between Chorleywood and Chalfont, we crawled along and finally stopped. There was smoke pouring out of the resistors, as the speed was so slow – a phenomenon that occurs if the train goes slowly for too long. The driver did what one was supposed not to do to keep going: roll back a few feet to clear the conductor rail and then drive forward until the train stalled; then repeat the process. I had checked the taillights, as we were taking so long to go through a signal section. Looking out, I found a train coming up behind. As we had cleared the snow, it had made good progress. We stopped and it coupled up to us. We then moved forward, all 16 cars together. The electrical connections did not then work to open and close the passenger doors or ring the bell, so I had to work the doors from the outside of the individual cars and wave the green flag to signal the train away. That was the only occasion I ever used the green flag which was kept with other items in the emergency equipment box. We eventually arrived at Amersham about an hour and a half late.

Another week, whilst a driver, I drove my train south to London. To try and keep the rails clear and to keep trains from stalling in the falling snow, all trains were using the Met 'Local' lines, including the limited stop trains. The BR diesel trains were using the 'Through' lines. We struggled up to Baker Street, arriving there about three quarters of an hour late. There, I was given the signal into one of the terminal platforms, even though I was supposed to go through to the City. Looking ahead, I could see the northbound platform packed. The signalman told me to accept the signal. There had been no northbound train for ages, so our passengers had to change to the Circle or Hammersmith & City lines to go onward. I actually had two passengers thank me for getting the train there. We seemed to be one of the few trains moving on the Met main line and soon we headed back north.

On another such day, with few morning trains, management cleverly decided they would work a full evening peak service, but without clearing snow off some sections of line that had not been used all day, despite the fact that half the punters had stayed at home. Within 15 minutes, trains were stalled at three locations, necessitating rescues. This was typical of the ignorance of some top managers, who should know better.

One winter morning, I took a train from Wembley Park to Uxbridge. I was supposed to go to Uxbridge, then Baker Street, then Uxbridge, then to Wembley Park again. After an hour or so, I had not got to Uxbridge the first time (usually about 30 mins journey). There were about six trains working the Uxbridge service at that time of day and they were all west of Rayners Lane. The first in the queue of eastbound trains had gradually lost all its current pick-up shoes in the snow and was being pushed by the second train. The third was just behind them. We were amongst the other three, still trying to get into Uxbridge. I eventually got off the train at Wembley Park twenty minutes later than I should have done – but having only done about a fifth of the mileage I should have.

The leaf-fall season could produce excitement.

One morning, a driver applied the brakes for the stop at Moor Park and most of the train slid through the station. He reported the matter and was taken off the train for interview by the Area Manager. He had just finished writing his report when the AM returned to the office, screwed up the report and sent him back to work. "Two more trains have just done the same," he said. That was leaves or - more likely at that spot - pine needles.

A minor incident in which I was involved was a journey of 36 minutes up hill from Chesham to Chalfont, which is timetabled at 8 minutes. The rails were covered in leaf-mulch and I suspect there had been a slight shower – enough to wet the rails but not wash any leaves off. Anyway, the train went slower and slower, such that I could have got out and walked quicker. Steam was again coming out of the resistors. If moving slowly, one is instructed to shut off and coast for a few seconds every minute or so. But I dared not shut off power, or the train would have stopped, probably with no hope of moving forward again unless I had allowed the train to go back down the hill for a 'run' at the gradient (this was my 'Plan B'). Anyway, the wheels kept spinning, but eventually we arrived. The next trip took the usual time, probably because all the mulch had been cleared off the railheads by the spinning wheels.

The next incident – or rather series of incidents - was one of the most impressive I have ever seen or taken part in. I was mainly an observer, because I was the driver of the Chesham shuttle train that evening, which was 5th November. I came to see a lot, as we spent much of the evening at Chalfont, awaiting connections from London.

I was due to travel to work on the dmu (diesel train) for Chalfont and Latimer about 16.20, but I went on the previous LUL train, about ten minutes earlier. This was as well for me and the driver I was relieving, as will become clear. My journey was without event and I took the train over – and I waited for the dmu I had been due to travel on, as we were the connection to Chesham for it.

After some time, I was told to go to Chesham without waiting, as the dmu was late. And how! It still had not arrived when we got back from Chesham half-an-hour later. Leaves were more of a problem for the dmus than the LUL trains, which had a better adhesion co-efficient. Out of four cars, only four sets of wheels on the dmus were powered and the cars were fairly light, whereas the Met trains had eight sets of wheels powered per four cars and were heavier. The station staff at Chalfont took sand from the station and began to put on the rails of the northbound line. Eventually, the dmu crawled into sight at about 5mph, its driving wheels spinning wildly. On reaching the piece of track which the staff had sanded, the train shot forward, as its wheels gripped.

It managed to get into the platform, the passengers for Chesham boarded our train and off we went. Arriving back about 25 minutes later, the dmu was still there, having failed to leave the platform. Eventually, another 4-car dmu arrived from the south and coupled up. The 8 cars then headed north again with difficulty. We heard later that the train expired between Amersham and Great Missenden and had to wait for the following 8-car train to arrive, whereupon the 16-car train made a triumphal run to Aylesbury. It seems that the constant spinning driving wheels played havoc with the drive shafts.

I need explain that getting a dmu to help a dmu south of Amersham was not easy. Normally, the next train behind a dmu would be a Metropolitan train. Met trains have LUL auto-couplers and no conventional buffers, so the two kinds of trains are incompatible. There was an emergency coupler on the LUL breakdown lorry at Neasden and, in dire emergency, a sleeper could be put across the front of a Met train, to try and meet up with the BR buffers. I do not recall either of these options being used in my time, however. I can only assume that the Met trains were being held at Rickmansworth and, when the dmu was found to be in trouble, put in the sidings, so the next BR train could go up behind it.

The first of the dmus had been carrying school children home. The parents were waiting at Great Missenden and points north for their offspring to appear. They were told the train was at

Amersham and many made their way there, only to find that the train had then left. So back they went. Just one of the farces played out that evening.

Whilst we were waiting at Chalfont, a BR Class 25 loco hurried southward through the station. We found later that a spare crew at Aylesbury were put on it (it was in the yard for weekend engineers' trains) and sent post-haste to Rickmansworth, to act as a banker[17]. Sure enough, not long after, an 8-car dmu arrived, with the 25 burbling away at the rear. Its departure was one of the most amazing displays of pyrotechnics I have ever witnessed. The dmu had its wheels spinning helplessly, with columns of smoke pouring from its exhausts, whilst the 25's driver applied full power plus sand. A dark column of exhaust erupted and sheets of sparks flew out from under the loco, rather like a rail grinding machine at work. With a deafening roar, sparks flying and clouds of sand and exhaust, the train powered out of the station at a rate of acceleration I have rarely witnessed for a diesel-powered train. It was quite a sight as it disappeared into the night and it shook the station as well.

Off we went to Chesham again and the service at Chalfont began to settle down as the rush-hour came to an end. Each up-hill dmu from then on had the Class 25 at the rear (the off-peak service was hourly in those days). That cured the problem. The banker stood by at Rickmansworth the next day, and, for the next year, a number of the dmus had sanders fitted. LUL were not very keen on sand, as they said it got into the block-joints and affected the track-circuitry[18].

That night, I travelled home in a 4-car dmu with the Class 25 banking. The speed up-hill was the fastest I had ever experienced until the new generation Turbos came.

---

[17] Banker = a locomotive that assists a train up a gradient by pushing at the rear
[18] Simply stated, this is a system in which the rails are literally cut into insulated pieces with separate electric current circuits, to co-ordinate with the signals. See also in Chapter 2 re Signal Operating Staff

Later, I heard of the other comedy that was enacted in the Moor Park/Croxley/Rickmansworth area during the course of the evening. The diesel loco had to come onto the rear of each dmu at Rickmansworth and be coupled up, including the brakes. This involved the BR guard or second man getting down on the track near the negative current rail. Evidently the crew would not do this with the current on. So the SM had to go and 'phone up to get it turned off for coupling up. Whilst this was happening, an Amersham train arrived at Moor Park (on the local line) and then at the junction for Watford. When the current went off, the signalman diverted the train to Watford. The already-delayed passengers arrived at Croxley (the first station along the branch) in a rage. They trooped back to Moor Park. When the next Amersham train arrived, they demanded to be assured it was going to Amersham. They were. But, when it got to the junction, the same thing happened again. It has its funny side now - but not at the time - especially as this was Guy Fawkes' Night and dads were expected home for the parties.

One last absurdity. After the SM had gone to the 'phone, on one of the occasions that the BR crew demanded the current to be switched off to couple up, my previous driver (when I was a guard) got down on the track and coupled up with the current on. He'd been a guard in the days when electric locos were changed for steam at Rickmansworth, and so had done it hundreds of times in his life and knew what he was doing. I remember that SM well and still can't resist a laugh when I imagine what his reaction must have been when he returned to say the current was off and found the train had disappeared ...

All these things were no fun for the passengers, of course, but it made for interest and a challenge, which helped the days go by.

Some other incidents

I came across a few serious accidents in my career. Probably the worst was the Kilburn incident.

This was a very sad affair, which occurred when one train, driven by a new driver, on his first day 'solo', ran into the back of a stationary train in fog. The new driver was killed.

This young driver was one I had trained some time before, when he started as a guard. He had done quite a bit of his promotional driver training with the Asian girl instructor I mention later, who was very conscientious. As it was foggy that morning, she offered to go with him for the first few miles. When he said he felt confident, she left him to carry on. It seems that, shortly after, he over-ran a red signal in the fog. What happened next is disputed. Some said that a signal on an adjacent line, that was showing green, was taken to be the signal for his train. For whatever reason, he started off again at normal speed, instead of the severely reduced speed he should have done. He ran into the back of the train ahead, which was waiting at a signal. He probably died instantly. This was one of the worst accidents on LT for many years and one of a number that have occurred when drivers fail to follow the correct 'stop and proceed' rule correctly.

When the extent of the damage was appreciated, BR was asked to provide a breakdown crane, a suitable one being available at Old Oak Common (OOC) depot in West London. At that time Old Oak had Brush Class 31 A1A-A1A[19] locos that were used on empty stock work around Paddington. It seems they had come on the Met on odd occasions. LT expected one to bring the breakdown train. What they got was a Brush Class 47. This 'monster' (probably the biggest loco to get on the south end of the Met for decades) took the train from OOC to Ruislip Depot, where it went into Ruislip Siding, with the loco at the rear, and reversed. The engine, now at the front, with the LUL crew conducting (guiding) the BR crew, made its way along the Uxbridge branch to Harrow, allegedly shaving the platform edge at Rayners Lane. It continued slowly to Neasden, where some of the vehicles of the train were removed in the depot, as the train was too long as it was. The train then went southwards down the southbound Jubilee Line to Willesden Green, where it went into the siding just

---

[19] *See* Appendix.

north of the station. It then backed down the northbound line until it got to the scene of the accident.

A guard I knew well was working on the special shuttle train that was working backwards and forwards on the only track still open between Finchley Rd and Wembley Park. The passengers were moaning like mad about 'another underground hold-up', until the train went slowly past Kilburn. Suddenly the chatter stopped and a hush prevailed. The fog had lifted and they had a good view of the mess.

I saw the scene at Neasden, where a new 1983 Jubilee Line train displaced a conductor rail, which flipped over onto the southbound Met Line, as a Met train approached. Fortunately, it caused a short circuit and, as the Met train was reducing speed for some points, it stopped in time. Amazingly, the incident never made the TV news, as it was a Sunday. With a slight variation of the factors, there could have been a serious incident.

On another occasion – it must have been about 1980 - a driver accelerated his train into a siding and the leading car leapfrogged over the buffers. Some of the wheels of the first car moved back under the second. It was quite a sight. The driver was unharmed. I never found out what really caused it. Not long after, the driver was promoted and later became a Station Manager.

Sadly, LUL had a number of accidents that can never be totally explained, as the drivers involved were killed. One drove into a wall at the end of Tooting Broadway siding, but, like the similar incident at Moorgate, there has never been a proper explanation.

A very different accident occurred at the north end of the Met that was repeated almost identically on the West Coast Main Line[20] 20 years later. An inventor had constructed a new sort of machine for working on the track (a 'tamper') and it was being tested by LUL. As it was too light to ensure the working of track circuits, it had to have a wagon attached. This wagon was uncoupled when the machine was working. One night, the wagon was left at

---

[20] The line from London (Euston) to Glasgow

Chorleywood station and the machine went on down the gradient toward Rickmansworth. It made a lot of noise when working and the crew of four were standing on the track behind it when the wagon left at Chorleywood hit them and killed them. It seems that, although the wagon had three independent brake systems, none had been applied properly. The wagon began to move, picking up speed down the steep hill, and mowed them down. I had seen the men one night: 24 hours later, they were dead. A tragedy.

Fortunately, many incidents were not so tragic.

One evening, the crew left a train in a siding. It was not secured and moved, crushing a small track trolley. Another track trolley ran away one morning. It roared through Rickmansworth, pursued by the crew on foot. It ran toward Moor Park on the rising gradient, stopped and then began to run backwards, but was 'recaptured' without injury.

There was a washing machine at Neasden – similar to a car wash, but big enough to wash trains. The one at Neasden had a refinement. There was a detector to check if a small, tube-size train was passing through or one of the larger-dimension, surface stock[21] trains. If the latter, the top brush would be set higher. One night, a driver was driving his (large-size) train through the washer, when he heard a loud bang on top of it. For some reason, the machine had thrown a fit, changed to tube-size mode and disintegrated on top of his train. He stopped the train immediately and called the depot staff, who told him to leave the train where it was whilst they sorted out the mess.

About one o'clock one morning, a staff train was heading to Neasden. Some track staff had put their trolley on the wrong line. There was an almighty crash as the staff train hit it. Fortunately, it was an old "T" stock train, built like a tank, or the result might have been different. The train stopped safely. After his initial shock, the driver was somewhat forceful in his comments to the track-workers. The Foreman of the gang decided to approach the

---

[21] See Appendix

guard. "Do you think your driver will have to report this?" he asked. The guard, an old-timer, pointed to the pile of scrap wood and metal wrapped around the front and underside of the train, being all that remained of the trolley. "What do you think?" were the printable elements of his reply.

5 - PERSONS UNDER TRAINS

Unfortunately, many people chose to try and end their lives under the wheels of a London Underground train. The subject seems to fascinate outsiders, possibly due to morbid curiosity. I understand Westminster University did a study of the phenomenon, although I have never seen their findings. For some years, attempts averaged two a week and I imagine it is much the same today.

Whilst most of these incidents were seemingly the result of a deliberate act on the part of the person under the train, there was one case where a mother and her daughter had a row. The girl stormed out, followed by her mother, and ended up dead on the track at a nearby station. It was alleged the mother pushed her off the platform. Often, one would see groups messing about on the edge of the platform as a train arrived, pretending to push someone off the platform. On one occasion, this succeeded. The second person fell as he attempted to stop the first. I mention a similar event below. Apart from being very dangerous, those incidents could give the train driver a nasty shock. With more and more deranged people now at large in society, deliberate pushing is more of a hazard. I also know of one senior transport person who is reluctant to travel by tube in peak hours because of the crowding on platforms.

As not all incidents were proven suicides, they were officially known in LUL as "Person Under Train" incidents, "PUTs (Pee-You-Tees)" or, more commonly as "one-unders", although the term 'suicide' slipped through at times.

Whilst I am not immune to the cases of the people who are injured or died under trains, you will appreciate that my main concern, both when I was train crew and later as a manager, was toward the staff involved, that had to deal with the incident and its aftermath.

Whilst not all drivers had breakdowns or became shivering wrecks after a PUT incident, it is reasonable to suppose that none passed through such an experience unscathed. Some seemed to 'brave it out' better than others. But there was often the 'macho' instinct and I suspect many drivers were more affected than they cared to admit.

Many drivers are shocked and stressed for varying periods by these incidents. One driver had had three PUTs and was deeply affected by the third. He stopped his train, but not before the man attempting suicide had an arm and leg cut off. The man then crawled out from under the train, dragging his mangled limbs, as the driver looked down. He was a generally sensible chap, but one could see from his eyes weeks afterwards how shaken he was. Many drivers never get over the experience although, of course, the suicidal person probably never thinks of that aspect. Some drivers never drive again.

It was not only the driver who was affected. I recall one guard of a train, whose driver managed to stop short of a young woman who threw herself under the train as it approached an island platform (that is, a station platform with a track on each side). The guard helped the lady off the track. She asked him to get her handbag, which was still between the rails. As he did so, the woman ran across to the other side of the platform and jumped under a train approaching from the other direction. This time she was killed.

The shock aspect of one-unders is very important. As a manager, I always made a point of trying to speak to the driver as soon as I arrived at the scene, for humane reasons, if none other. Quite reasonably, many station staff thought that the driver's situation was dwelt on to the exclusion of the effects on them, as they often got involved in the incident. As well as a personal account as a driver, I'll give a specific example of a Station Foreman a little later.

The first week I was on late duty as a trainee manager, it seemed my first chance to be involved in managing such an incident had arrived, when a report of a one-under came from the Controller. Shortly after, however, this was amended. The person was not under the train but on top of it. Some inebriated person had managed to climb on top of a train, but he was removed by the police before he came to any harm.

Later, 'surfing' (riding on the outside of trains) became popular and a number of youngsters died or were badly injured falling off trains which they had been riding. Mind you, surfing was not new. A driver I worked with admitted that, when he was a boy, he and his school-chums used to walk along the outside of Underground trains on their way to and from school (this was when there were old trains with a wooden framework on the outside, on which one could get a foot-hold). Other deaths occurred with people wrongly on the line, such as graffiti painters.

One day, the subway from the platform to the depot at Neasden was flooded. Someone was supervising staff crossing the line on the level. Unfortunately, a lady member of the canteen staff saw others crossing and went to do the same, but was run down by an approaching train.

In my career, I was probably involved in about 25 or more PUT incidents. In one, I was the driver of the train that killed the person; in a dozen or so, I attended as the investigating manager; and in the rest I was involved in some way, possibly obtaining information, writing up the report or overseeing in the Control Room

Like all staff on LUL, I was aware of the situation regarding these incidents on the underground. On our initiation course, we were told that LUL did not give specific training on the subject, as they found people tackled the situation differently. I'm not sure if that was the true reason, but little was said. As most incidents happened at stations and most stations had a minimum of two staff on duty in those days, help was usually to hand very quickly, if an incident occurred. One tended to hear stories from other staff who had been involved in incidents and my attitude was that, if it happened to me, I'd face it then and there.

There were a number of stations that had a higher than average incidence of these happenings, because they were near to psychiatric institutions, where the patients were free to leave if they wished. There was one in Tooting and Northwick Park was another.

I had no encounter with such an incident until the day I was involved directly. It was on Friday 13th, I was driving Train 13 at the time and it happened at about 13.55 – although I only mention this in passing, as I am not a superstitious person. I was also not the rostered driver and the guard was not the rostered guard: we were both on the train, due to the rostered staff being absent. And we were four minutes from finishing work when the incident occurred.

I was driving a train southbound at about 30 miles an hour and we were coasting, prior to stopping at a station. I saw this lady near the ramp at the north end of the platform. She scuttled (that is the best word to describe her movements, which were like a mouse or spider) across the platform to the edge and back; then she ran down the ramp and jumped under the front of the train, when we were about 6 feet away. I heard the bang as she hit the train. Subconsciously, I had already applied the emergency brake before my conscious was fully aware of what was happening. When I went to apply the brake, I found I had already done so and we stopped half-way down the platform.

For a minute or so after we had stopped, I just sat and took in what had happened. Then I blew the train whistle and a lady station person came immediately. I asked her to get the Station Foreman, as we had just killed somebody. She gasped and headed off. I applied the front handbrake, to ensure that the train moved no further and then contacted the guard on the telephone, telling him what had happened, to apply the handbrakes at the rear and middle of the train and to detrain the passengers *via* those doors that were actually in the platform. I asked the waiting passengers if anybody had seen anything. Immediately, the sense of 'hear no evil, see no evil' of the British public hit them. I shouted at them sarcastically: "Oh yes, so no-one saw anything, as usual." At that, a man stepped forward, somewhat shamefacedly, and admitted he had seen the incident. I asked the lady member of staff to take his name and address – at least we should have one witness. The Foreman returned, saying he had informed the Line Controller, so additional help would be on its way and the emergency services would be informed.

I walked toward the rear of the train. I was met by an off-duty police officer, who realised something was amiss and offered help. I said that a woman had gone under the train, but we couldn't see her now. I then telephoned the Line Controller, gave him an update, asking him to switch off the traction current for the line on which we were standing, so that we could look under the train. I could do so without switching the current off, but I was not allowing the police officer to come with me without taking that precaution. And the ambulance crew were likely to be there soon. I also asked for protection from trains passing on the adjacent line, as we were blocking one line and trains could only proceed southbound by using the 'fast' line to overtake. We still could not see the lady, although her handbag was lying on the track. We carefully walked along the side of the train, as the next southbound train passed slowly by. Having located the body, we returned to the platform and met the ambulance crew and two Area Managers, who had arrived very quickly on a northbound train. We put the waiting passengers and those from our train on this northbound one, so that they could go back to the previous station and catch a southbound train that could pass us on the 'fast' line.

We could then tackle the body. Once I had ensured that the air brakes were charged, we released the handbrakes. I would allow the train to roll southward on the falling gradient for about four car lengths, by which time, the train should be clear of the body. Often, the body gets entangled in the train and this is not possible. The guard had to go into the rear cab, to stop the train when it was clear of the body. He was not too happy about it, but that was his job. Fortunately, the lady had hardly a scratch on her and so there was not some gruesome sight.

The current had been switched on for us to move forward (even though we were coasting, as the brakes would need re-charging by the air compressors). It was switched off again and the ambulance crew picked the lady up. I made a point of going to look at her, as I felt it was best faced. The poor lady looked asleep. The current being switched on again, we took the train on empty, until we were relieved for interview and the train went to depot for inspection and any necessary cleaning.

The interview took place in the Area Manager's office. We were offered tea and "something medicinal". I was told that the police were there and there would be no suggestion that I had drunk anything before the incident. I said "no" – a good cup of tea would do. I did, however, ask that my wife be telephoned, as she was expecting me home and I was likely to be somewhat late. (In fact, LUL could not find my home address or telephone number. Someone did, however, speak to my local station and the Foreman kindly dropped a note in my door). Normally, driver and guard are interviewed separately, but we were interviewed next to one another. I was asked what I had done. Had I put the handbrakes on and when? I said I knew I had, but could not remember when. At this point, the guard interrupted and said that, when I had told him to put the handbrakes on at the middle and rear of the train, I told him I had done so at the front. I think this shows the importance of good communication between the members of a crew, as so many problems can be overcome.

Normally, train staff who had been involved in a PUT incident were given three days after the incident without having to work on a train. Officially this was so as to be 'available for enquiries', but it was largely supposed to give a few days to get over the event. I happened to have the weekend off after my own incident as a driver. As I walked in on my first day back at work, the SM abruptly informed me that I wasn't getting three days off as I'd had my two rest days. Technically, he was wrong, as I should have had three days, but I wanted to get back to driving without delay, so I said nothing.

A few days later, I received a letter from the lady's family, apologising for the incident, wishing me well, with the hope that I did not suffer ill-effects. That was quite unusual in such cases. It transpired at the inquest that the lady was a Jewess, who had come to Britain about 1938. She had attempted to take her life a few times before. Who knows what sadness was in her life all those years?

The Coroner's Inquest was interesting. A few minutes before the start, a British Transport Police Sergeant rushed up to me. "Are you OK with this?" he asked. It seems I should have had a briefing on how to present my case and so on but it had been forgotten. I really didn't need it and he disappeared with a relieved look. But one curiosity was that, just as the coroner was finishing his rather superficial questioning of the one witness, he seemed to think he should ask him if he thought I could have stopped the train quicker. The man looked surprised and said "No". How on earth the coroner expected him to know how quickly I could have stopped the train is beyond me. And what if he had said I could have stopped much quicker and not hit the woman? Would I have been arrested for careless driving? It was nonsense, leaving me with little faith in that coroner. Incidentally, on my way home, I narrowly missed being hit by some bricks that fell from a station roof! Quite a traumatic day.

Strangely, that first PUT incident originally shook me for only the first minute. Then the adrenaline and training hit in and I got on with sorting the matter out. But, about six months later, just as I was approaching Harrow, an old man ran down the platform ramp as my train approached. That shook me more. I think the man may have been going to kill himself and then had second thoughts. Within seconds, the Station Inspector and (I think) a relative rushed up and took him away. We carried on and I later found that there was an LUL manager in the front car of the train, keeping his head down, as he didn't want to become involved. A few months later, I was driving a train down hill at about 65mph, when someone walked through the arch of a bridge at Neasden, just ahead of me, turned and crossed the adjacent BR lines. There was no preventative action I could have taken beyond making an emergency brake application. But, by the time we stopped, the man had got off the track and we were stationary in Neasden platform. I then saw him make his way to a BR loco in the Neasden coal yard. That incident affected me even more – I don't know why – possibly a delayed reaction. I was literally shaking and I asked to get off the train at Wembley, where I had a strong cup of tea. After that and something to eat, I was fine and I have never had any further reactions. Different people react in different ways.

As a postscript to the PUT incident, a couple of years later, when being interviewed for promotion, I learned I had been given a commendation for my actions. I'm afraid that it was typical of LUL that adverse criticisms came quickly, but commendations were low priority. As I say elsewhere, 'thank you' was not a valued commodity.

Some years later, as a manager, there was a Saturday when I was involved in two PUT incidents. I was at the north end of the line, overseeing a return football special in the afternoon, when a person jumped under a train a few stations down the line. I went there, but two of my colleagues had the matter in hand, so I left them to it. That night, I was cooking the meal. This was a fairly normal feature of Saturdays. There were fewer AMs on duty and those that were normally got together for breakfast on the early shift or dinner in the evening, to talk over matters of common interest and so on. Either somebody cooked or went out to get a fish and chip supper. We had just finished the meal when a colleague said we had a person under a train elsewhere. As he was noted for his 'wind ups', I told him to go away. "Seriously," he said. It was true and, since it seemed set for a long job and as I was the 'dead late' shift man, off I went. This was a less usual case. There had been horse-play by a group of young people waiting on the platform, a number of whom had been drinking. A pushed B and B pushed A, but B pushed too hard and A went under the approaching train. It stopped, but A had been killed. B, stunned into sobriety, jumped down onto the track, scrabbling at his friend to get him out, but it was all too late. The whole group was arrested by the British Transport Police, pending enquiries. We spent two hours sorting things out. Literally seconds before we had the train moving again, the Metropolitan police turned up, stating nothing was to be touched, as they were declaring a crime scene. This was typical of the friction between the BT and Metropolitan forces at the time. It was thus four hours before we had the train moving and we were just able to run the last two or three trains on time. One poignant aspect occurred later that evening. The girlfriend of one of the men turned up at the police station, demanding that her boyfriend be released. The list of arrested people was checked and he was not on it. She was about to be told there must be a mistake, when another police officer whispered to his colleague that the reason his name was not on the list of arrestees was that he was lying dead in hospital. Someone had to break the news to the girl.

I was fortunate in that, in most of the death incidents I attended, the body was not too mutilated. A few were, however, and one was picked up in many pieces. Another time, a colleague had the unenviable job of walking along a tunnel, helping an ambulance crew pick up arms and legs and other items. Whilst not a pleasant job, I did not become badly affected by it. I remembered that, bar one, all the people had wished to be dead – not that that is a happy thought. One suicide had killed her two children in her flat and then jumped under a train.

Amazingly, many people survive their jump. One, I remember, was hit by a Victoria Line train at 30mph or more. When the train stopped, the Station Inspector went to see what had happened. He was greeted by her shouted demands to be got out. Incredibly, she had virtually no scratches.

I went to one station after a 'one under' incident. When I got to the Station Foreman's office, there was the Foreman and another member of staff there, the ambulance crew, a police officer and a young fellow, whom everyone was addressing by his first name. I found he was the 'victim'. He had come from the local psychiatric hospital. The train had stopped just over him. The Station Foreman got down into the 'suicide pit'[22] and lay on top of him whilst the train drove over them both. He then got the lad out. The hospital took him back. When the nurses heard how he had tried to do a cartwheel onto the track in front of the train, they said they now realised why he had been turning cartwheels in the ward the preceding week; he'd been practising. I thanked the West Indian Foreman for what he had done, which required a lot of guts and a cool head – especially if the other person had started to struggle – as there were live electric rails nearby and a moving train inches above his head. "No problem, Governor," he replied,

---

[22] More correctly known as the invert, this is a trough between the rails at tunnel stations on tube lines. Some people fall there. It is also useful for staff dealing with some train problems, when they need to access the underside of the vehicles.

"I'm used to it - it's my seventh." True. It was a common occurrence at that station. The Foreman was well over 60 and he retired not long after. Should one expect such actions as part of a day's work at his age? Yet that Foreman was typical of the many unsung heroes of the Underground, who just do their job consistently well, day after day, not asking for more than the occasional "thanks" and their pay at the end of the week, but who often get verbal and physical abuse instead.

One more amusing PUT incident occurred at about 14.45 one Saturday afternoon, when a vagrant jumped on the track in front of a train. The train stopped and the SM jumped down to speak to the vagrant. In a few well-chosen but unrepeatable words, he told the vagrant to remove himself immediately, as he (the SM) was off-duty in 12 minutes and had no intention of staying late to write a report. I was only 10 minutes away, but the trains were running again by the time I arrived, getting the gist of what had happened as the SM grabbed his coat and headed for the office door. If I remember rightly, there were a just few terse words in the Log Book.

6 - OTHER PERSONS ON THE TRACK

Britain is unusual amongst railways world-wide, in that the railway is normally fenced in. As a result, there is a bit of a phobia about people on the line. Whilst a railway is generally a safe environment, it is a dangerous place if you don't know what you are doing. Apart from those seeking to kill themselves, people will decide to go on the line for various reasons – some without any evil intent.

There are those who get on the railway because they have found a short-cut from one place to another and cross the line or walk along it. Often, this entails making a hole in a fence and there is then a danger of small children getting on the line and being injured or even killed. Others find that by nipping through a hole in a fence or something similar they can avoid passing a ticket barrier. And there are the vandals.

One incident I recall was when I was still driving. Approaching the platforms at Watford, I saw a little boy of about 3 - 4 years of age walking toward the platform end. He went down the ramp and headed off along the line. The train was going slowly and I stopped it quickly. Fortunately, by then, we had 'handbrakes' which were applied with a push button (they are now called 'parking brakes'). I applied the emergency brake and the parking brakes and got out of the cab as soon as possible. I called out "little boy, come here," hoping it would not drive him away. I knew he could not be run down by a train, as we were blocking all lines, but, for a young child, touching the current rails can be fatal. Fortunately, hearing my voice distracted him enough to turn to me and I grabbed him. I was going to get him into the cab and take him to the platform, but, at that moment, the Station Foreman and the boy's father came racing down the platform. It seems his father was visiting the station and the child was looking for him. Naturally, the father was in panic mode and the boy was whisked away.

I have always said there was only ever one incident in the whole of my career that I never ever wanted to repeat. I was called to one of our depots to a fatality. It seems that some mentally disturbed person had lured his neighbour's child to some nearby woods and sexually assaulted him. The child, without any clothes, had crawled to the lineside and been electrocuted. When found by the crew of a train, he was just alive, but died before help came. I have never forgotten him lying there beside the line, as if he were asleep. Poor little kid. I have often thought - if only he had been found just a few moments earlier. Help was on its way, but came too late. Tragic.

Sadly, drink and high spirits can wreak horrible results. Another young man had been out drinking with some others, whilst his girl friend thought he was at work. He followed some of the others down to the platform. They had got on the train that was just leaving. He decided to run along the side of the train, trying to attract the attention of those on board. But he failed to realise that he was near the tunnel entrance. The train dragged him into the tunnel, he fell down where the platform ended and lost parts of both feet. He later sued the Underground for negligence.

Of course, most of the people on the track are (or were, in those days) LUL staff; ones who worked on the line. Most of them were sensible and realised their lives depended on the vigilance of themselves and others. I was involved in a few unusual incidents with them.

One night, heading northwards, I saw a gang working on the adjacent line. They had all their kit out, well before they were supposed to start work. I knew they should not be there in the dark. I stopped the train and ordered them on board. After some argument, when I explained we were going no further with them still on the line, they got in and alighted, still complaining, at the next station, where I informed the Line Controller what had happened. I found out later that, immediately I left, they had returned to the site and carried on with their work. Shortly after, another driver found them on the line in front of him and the current went off. They had damaged the track. Eventually, that train had to go back to the previous station and the passengers put on another train. I never heard the end of that one.

One particular track-worker was a pain. Track workers normally wanted to finish their work as soon as possible. They thus tried to get as much work as they could do between trains. They were notorious for taking 'one more hit' with their hammers. This man took far more than one extra strike, remaining on the track repeatedly until his life was in danger. More than once, I had to make an emergency brake application and he would then stroll clear. He took no notice when I told him and even continued after he was reported to his boss. One day, as I approached a junction with a fast train, he nearly ended his career. He was standing on the fast line, as a slow train was entering the station on the adjacent line. The slow train was making so much noise over the points and he was standing so close, he neither saw nor heard my train approaching, whistling, until the last seconds. I could not have stopped in time, but suddenly he saw or heard my train and made an amazing leap – literally for his life – and got clear. I think this was the point at which I reported him – for his own good. Amazingly, he was still alive and working on the track 10 years later.

A very conscientious driver told me of an incident when a track-worker was travelling with him in the cab. He had to apply the emergency brake when some workers failed to get clear until the last second. The train stopped where the workers were. After a few well-chosen words were spoken to the men, he drove on. He then noticed the face of the track-worker in the cab: it was white. "Couldn't you have stopped sooner?" he stammered. "You must be joking," was the reply. The man uttered some expletives: "We were told you could stop on a sixpence." Nonsense: but it might explain how these men sometimes acted.

On a bright and clear day, I was approaching a junction. I saw two workers standing in the middle of the track, examining something, not far ahead. Neither was looking out. I blew the train whistle, but they didn't seem to hear. I knew the men, so slowed the train to a stop (we were already going slowly over the junction). I called out from the cab to ask if they would kindly move to one side, so I could get by. Only then did they see the train, stationary, a few feet away from them. Their faces went white and they sheepishly moved off the line. We often saw one another and spoke afterwards, but that incident was never mentioned again.

Once, reversing at Amersham, I saw another group of track workers clearing old vegetation. I could see no lookout man[23]. The hourly BR train was due and often flew around the corner with hardly a sound on the falling gradient. "Where's your lookout?" I asked. The man pointed down the track. The lookout was helping clear the vegetation, to get the job finished quicker. Fortunately, they were all clear as, a few moments later, the BR train rushed past.

One morning, on my way to work, when I was still a driver, I saw a man, covered in blood, waiting on the platform for the same train as me. In typical British style, everybody was ignoring him. Not knowing what it was all about (he could have just murdered someone, for all I knew), I telephoned the signalman, asking for him to have the police meet the train at the next station, where the nick was. In fact, after he got on the train, a manager on his way to work saw his condition and, understandably, took him off the train. One way or another, the police were re-directed to where he was and he was picked up. The story that came out eventually was that he was a track-worker. The previous evening, he had been sent home from work – allegedly for being under the influence of drink. He should have taken the staff train, but decided to walk along the track in the pitch dark. The staff train came along and, it seems, hit him a glancing blow – hence the blood. The staff train had its tripcock activated and the brakes applied between signals. When it stopped, the driver could see nothing. It was assumed that a fox or something might have caused it (not an unusual occurrence) and so the train continued. The man lay by the track most of the night and eventually recovered. The driver of the morning staff train (in daylight) saw him leaning against a post, but merely thought it was rather early for the track patrolman to be out and about. The man then walked the few hundred yards to the station – which was where I came in. There is little doubt that he was lucky to have survived that incident.

---

[23] Someone whose sole (and vital) job is to lookout for approaching trains and warn the workers.

As an aside, one of the track staff on our line lived a strange life. If one were to see him in the morning, on the way to work, you would think him a well-off executive. He was very smartly dressed, with a fur-collared overcoat and brief-case. He would walk off the end of the platform at a certain station and into the track staff's hut. Not long after (like Mr Ben in the kiddies' TV series), he would emerge a totally different character. He would be dressed in his dirty orange track-workers' gear and would be about his duties until the evening, when he would change back again. The tale was that he was married to an oriental lady and lived in a small mansion in the Surrey stockbroker belt. I cannot confirm the story, but I saw his changes of appearance many times and think that it was more-or-less true.

Other staff whose work took them out and about on the line included the AETs (Automatic Equipment Technicians, often called Linesmen) who dealt with signal and associated problems and who wore maroon boiler suits; and the Car Examiners (often called fitters), who attended defective trains and wore green boiler suits. The former would often ask for a lift to the site of a problem. Depending on the circumstances, one would wait for them to change a bulb or whatever or drop them off to tackle their job. The fitters would attend if the train had a defect. Some they could rectify, some just confirm and put down for attention that evening or, if more serious, they would arrange for the train to be changed as soon as possible. Investigations might involve them checking parts of the train whilst it was moving or going under the train (whilst it was stationary!). If it was a small job, such as changing a light-bulb, I would sometimes use a spare from the train, get a replacement when we passed the fitter's office and he would then 'book' the job without having to leave his post. The time they spent in my cab was used for improving relationships and also added to one's store of info about aspects of the railway. It certainly helped me over the years.

7 – A STEP FORWARD

As time passed and I became more *au fait* with the running of the railway, I felt I could make a career of it and sought promotion. The 'seniority' criteria then held sway in LUL, which meant that the normal line to Station Inspector and then Station Master would take many years. But there were other jobs. The job of Area Manager, with the possibility of one day becoming a Traffic Manager, was attractive to many of us.

I applied for the position of Area Manager many times. Once or twice I got interviews, but other times I was rejected out of hand. Once, as I answered the questions, I realised that I could say the moon was made of green cheese: my questioner had lost any interest in the interview he may have originally had. Perhaps I got nearer the problem on another occasion. The person who interviewed me (who was my boss at the time) said he would not allow my name to go forward because he thought my religious beliefs would prevent me being a good manager. Indeed, I did not progress in any of my applications until, about a year later, he was seriously ill for some months, away from work, during which time I was offered three different promotions for which I had applied – one being that of training for Area Manager. I pursued the Area Manager job, which was the one I wanted most, and was successful. I'll never know if my boss' absence and my successful application were connected.

The training course for Area Manager was comprehensive and, in my opinion, very well targeted for the job. The 'indoor' part was for three weeks, two back at the Training Centre at White City and a week at good old Flagstaff House[24].

One of the first sessions was on rates of pay. It seems that it had recently come to light that some of those on a previous course had (allegedly) been 'massaging' their timesheets. We were given a

---

[24] Flagstaff House was the LUL management training centre in leafy Weybridge. This was a very nice place, with excellent food. I was glad for any excuse - I mean opportunity - to go there!

thorough briefing on pay and had to sign a form to say we had been so informed and understood (a bit like signing the Official Secrets' Act).

The course went on to cover practical issues such as the ticketing and accounting system, writing reports, reviewing evidence, the security for engineering work on the track (much of it at night), signalling, control, answering public letters, approving staff for promotion, Trade Union (TU) relations, equal opportunities aspects (then in its infancy, but later to grow into a monster) and mock disciplinary interviews with rôle-play.

These last were most enjoyable. They included one of the senior staff relations' managers, who was not afraid to rôle-play humble parts. One he played was a Station Inspector with a drink problem, trying to deny all the accusations against him. He finally admitted in the rôle-play that he'd "just had a little drink" on duty, but the trainee manager group interviewing him were, at the time, trying to ascertain some other point and failed to notice his 'slip of the tongue'. There were hoots of laughter and groans (from the respective teams), when the rôle-play video was played back later. But there was comparatively little on the soft skills of dealing with staff, although they were touched on in the rôle-play.

We were told that we must 'be your own man' and not try to copy other managers. To illustrate this there was the (possibly apocryphal) story of the rookie AM, who was with an experienced AM at White City for training. A train was reported as having lost time from Liverpool Street. The two men went down to the platform and the older AM remonstrated with the driver in very basic English. The driver gave a mouthful back and, after suitable words from the seasoned AM about future conduct, the train left. The next day, when a similar report was received, the rookie was sent down to investigate on his own. He started to harangue the driver immediately, as he had seen done the previous day. But this driver jumped out of his cab, threw his control keys on the ground, explained in graphic detail whereabouts on his managerial person the new AM could put an 8-car Central Line tube train, grabbed his bag and stalked off to the Mess Room. The rookie was left with the train, a crowd of disgruntled passengers and bells ringing all over the place until his mentor came to sort it all out.

There was a number of examinations and a pass mark of 90+% for each was expected. I managed this, except for one mark of 89½%. This score was given by an examiner on Booking Office procedures, who, I think, was trying to prove a perverse point. I wondered if his own application to become an Area Manager had just been turned down and I found later that I was in fact correct on the item he marked me down on.

By the end of the course, one of the eight of us was dropped and did not go out to a Division. After the exams, I was sent to a line where the Divisional Manager was a man of whom I had fallen foul at the Training Centre whilst on a course a year or so before. I guessed the original plan was to give two trainees to each Division, but now one Division - his - would only get one – and it was me. So, out of a chance of 1 in 7, I got sent to his Division and had to deal with him again. I had had to report to him each month, which I detested. I got the impression he was playing cat and mouse with me. I suspect that he would like to have had an excuse to drop me, but he would then have had no new blood. I wonder if that influenced him. He was one of the very few people in LUL with whom I felt it almost impossible to work and I was glad when he retired very soon afterward. Mind you, I think the dislike was mutual and he seemed generally unpopular.

Before taking up my place, I was kitted out with a pair of winter-weight trousers and a summer-weight jacket, two white shirts and three ties. How on earth two white shirts were supposed to last a week in the tunnel environment, I cannot imagine. Presumably some office *Walla* had an allocation and that was that. Then there was the semi-official jacket that all AMs had. And I got my black mac![25]

I was put with a succession of full-time Area Managers, to continue my training – now out and about 'on-the-job'. My first shift placement was at 05.00 one morning. The trainer was a good

---

[25] *See* Appendix

mentor and knew the practical aspects well, although he had come from a 55 Broadway office background. I particularly remember the way he telephoned all over the line without consulting a telephone directory. I wondered how he could recall so many numbers (not in any logical order) instantly. But, despite my qualms, I found I soon picked them up too.

It was subsequently stated that I probably had one of the most instructive periods of any trainee, as we had a very high number of serious incidents to deal with whilst I was training, whilst some trainees had few. On the second Saturday evening, we were undertaking the last shift of the day. This was due to finish at 01.40, when the last train was stabled for the night. We were about to leave, when we heard that the last train had been halted between stations out in the open. I can't recall what the cause was, but the current had been switched off. If this occurs about the time the last train is due to run, the track workers may think that the current has gone off normally and that all is OK to start work on the track. So, if the current does get switched off about then and needs to be switched back on, it is important to find out if any track staff are working in the area and, if so, warn them or clear them off the line before the current is switched on again. Anyway, we had to go to the train, by which time some passengers had got out onto the track. We had to persuade them back on to the train. I then said I'd walk to the next station, to see if any of the track workers were on the track, whilst my trainer stayed with the train. Fortunately, I found the one track worker who was in a potentially dangerous situation and got him to come with me to the next station, where he could telephone to confirm he was safe and clear of the track. The current could then be switched on and the train finish its journey. All this took over an hour and we then had to start writing the report. At that time, Mrs Thatcher was the local MP and there were many influential people living in the area. It was expected questions would be asked and so the report had to be made pdq. We finished about four in the morning and my trainer drove me home. Fortunately, he lived in that direction. I was due to work later that Sunday and took the report in with me that afternoon. We thought it would be in order if all the facts were available by Monday morning, but it seemed that the telephone wires had been humming already and I was asked why we had not brought the report in that morning.

One amusing incident occurred whilst we were writing the report in an SM's office about three in the morning. The SM needed to print out the pay-sheets for his staff, but he accidentally pressed the wrong button, whereupon the machine started to spew out the sheets for the staff on the whole line. They were those older green and white sheets and the floor gradually filled with paper. The system was new and no-one knew how to stop the printer without taking the plug out and doing unknown harm ...

I subsequently went with other AMs for two weeks each, for a couple of months. Each of those postings went fine. They were all good teachers and I learned a lot.

However, I was then put with one AM for four weeks to get to know the Victoria Line. This was different in many ways, as it was then the only one with automatic working, apart from the Central Line Woodford – Hainault 'test-bed', which was still operating automatically with the Cravens[26] and occasional 1967 Tube Stock. This AM knew his job, having been part of the team that set it up. But he was a tartar and continually goaded me. I wonder if the idea was to see if he could break me. If I survived him, then I would have proved myself. But he certainly taught me the Vic Line 'ropes'.

At the time, there were many problems with the escalators at Victoria. Victoria was under-provided with escalators. The traffic-growth had been grossly under-estimated. Also, the escalators were continually breaking down and it was rare to have them all in operation at one time. This AM had made great efforts to get a defective escalator put right as a matter of urgency and each morning we went to the station to assist in crowd control. One morning, he found a second escalator was out of action,

---

[26] Cravens was the name of an engineering firm in Sheffield, who built railway rolling stock. They built some prototypes for LUL, which were officially 1960 Tube Stock (see Appendix), but commonly referred to as 'Cravens'. There were no repeat orders and the prototypes were converted as the first automatic trains.

causing worse congestion. In disgust, he said we would go instead to Netherton Road Fan Shaft. This was not only a ventilation shaft on a long inter-station tunnel on the Vic, but it had stairs, so that the emergency services could reach a train or passengers could be evacuated.

On another occasion, there was considerable disruption when trains between Vauxhall and Stockwell were being repeatedly 'Code Tripped'[27] and stopping in the tunnel. If a wrong code is received by the train, the equipment trips and the train stops as a safety measure. The drivers had to drive the trains manually and the timetable went to pieces. He ordered that the two sub-stations at either end of the section be shut down in turn. This produced a remedy to allow trains to run during the day, but the reason for the problem remained a mystery. That night, the two substations were put back to normal working, whilst we drove a train up and down. Suddenly, someone saw that, as soon as the train began to move, the code reading (on the driver's control desk) changed to a false command and the train slowed. The moment the train's control mechanism switched off power, the fault stopped and correct code showed again. No driver had noticed the 'wrong' code showing for a few seconds, since he was looking ahead, not at his desk. It was discovered that there was a defective diode and ac and dc current were wrongly being fed into the track, but only when the train was drawing power. This AM had sussed out the problem before any of the 'experts' had.

On our last day together, his attitude toward me changed. The thing that impressed him was that, when he told me that he had been a steam loco fireman at Stratford, he found I knew what a *'Bongo'* was[28]. If only he'd found out sooner, I might have had an easier time with him.

My last two weeks were with another AM who had come from an office background. But he also had an interest in railways. He

---

[27] Codes were electronic pulses in the rails that made the automatic train move and stop.
[28] *'Bongo'* was the staff nickname for the LNER B1 class of steam loco, many of which were named after antelopes, including the *Gnu, Nilghai, Kudu, Wildebeeste* - and the *Bongo*.

admitted that, on a university trip to Glasgow, he had managed to wangle a visit to the then-closed Glasgow Central Low level station. By that time, I was largely left on my own and he was really letting me do all the work as a last test. Some of the staff were wary of him, because of his dry sense of humour, although he was actually a good manager and I enjoyed working with him. I found the secret was to answer him back in his own kind. One night, I needed to speak to three members of staff. That is not easy when they are train staff, as they could be anywhere on the line – if still on duty. I found that, by clever manoeuvres, I could travel a few stations and back and see the two guards and a driver. He was amazed when I walked back in 40 minutes or so later with all the info I needed. But, before I went out, he asked me if I ought to tell the Controller where I was going. "If you weren't asleep, you'd have heard me telephone him", I retorted. He just smiled and settled back in his chair. I felt then that I was probably over the hump.

A day after this last incident the Divisional Manager called me in for the last time. He told me he had asked the Traffic Manager if he thought I would be OK as one of the team and he replied "yes". He asked if I felt I would manage on my own the following week and I said I could. So I was told that, from the next Monday, I would become a relief AM, covering holidays and the like.

8 - MANAGER (at last)

I was given a 'middle' shift AM's job for a couple of weeks. This meant that I would not be on duty totally on my own and was within shouting distance of the Traffic Manager if I needed support. In fact, I never had to call for help, other than to get the normal information that I needed to do my job.

After a couple of weeks, I was allocated shifts when there was no-one close to call on. The only time any extra care was shown was when I went to manage my first 'one under'[29] on my own. A more experienced AM turned up. He was frankly apologetic and said he'd been sent as it was my first 'solo'. Ironically, he did find the answer to a question that puzzled me. The driver said he had stopped as soon as the incident occurred. Most people jump at the end of the platform the train arrives, as the train is faster there. But the train was fully in the platform when I got there. The driver said he had not moved the train, but later, speaking to the other AM, he said the Station Inspector had asked him to move the train, so that they could get at the body. He'd simply forgotten with the shock. I'd have found out eventually, when I questioned him further, but it solved the mystery. It just shows that such incidents need careful handling.

I then settled down to an enjoyable 18 months as an AM, before LUL got rid of the grade.

If you were an AM, it was not expected that you needed to be told what to do. I knew in theory that I was now a manager, but it came home to me when, a few weeks after I was put on my own, there was a derailment in a depot. I investigated and found the cause. Although a cure would have to await a new piece of equipment, as long as the problem was recognised and staff watched for a possible repeat failure, all should be well. I went to the Traffic Manager and said that I thought X should be done. He looked me in the eye: "Who's the manager in charge?" I knew he

---

[29] *See* Appendix and Chapter 5.

meant me. I took the hint, realised the authority I now had, went and arranged it all myself and never had to ask again.

Incidentally, I think that derailment was the first time I had come across one of the 'breakdown gangs' (Emergency Response Units, as they were later called). They arrived in their van, with ropes, chains, jacks and assorted lumps of wood. Then they would take over the derailed train and would burrow about underneath it. On one plane, what they were doing looked easy, whilst, on another, one wondered what they were up to. But I respected their abilities. After giving them a short while to assess a situation, one would ask for an estimate of a 'time to fix' and they were normally on the button. A lot of shoving and pushing and hard graft and the train would lift and slide and be back on the rails, ready to be taken away to be checked over and, if necessary, repaired. Soon, they'd pack up their kit and off they'd go again in their van. Whilst many of their jobs were in the open, as this one was, in the depot, it could be a different story under a train in a cramped tube tunnel environment. One of their least palatable jobs was to lift a train and get lumps of human body out when someone became mangled up in the wheels and motors. They were just some more of the unsung heroes of the railway.

As a manager, I went to more of those meetings that managements love. Personally, my criterion of a necessary meeting was when one ultimately saved me more time by being there than the actual time taken for the meeting. Of course, that's not always a satisfactory equation, but it's a good test.

One of the first meetings was one where, under one of LUL's continual new initiatives, we were told of things that the public wanted. It sounded 'off' to me, so I politely asked the speaker if this was what the public had said they wanted or what LUL thought they did. A wave of his hand and the talk continued. I think I had my answer. You will see later that LUL preferred answers they wanted, rather than the actual answers, if the latter did not fit in with their ideas. Who was it who allegedly said: *"I have my theories; don't confuse me with the facts"*? That concept is alive and well in LUL.

On the plus side were meetings with more people on the engineering side. For some reason, they did not seem to be getting rid of their older managers and many of them were long-term in the job. I found it very satisfying to sit with people, discussing a subject that they enjoyed and in which they were obviously competent. In those days, we had direct and frequent contact with the engineers who managed the track. If there was a problem, I could contact them and get matters sorted out quickly. We had mutual respect for each other. It was far less debilitating than the subsequent wranglings that came about after the management changes around the time of the 'Company Plan'[30], as to who was responsible for what, which became akin to swimming through treacle.

An initiative was to send all managers on those 4-day team-building exercises in the countryside. Ours was in Wales (not far from my family home) led by an *ex*-Lieutenant from the army. Chatting in the bar one evening, a number of us exchanged experiences with him. We realised that management of people is much the same in whatever walk of life one is. The man impressed me. He was obviously of a different social class to many of his men, yet one could see from the enthusiasm he engendered what would make men go 'over the top' when inspired by someone like him. It was interesting when I first met a colleague soon after we got back from the course that he said how he thought that LUL would do well to get *ex*-military men like him into our management. I thoroughly agreed. Indeed, one of the colleagues I later admired for his managerial techniques came from a military background. Unfortunately, LUL top management didn't seem to agree with that view!

By the way, LUL seemed to love throwing money away on things like those courses. I doubt if they would show up positively in a cost:benefit analysis. There was an argument that it was good to get staff away on jaunts of that kind – but they would probably have preferred a week-end in Dubai, such as offered by a firm I know!

---

[30] *See* Chapter 10

Unfortunately, "thank you" was an expression that often got overlooked on LUL. When I arrived at an office one week, to cover another manager's holiday, and started to look through the 'in' tray, I found a letter of thanks about one of the ticket collectors. She was a terror. She seemed to fear no-one and used to (literally) man-handle some of her supervisors. She had helped an elderly woman passenger from the West Country a few weeks before and the lady had now written a letter of thanks. I took the letter to her and asked if she knew about the incident. She remembered it and grew six inches taller to think that the woman had bothered to write. She remained a terror and she'd never change. But she deserved her letter of thanks and to know it had been noted. Anyway, saying "thank you" to staff also provided a basis if one had later to take disciplinary action. Staff couldn't accuse one of only adverse criticism. I'm convinced that "thank you" is a very under-rated thing, as well as being a positive side of discipline[31].

A lot depended on one's personal credibility, which had to be built on. Most AMs were respected, but a few not. One I knew was disliked intensely. He would lie profusely if needed. It was said he once told a supervisor to do something and then, when it went wrong, denied it and let him carry the can. I'm sorry to say I can believe it of him. I made it a point of honour never to lie to staff. If I had to hold something back, then I would say nothing. But discretion is different from lying.

One day, I met a Station Inspector I had not met for a year or more, having changed jobs. He spoke to me quietly but firmly, saying that he was disappointed that I had 'shopped' him over some incident over a year before. I assured him I had done no such thing. He said I had told him to do something and then denied it. I replied that I had not told him to do it and could not think what I might have said that he could have misconstrued. I felt bad about that as he was sure he was right. To this day, I cannot understand what caused him to get the wrong end of the stick as he was otherwise a reliable Inspector, yet what he had

---

[31] *"The worst mistake a boss can make is not to say 'Well done'".* John Ashcroft.

done was dangerous. Fortunately, no harm resulted, apart from my dented reputation. But I suppose such misunderstandings are inevitable in life, how ever hard one tries.

Attitude to staff is very important. Much later in my career, when shopping in Tesco, I used to bump into a lady who had been a ticket collector at a station I had previously managed. Once, turning to her husband who was with her, she said that she had always respected me, because, however busy I was, I always said "hullo" to her and the other staff as I passed – "unlike some managers I could mention," she added darkly. I wondered whom she meant. Having respect for staff seemed a basic issue to most of those I worked with. Most staff would reciprocate, if treated with respect. Apart from that, having a good relationship with staff could come in useful when one needed help – not that one did it for such motives. On more than one occasion, a member of staff tipped me off about something, which saved me a lot of work.

There was rarely a dull moment for an Area Manager. One morning, I went to four serious incidents in four hours, having to leave each of the first three before managing to tie up all the loose ends. After the fourth, I went back to the third, then second, then first incident, finishing them off, finally returning to the office to face the paper-work for all four.

You must bear in mind that AMs did not rotate on shift with a fixed group of staff, as I believe happens in the police and fire service. One had to deal with all the employees on two different lines at different times.

After a late shift, I would sometimes find it difficult to relax immediately on my return home. Often, a cup of tea and a fry-up would be in order. However, I'm glad I never got to the same state as a younger colleague, who admitted he needed a stiff drink as soon as he got in. He was a nice chap, but I felt it could be the start of a slippery slope.

One very busy Saturday evening, we were investigating and writing up a series of incidents. The person nearest the kettle kept making coffee and I was too busy to get tea. When I got home, I found I was twitching. I wondered what was happening until I realised I had drunk more coffee in a few hours than I normally did in a month.

As I said, there were only enough Traffic Managers to cover their normal duties, so an AM often covered the TM's job at holiday times or if there was sickness. Sometimes, instead of the TMs having two shifts, they would work 10 till 6 or thereabouts. In any case, the AMs were supposed to undertake any TM duties when there was not one there. This again gave variety and opportunity for further experience.

Early morning and late at night, there were other jobs to cover, as well as that of Traffic Manager. In those days, there was a complicated agreed pecking order of who should get a Booking Office job if someone failed to turn up for work. Normally, the Cover Clerk arranged this, but there were times when the AM had to make some arrangement at short notice and one soon found out if one tried to give a job to the wrong person. THEY knew who was available and who should go first ...

One evening, when I was covering the late turn TM, I received a telephone call from an irate member of the public. The nurse to look after his wife had arrived late, stating that she had been trapped in a tunnel for 25 minutes. I knew immediately, when he told me the time of the alleged incident, that this was well-nigh impossible. Although, at that time, I had been elsewhere, I could not have been anywhere on the line without feeling the effects of such a delay. I told him so, but said that I would confer with others who could confirm it. I spoke to the Controller and the Signalman and they did so. I borrowed the signalman's log sheets and 'phoned the man back, giving him the times of all the trains passing through the place the nurse had mentioned and saying that there was nothing like such a delay (it had actually been a very good evening peak service.) There was a pregnant pause and deep breath at the other end of the 'phone and the man said he would speak to the nurse. It was obvious he realised he had been lied to. The underground was fair game as an excuse, but she'd been caught out.

Late another evening, I got a call ostensibly from a hospital A&E department. A man had been brought in, apparently the victim of a mugging. They had his LUL Pass, which showed he was a member of our staff. They said they needed his address. I immediately smelt a rat, said I'd have to look into it and asked their number to 'phone back. They said they had no outside line, which strengthened my suspicions. I asked them to 'phone back in 20 minutes, whilst I made enquiries. Meantime I telephoned the BT Police[32], as I wondered if someone had been mugged and was lying somewhere, injured, whilst his attacker was trying to capitalise by burglary, by using his keys to enter his home. The police called at his home and established he was safe. He realised he had lost his ID and was going to report it next day. It was better to be safe than sorry; but there was obviously dirty work planned and, hopefully, squashed. The caller never did 'phone again, of course.

About the time I came into the job, many of the older managers, most of whom had obtained their positions through seniority, were looking to leave. Quite a number of them did not find the new systems palatable and were glad to take retirement on whatever basis they could. One manager had a whiteboard behind his desk with the numbers counting down the days to his retirement. When a fellow manager walked in, they were immediately greeted with "Two months, two weeks and three days to go ..." or whatever it was. One could hardly expect standards to be kept up with managers just waiting until the minute they could get out the door for ever. It was a tribute to the way many of the staff just kept 'doing the job' that things went as well as they did.

When I first started, there was no Controller-to-train radio, so it was vital that one kept in touch with the Controller at all times. Anyone who wanted you 'phoned the Controller to see where you were. A message would then be sent ahead to the next place you would be, to await arrival or to find you there already. If one forgot or got way-laid, one had to 'phone in as soon as one arrived. The advent of train radio was allegedly a boon to one of

[32] The British Transport Police, who had a special responsibility for policing transport in London.

our managers. His house backed on the line just near a station. It was said that, if all was quiet, he would pop home and leave his personal radio switched on. If the Controller called him, he responded, said he was at a certain station and nipped around to it, double-quick.

Mentioning radios and allied equipment reminds me: The radios were not fool-proof and the 'carrier wave'[33] equipment then installed on the Victoria line was far worse. Attending an incident one day, I arrived at the approach to the station on a train. The train could not get in to the station, so I had to walk and sent a message by carrier wave to tell the Controller what I was doing. But he failed to get all the message. I then 'disappeared'. When I got to the station, the 'phone on the platform was not working and it took ages for me to make urgent contact. At this time, it was a common fault – vital kit was not being repaired quickly enough.

One of the responsibilities of my new rôle was 'passing out' new train crew. This involved reviewing their training and ensuring that they were able to translate what they had learned from a classroom environment into the real world of the railway. That was not easy for some. A weakness in the LUL training system was that staff could learn the job merely by rote. Also, they tended to be taught in subjects, whereas real-life situations were rarely text-book and involved lateral thinking. In my time as a driver, I think I had only one defect that was clear-cut. Following the procedure led me to finding and curing the fault in a couple of minutes. Virtually every other time, there was a complication that distorted a quick diagnosis.

I always tried to see if trainees could think laterally. For example, I might ask what could cause a train to stop with an emergency brake application. What had to be done to cure it? Then I would move to how to protect the train and how to deal with impatient passengers and so on. Some just could not think except in straight lines. One AM I know used to ask trainee guards if they should take any action if they saw someone fall off a platform behind their train. One guard immediately said he would stop the train.

---

[33] So called, because it used the rails to transmit (carry) the message.

"Why?" he was asked. "What has it to do with you?" "Well, if I can stop my train in the signal section, it will keep the last signal red and stop the next train entering the station and running the person over." The AM gasped. "You know," he said, "you're the first guard in ages to see that."

AMs were also in charge of Booking Offices, although most of the day-to-day work was done by the Chief Clerk. Procedures were freer than today. One evening, a passenger came to me with a complaint that he had been given a wrong season ticket at a different station. I had the local station issue the correct ticket and put it down as awaiting credit, 'phoned the other booking office and told them not to bank the cheque passenger had given them and account for the 'wrong' ticket they had issued as awaiting credit. The next day, I took the incorrect ticket back to the issuing office, where they cancelled it to balance their books and took the cheque to the office that issued the correct ticket, so that they could pay it in and balance their books. And this was all on my personal say-so. That was the way it worked.

Another time, a colleague and I found a tourist travelling on an out-of-date weekly ticket belonging to someone else. He admitted travelling on it for four weeks. We got the Booking Office to issue four weekly tickets, charged him for them all, gave him one of the tickets for the rest of the week and put the others in the 'used ticket' bag. Unorthodox, but it would have been useless to prosecute him, as he was about to leave the country and, in any case, he probably wasn't fully aware of what he was doing.

One example of how things can go wrong occurred one Bank Holiday, when I was covering for the regular AM. I found a message saying that a couple of Booking Clerks were not to be allowed to enter the Booking Office at their station, but were to be sent home to await further investigations. It seems that some malpractice had been discovered, but what I did not know. I had the two clerks sent to me individually and I explained to them as much as I knew – which was virtually nothing. One clerk accepted it in a matter of fact way. The other was most distressed. How could he go home? - What would his wife say? - *etc.* I understood his feelings, but I was at a considerable disadvantage, not knowing what was really happening and not sure how much I could have said if I did. When I went back to that office a week later, I asked what had happened to the two clerks. It seems there had been an incredible mix-up: they were the two clerks NOT under suspicion; two of their colleagues were. I'd been told to suspend the wrong clerks. Astonishing, but there we are.

One evening, I went to give a Booking Clerk a 'follow-up' assessment. I found him in his office with a huge dog. It was probably wrong of him, but, such was the situation in that part of London at night, I had a bout of diplomatic blindness. If it gave him security in a dangerous area, why not? In my opinion, selective attacks of deafness, blindness and ignorance are essential qualities of a good manager.

On the other hand, one should not overlook important 'little' things, which are not little. One afternoon, when training a new Station Manager, I saw a guard with a newspaper in his hand, whilst checking passengers on and off his train. I quietly told him to put the paper away. Even if he wasn't actually reading, it gave a very slack impression to the public. Afterwards, this trainee manager told a colleague what I had done. "I wouldn't have bothered," he boasted. To me that showed his lack of ability for the job: he didn't realise it was important and thus showed his lack of managerial expertise. It was a sign of the changes for the worse that were occurring in management.

Early one morning, I was told that a train had nearly run down about 20 men in a tunnel, where they were just walking back from a job. A train had been allowed to enter the tunnel before they had given the 'all clear'. I was new to the line and it possibly made me see an obvious loop-hole in the procedures. I wrote out my recommendation for a change. No-one ever said it was a good idea, but I had a wry smile when, a week or so later, my recommendation - almost word for word - was published system-wide, but signed by someone else.

My early experiences as manager on shift included the arrival of the Guardian Angels and an increase in begging on trains.

The Guardian Angels were a vigilante group. The concept originated in the USA, where groups of (generally) young people of about 20 years of age, travelled around on US metro systems. Each wore a maroon beret and an inscribed T-shirt. They usually went around in *posses* of 4 or 5. The idea was to provide a visible presence to assure travellers in what was perceived as a dangerous environment. LUL's official line was that they didn't like them, because it enforced the perception that the London Underground was a dangerous place, whereas it was much safer than the streets of London! We were told to be neutral toward them, unless they interfered adversely. We just used to tell the Controller when and where they were about.

With the war in the Balkans, more and more people from thereabouts came to Britain. Women used to beg on trains. They usually had a baby with them. All this was discouraged as far as possible. One day I encountered a pretty girl of about 17-18 with a tiny baby. I escorted her to the booking hall and awaited the police. I was accosted by a young man of Asian appearance, who had the ID of a Home Office immigration official. He said that the UK government paid these people an allowance. But they sought more money, to send back to their country of origin, often to fund criminal gangs. He had to leave, but, as soon as he did so, the young woman reached into her dress, brought out an attractive breast and began to suckle the child. Whether this was an innocent act, or she sought to intimidate me, embarrass me in front of the public or whatever, I don't know. Anyway, the police arrived within moments and took her away. I expect she was back again quite soon. In fact, few passengers were well-disposed toward these beggars, except for visitors to London, who often spoke against LUL staff when they tried to stop the beggars' activities.

We also had a lot of Irish ladies, all called Mary Malone or Mary O'Connor, according to the police, who used to sit with young children, begging on platforms for hours on end if we let them.

Variety in the job was almost endless. One evening, I was asked to interview a young guard, who had been Superglued to a staff toilet seat. He said that he accepted the ribbings he got, but the most embarrassing thing was that both the ambulance staff who came to release him were female (a rare event at that time). They had to disconnect the seat from the toilet pan and take him, with the toilet seat fixed firmly to his bottom, to hospital, where they managed to detach it. It was a bizarre affair. Superglue dries very quickly and I sometimes wonder how it all came about. He did seem to get himself in some odd - or should I say sticky - situations!

Often the AM's job was 'fire-fighting'. If an incident occurred, the AM sought to get there and oversee at a local level, whilst the Controller and Traffic Manager oversaw from the Control Room.

Much of one's ability was as the result of 'gut feeling'. This was an unpopular concept in the 'new' LUL. One was expected to explain why one did what one did. But I believe that what one calls gut feeling is actually the brain working at a very high speed, reviewing experiences as quick as a flash and giving insight into probabilities. I found it frequently held me in very good stead and I can't recall it ever letting me down.

Three incidents in particular spring to mind.

The first was when I had just finished dealing with an incident at one end of the line. I heard that there was another Fire Brigade incident[34] half-an-hour away. Yet, although common sense said that it would all be over when I got there (it should have been), I kept going past my office until I reached the incident. It had been badly handled by a new manager from another line and I was just in time to stop it badly affecting our service.

On another occasion, there was a security alert at an important station. I was one station away, when we were halted because the police had evacuated the station ahead and left a train stuck in a tunnel outside. I waited for the 'all clear'. Three times I was told that the police had said it would be "five more minutes". At the third announcement, I said I was going to get the train out of the tunnel. I knew that that would take 20 minutes or more, so if this

---

[34] I mention more about these in Chapter 16

third "five minutes" became a reality, I would have caused a longer hold-up, because, once started, it would be almost impossible to stop the 'rescue'. I walked down the tunnel and up another to the train. The driver had been advised by radio and, as soon as I arrived, we told the passengers what we were doing. I conferred with my colleague in the Control Room and we started to drive the train backwards from the rear at about 5 mph. This all went well and all the passengers got off at the previous station or waited there: at least they had the choice. It was still some time before we got the 'all clear' – far more than the repeatedly-promised five minutes.

The third incident occurred one Sunday evening. We heard that a train had stopped in a tunnel approaching a station 30 minutes or more from our office. It had a problem. As soon as H (there were just the two of us on duty) heard the name of the driver, he said he would go immediately to the incident. I pointed out that, by the time he got there, all should be sorted out, one way or another. "No," he replied, "I've got a feeling about this." He was right. When he got to the train (the traction current had to be switched off to ensure the train would not move, so he could walk down the tunnel to it from the nearest station), he found that the driver had got in such a mess that it took him some time to help the driver put it all back together. The train then went perfectly well. The driver had lost all sense of what he should do. If he had set out to sabotage the train completely, he could hardly have done a better job. A manager's gut feeling again.

I'm sure many of my colleagues could tell similar stories.

When one went to an incident - a derailment, signal failure, person under a train or whatever - one met two basic responses from the staff. Either they immediately breathed a sigh of relief, took two steps back and let you take control, or they gave you a look, as if to say "Look, Guv, I'm handling this quite OK without your help, thanks." One had to be sensitive, judge the situation and respond accordingly. It was a fact that, though I was 'the boss', many of these people were more experienced in length of service or time at that location than I was. They were often more than competent to do what was needed. I would then just keep a 'watching brief'.

To interfere would have been an insult. Also, when a time came when I needed their input, they might have said as good as "You didn't need me before; why now?" And understandably so. I had a number of very well-qualified supervisors, whom I wouldn't dream of stopping, when they were stuck in to an incident. But neither would I walk away and leave them. I was there if needed and would do what was required: make the tea, if necessary. That was not dodging my responsibilities, just using discretion. If it all went wrong, it would be down to me.

I think I also came to distinguish between the two types of supervisors and managers that seemed to be doing nothing. Some were doing nothing because they were lazy. But they were also the type that tended to "look busy: the boss is coming". The other sort might be found drinking tea or having a smoke in their offices. They were the ones who were having a breather because they had the situation under control. They would get stuck in with gusto if the need arose and otherwise just made sure all was as it should be on their patch.

Personal *rapport* with staff was crucial. When I came on duty each day, I would normally telephone a few key points, to see who was sharing the shift. If it was certain people, all well and good, I knew we were in good hands. If it was others, then I knew a more hands-on style would be needed. If there was a problem at F when George was on duty, no hassle. Just wander there at moderate speed and have a cuppa, whilst he told me what he'd done. Then I just wrote it all up. He knew he was good at his job; I knew it and he knew that I knew it; there was mutual respect. I liked it that way, but, of course, it was not always like that.

Some staff wanted to refer anything and everything to you. One Inspector would 'phone at least once every shift with some matter or other. Often, he just needed reassurance. Others would just say, on the next visit to their station: "Oh, by the way Guv, X happened the other day and I did Y: just thought you'd like to know. Normally, that was enough. Sometimes, three people would 'phone to tell me the same thing. I tried never to say that I already knew. Better to be told three times than not at all.

Then there was Mickey, the Inspector who was the absolute whiz-kid on lifts and escalators. He was happy to get his hands dirty – and he had a motor-bike. "If I'm around and you have a problem on lifts or escalators, just give me a call and I'll be there", he said. He had forgotten more about lifts than I was ever likely to learn. The old ones were gradually being replaced, but, in the meantime, each machine seemed to have had some unique feature added over the years – and its own idiosyncrasies. He was another solid member of staff who was totally reliable, never asked for more than his pay for his work and never let me down.

I well remember the first time I met Paul. He was sweating profusely at five o'clock in the morning. The Booking Office facilities at his station were being renovated in connection with the new Underground Ticketing System (UTS). The painters had painted the Booking Hall and passage floors, not in quick-drying matt paint but gloss. It was still tacky and would take ages to dry. He was trying to put down planks and sheets of cardboard for people to walk on. There were painted footmarks all over the place. In the end, we had to shut the Booking Hall for the morning and divert everybody in and out of the station by the emergency exit – and no tickets were sold. Typical of the mess contractors left the railway in when they went home about 4.30 in the morning.

I came to find Paul to be one of the best front-line supervisors I knew. He seemed to have an incredible 'feel' for the job and the staff. If a serious delay occurred at 18.00, you would see him preparing for the ramifications that would follow two or three hours later, when the crews needed to take their breaks, whilst other supervisors would go from crisis to crisis for the rest of the evening. Mind you, the way Paul spoke to staff and the language he used would not please PC[35] managers today. But he used words the staff understood ('industrial language' it has been called). The staff liked and respected him for it – and often they would speak back to him the same way. It was rare for him not to wheedle his way out of a problem by his wits or getting a favour

---

[35] Politically Correct

done or paid back. Paul was a great example against treating all supervisors and managers as equal.

As a supervisor, Paul was one of those men who did 'over and above' his job. He was noted for his nocturnal tunnel walks. These were done every so often, when new staff came to the area. Camden Town was a station on a knife-edge - not just for possible congestion, but with the complicated and vital junctions just south of the platforms. If a train over-ran a signal at danger in that area, other signals went to danger, to stop a collision in the confined tube tunnels – not a happy possibility When this happened, the rules stated that the points ahead needed to be secured by 'scotch and clip'[36], so that the trains could proceed safely. This was time-consuming for all concerned, including the passengers stuck in the tunnel. But, under adequate local supervision, it might well be possible to put the train in reverse for a few feet to the place it should have stopped, thus unlocking the signalling equipment, allowing a swift return to normality. Paul knew where all the 'bolt holes' between tunnels were and the quickest ways to get there, either on foot down another tunnel or by another train, without putting the staff in danger. (By the way, this emphasises how important it was for a driver not to move his train without authority – someone could be walking down the tunnel to meet him (*see* later re SPADs[37]).) So, every few months, Paul would organise these excursions to acquaint the staff with (literally) the ins and outs of the area.

I was very sorry to hear recently that Paul had died after a long illness. He was a great character …

Camden Town was not a salubrious station, with vomit and vagrants about. Incredible things were viewed on their security CCTV monitors, including one couple copulating on a sand bin, whilst a baby sat by them in a buggy. It was (and probably still is) an amazing place to work. But the staff there accepted it all as a daily challenge. A manager recalls one of his first visits there. In the corner of the small office, a pretty young female member of

---

[36] Explained in the Appendix

[37] SPAD = Signal Passed at Danger – *see also* the chapter on that subject.

staff was holding up her new skirt to stop it falling down, whilst the inspector made an extra hole in her new belt to fit her trim waist. Of course, the young male members of staff were making saucy remarks about her need to hold on to her skirt so tightly, which she took in good part. But this was just part of the *esprit de corps* of the staff there, who often chose to stay, rather than move to an apparently better location. I know this young woman always expressed relief to be back there, after she had had to 'fill in' temporarily at another station. Another lady, Joan, was a very solid part of the team, and I suspect she kept a motherly eye on them all. The Camden Town staff was a bunch that any manager would be glad to have to run his patch.

I remember one of my supervisors-made-manager, who had been good as a supervisor, but never made the mental change to managerial status. On the other hand, he was excellent if given the task of overseeing something like engineering work or other things where his supervisory expertise came into play. As time passed, he complained more and more and was obviously unhappy in his job. I asked what was the root cause of this. He mentioned his health. I spoke with one of our employment managers, who was an expert on retirement plans. She said she would speak with him if he wished. He had long service, was fairly comfortably off and I thought he really wanted a financially satisfactory way out. But a few hours later, I got a call from my boss. The man had complained that I was trying to push him out of his job. I explained my motivation, but was told to soft peddle, so I left it at that: it was his choice. Sadly, shortly after I moved on, he died suddenly at work. I wonder if he could have lived longer if he had taken the good retirement terms available to him.

An AM carried a lot of clout and it was amusing sometimes to find out its effects. One evening, visiting a major station, I went down to the platforms as part of my tour. I was most concerned to find so many passengers waiting on a platform that they were nearly falling off the platform edge on to the track, as there had been a long delay. I went to the telephone to call the Line Controller, to get him to warn the next train to approach with caution. The 'phone did not work. At that moment, a train arrived and the danger was averted. I went to the Station Supervisor, who showed me the log book, which showed the fault had been repeatedly reported over four weeks. When I queried it, I was told that there were no spares. I made it quite clear to the department concerned that this was unacceptable and demanded action *pronto*. The Supervisor 'phoned me at 10.30 that night to say a replacement 'phone had been connected, pending the arrival of spares. I used to find similar vital outstanding issues that were just not being attended to. If I 'phoned, I would be told (for example) that Mr X was on holiday and his work was on hold for two weeks. "Never mind," I'd say, "just put me thro' to his boss, please." There would be a horrified silence. "Oh, that's Mr Y. He doesn't normally deal with that sort of thing and he's in a meeting right now." "Could you interrupt him and ask him to speak to me, please: it's urgent." Another horrified silence. Eventually, a heavily-breathing Mr Y would be on the 'phone, denying he knew anything. A polite summary of his departmental short-fall and the critical situation that had been found would usually bring a satisfactory result in a couple of hours.

Unfortunately, that sort of thing shows that much of the job was being a policeman. Once, I was at a certain station and came out of a cross-passage to find the guard reading a paper whilst his train awaited the signal to leave. As he saw me, he said "We never know where you'll turn up." Shame. Another guard was fond of detraining passengers on minor pretexts and then driving the train. One day, I was told he was up to his old tricks and went downstairs, just as his train arrived, with him driving, whilst the driver sat to one side. He saw me and I saw his mouth frame a rude word. I stopped the train, turfed him out of the cab and back to his post. But I knew he'd soon be up to mischief again. The trouble with such people was that, when an investigation was made, we would often find a minor fault. We could not say that it should be ignored, because there was always the 1 in 1,000,000 chance of a more serious problem developing. The trains were getting old and tolerances were weakening, causing these niggling minor defects.

One class of incidents managers had to deal with was 'alleged door irregularities'. Put simply, that is when train doors do what they shouldn't, which is usually open when they should be shut –

fortunately a rare occurrence. In such cases, doors were capable of opening on the side of the train away from the platform or even when the train was moving. Sometimes an incorrect electrical feed could cause such a thing. At other times, it was actually a staff fault: the guard opening doors when he shouldn't or the driver driving off with doors open. Since the bell should not ring if doors were open, the latter was usually down to a driver error. Whenever an allegation of this kind was made, a thorough investigation had to be made immediately, to find if it was a staff or equipment error. If the latter, one needed to find out the exact problem and have it fixed.

Often, it was the train crew's fault; but it was unwise to assume this too quickly. One guard had a situation when some doors opened on the correct side of the train, but not all, and some doors on the side away from the platform opened as well. The guard complained he had been told he was responsible. This seemed incredible, as it would be well-nigh impossible for a guard to make that happen, unless he had re-wired a large part of the train!

One day, I was told of a train that had left a station with people still getting on. This was at a very busy station and the train's front doors were near an entrance to the platform. All the passengers had been taken off the train as soon as the incident was reported and I joined the train near my office. We headed off, empty, to the depot. I travelled with the driver, to get first impressions. (We always tried to do this before the crew could get together and concoct a story.) He swore he got the bell signal, indicating all the doors were safely shut. I said little, reserving my judgement. At the depot, we met up with another manager, who stayed with the guard. The tactics were to try and keep all electrical circuits as they were at the time of the alleged incident and keep the crew on hand to try and re-enact the scenario exactly – and so the crew could see the tests. The depot staff came aboard. I went back and held the first set of doors open and got the guard to press the bell-button. "Ding". I asked again and then got the driver to look. The bell rang repeatedly with the door open. The crew was cleared and the depot staff was able to find the fault (a broken electrical contact) immediately. Fortunately, there had been no injuries, only some shock. The driver thanked me for the way I never doubted his word. I didn't tell him, of course, that I had really only kept an open mind. Actually, I did have a feeling he was right, but I had to be sure.

In another of these incidents, the allegation was that doors on the rear car opened on the 'wrong side' at another station. Again, fortunately no-one was hurt. When we got to the depot, we could not reproduce the incident. I then asked the driver what position his control handle was in at the time the incident occurred and asked him to put it there. We then tried to open the doors on the correct side of the train, as the guard had said he had done. This time ALL the doors on BOTH SIDES of the WHOLE TRAIN opened. Again the crew were exonerated. But the fault only showed if the controls were in exactly the same positions as when it first happened.

Allied to this subject, a strange incident occurred when I was a driver. It was a very hot day and I had the cab windows open. My train arrived at a station and I heard the doors open. A few moments later, I heard a bell ring. It was the same tone as the guard's start bell. Subconsciously, I felt something was wrong. I looked at the platform. The Station Supervisor had just put down the telephone in the box on the platform beside me, making a single ring of just the same note as the door bell. Almost immediately the doors shut and the correct bell rang. I could easily have driven off with the doors open at the first bell. I read of a bus driver who did something similar. A bus stop was just by a greengrocer's shop and the noise made as an assistant put a weight on the scales (this was back in the1950s) was the same as the bus bell. As a passenger was injured when the bus moved off, the scales were taken to court as evidence of the similarity of the two sounds and the driver was cleared of dangerous driving.

A problem in dealing with some staff – *viz*, that they didn't always tell the truth! Strangely, LUL had rules about lots of things, but there was no rule to say that staff must not lie. Lying could be just trying to keep themselves out of trouble, but it could, in fact, be dangerous, as a genuine problem might go undiscovered. The setting up of a 'no-blame' reporting system was discussed, but not implemented in my time. Getting the truth could be a game.

Sometimes it was virtually certain that the crew were at fault and sometimes one couldn't prove it. If this was so, I would tell them. "Softly, softly catchee monkey" was often the tactic to follow.

As an example, a more serious incident occurred one day when I got a call from a signal technician. He said he had been called to an alleged points' failure at an important junction. When he looked, he found a fuse from a train jammed in the points, preventing them changing for the train to go to its correct destination. The incident was not, in itself, actually dangerous and the signalling equipment correctly acted to prevent an accident; it just meant the train had to return north early and that the crew went home early. But, the technician said, that exactly the same thing had happened a month previously. Technically, it was sabotage and it is not acceptable to have such actions on the railway. I knew the last time the points had changed correctly and looked at the names of the drivers whose trains had been there since. One name immediately caught my eye, as it was of a strange character. When I looked at the same information for the previous incident - lo and behold - there was his name again. We were talking of six people out of a total of about 600 or more and I was looking for a repeated name. It was too much to be a coincidence. I also remembered that, a few weeks previously, this driver's train had mysteriously become uncoupled at a terminus. I interviewed him and he denied it all. I told him I did not believe him, but could prove nothing, so would be keeping a lookout for any more strange happenings connected with his train. From then on, his working life was very quiet.

I recall an anecdote I read about the last stages of the career of the great locomotive engineer, OVS Bullied, whilst he held a top position in Ireland. A collision occurred in the work's yard between his brand new turf-burning loco and an old engine. After investigation, he called the two drivers into his office. "Gentlemen", he said, "I have read your reports with great interest. It seems that just before the collision occurred, both your locomotives were stationary." Obviously, failure to tell the truth was not a problem unique to LUL.

There were, as always, 'characters' among the staff. Bill (another one) was one of my guards. He was eccentric. He was always telling me about his hopes for promotion, for which he really was not qualified. He obviously thought I could 'put in a word' for him. One day, he came to me in an excited state. He said that, the day before, one of our directors had spoken with him whilst he was working on his train. "I didn't realise until afterward that it was you", he said cryptically. Before I had time to answer, he went on to say he realised that I had sent her to vet him for promotion. I tried to find a way of telling him it was not so, but he responded that he quite understood that I must keep quiet, but that it would be our secret. Then he hurried off. I was saved getting out of that problem by the sad fact that he died a month or so later. At his funeral, we learned he had been in show-biz as the manager of a theatre, but had then been in prison for embezzlement (a matter he had somehow kept from LUL).

Bill's funeral was taken by the LUL chaplain, Cliff, who was supplied by the London City Mission. He was a good and very genuine man. I know some managers used him when they had a difficult pastoral problem that they wished to avoid. He knew he was being used that way, but accepted the opportunities. He sadly died about a year later from a serious illness, which he also accepted with fortitude. Cliff was a good example of true Christianity. With others, I appreciated his visits and concern and was sorry when he died still fairly young. Even though some staff poked fun at him, one could tell that his genuineness made its mark.

I remember after one of the many changes in the level of management above me, being called to an emergency meeting by yet another new boss. He had been put in charge as a sort of caretaker, whilst the new system was put in place and permanent changes made. In his first week, there had been a series of bad days and he wanted to have a rant and rally us all to do better. He could then say he had told us what to do and hopefully cover his back, as he was probably hoping for a good job in the new setup. The delays were not our fault, of course, but more a series of unfortunate things that just happen in a business that had been allowed to run down as LUL had. When I arrived in his office, I found most of my colleagues had (wisely) found excuses not to be there - obviously, they had been to his meetings before. Even the Traffic Manager popped in to say he was tied up … Rather provocatively, I asked the boss what our plan was. "Plan, Andrew", he shouted; "I've got a crisis here. I haven't got time for a plan". I think that summed him up. The next two days were better days and so he soon found something else to occupy himself.

As part of the LUL Company Plan (*see* later), a new management structure was set up. A new General Manager arrived, together with four new managers. One of these turned out to be a rogue and a bad manager; one a lovable rogue and an excellent manager and very competent.

At the same time, my new boss (yes, another one) took the opportunity of the shake-up to reward a number of his chums with some of the new jobs. Unfortunately for him, some were not up to it and let him down badly.

One of the newly-chosen men, T, left his lady assistant to do much of his job. She was a very competent woman and tackled the routine with no problem, but discipline slid. He concocted a slogan: "We all work here, so let's all work together." This was so *facile*, it was almost unbelievable. Yet it appeared on official documents.

This manager had in his staff a guard with a drink problem. It came to light one evening, when I was advised that a man had complained that his daughter had been restrained from leaving a train by an allegedly drunken guard. When I investigated, I found the man had indeed acted under the influence of drink. I had him suspended immediately and he was lucky that the girl's parents decided after my visit to their home to leave the matter with me. I spoke to T the next day. He was obviously out of his depth. He had referred the man to our new alcohol and drugs advisory group and left it at that. I spoke to his counsellor, who said he had advised that the man be not promoted to driver, because of his 'problem'. He might not be safe, driving a train. I pointed out that a drunken driver would be stopped by the tripcock/trainstop mechanism[38] if his train passed a red signal and, if he went through a station without stopping, the guard would stop the train. On the other hand, as a drunken guard, what would stop him opening the doors as the train was moving (there was no system to prevent that in those days)? There was a pause and I could hear the counsellor swallowing hard at the other end of the telephone. "I think I may not have assessed his case correctly," he admitted slowly. "Send him back to me." The counsellor was a decent chap, but, like a lot of 'back room' advisory staff, didn't really understand what the work involved, so their advice was deficient. T, of course, should have known better, but he was more keen on being popular than being good at his job.

We had an excellent handbook produced for train staff on the Line. It was one of my boss's good ideas, produced by an *ex*-train driver and a train driver still in the grade. Being written from the front line, as it were, it met the staff's needs admirably. But when T retired in estranged circumstances, despite the fact that the Line had (seemingly) run out of these valuable tools, a large stock of them was discovered secreted in his cupboard.

Another newly-promoted manager only managed by walking in the shadow of a more experienced colleague. He had a habit, when challenged, of stating that he had left the relevant document in his "other briefcase". When the colleague on whom he depended retired, he beat a hasty retreat, becoming medically retired for some reason.

One of the managers was known as "X". He always had strong opinions on everything, especially on what he was going to do. He flitted from one job to another, but, after a while, his performance began to show cracks. When his boss telephoned his office, he would be told that X was at a site meeting or whatever. One day when this happened, the boss said bluntly to X's assistant, who was trying to protect him, to "stop messing about, get round to the so-and-so pub (where X spent much of his time) and tell him that, if he didn't 'phone back in 5 minutes … …" (You will appreciate that I have sanitized the language of this

---

[38] *See* Appendix.

conversation somewhat for publication!) Not long after, rumours circulated of missing funds and late-night assignations with a lady in his office. X was eventually required to face a Disciplinary Board, but I understand he never showed up, having resigned the day before.

Part of LUL's "making of many managers" included Line management. Where there had been Divisional management for two lines, now each line had its own managers, thus doubling the number – and, of course, there had to be twice the office space. On one of my first visits to our new office, I found all the doors of the Line mangers' offices had Latin inscriptions on them. One of the new managers was gifted in that language and composed apposite mottoes for himself and each of his colleagues. I wish I could remember them: they were very clever. I had little contact with him, but what I did have made me think he was an asset to the team, but he moved on before long.

On another visit, I espied a smartly-dressed, mature lady, whom I had never seen before, sitting at a desk, covered with papers. I seemed to sense a kindred spirit and introduced myself, asking something on the lines of what a nice girl like her was doing in a place like that. She answered me equally flippantly and we began to discuss what she was doing and the 'State of the Union'. She gave me a very succinct evaluation of the situation in the organisation as she saw it. I remarked that we needed people like her around, who saw things the way they really were. She said she was sorry, but she was just finalising the job on her desk and she was leaving on Friday. I never found out her background and I never saw her again. We lost so many able people like that along the way.

I had been selected to be promoted as a result of the management changes, but my boss wrote on my selection board decision "NO - he was a train driver a year ago," which was only half true. Although my new grade was ostensibly the same as an Area Manager, there were so many new managers that it did not turn out that way. I felt the demotion (because it was effectively such) keenly – even more when I saw some of those who overtook me. I knew I was good at my job and the appraisal of my abilities had agreed that I was suitable for promotion. One man's pique had stopped me again.

Over the next few months I was twice asked to stand in for someone of a higher grade than me. Once, I attended a meeting to discuss the ingress of water to tunnels. I found myself, with no preparation, remembering my 'O' level geography of 30-odd years before on the London Basin water table. On another occasion I was sent to a seminar on train driver's conditions as a stand-in for my boss, who had to be elsewhere – and he was supposed to be deputising for his boss! I soon realised that, of the 40 people there, only one other person beside me had any real idea of the situation. For example, incredulity was expressed by all but two delegates when train staff using tunnels as toilets was mentioned. At the end of the seminar, they needed someone to head-up a project. I was the only one qualified to do so ... and I wasn't even supposed to have been there. Anyway, I looked into the issue over the next few days. I came across someone who said "Oh, talk to D, I think he's doing something on that." I knew D from the past. I asked him and found he'd been undertaking the same project for two years. I 'phoned the person who had been over-seeing the seminar the previous week, to tell him. "I don't care," he responded, "I'm ****** off with the whole thing. Just forget it; nobody will ever ask you about it." True, to the day I retired, no-one did. But, over the next two years, two or three people 'phoned me to ask about identical projects. They seemed most upset when I directed them to D, who was still ploughing on with it. (There were TU and practical difficulties, but the project was eventually instituted about three years later). In a big organisation, some duplication was, I suppose, inevitable, but not on a project as big as that was. And how much time might I have wasted, if I had just continued with the project alone?

On a smaller scale, when I was in charge of area in North London, I found someone erecting some notice boards for drivers at the end of platforms. The very next day, another group of workmen arrived to do the same as part of another project. Neither knew of the other and I knew of neither of them until they turned up, despite it being my patch and thus I should have been consulted first. The two notice boards stood side by side on a number of platforms for some time, as mute testimony to this nonsense.

Twice, in the few weeks before I moved to another management job, I went to trains stalled in tunnels, where the drivers had done all that they should to get their trains to go. The drivers spent valuable time, questioning what they had done. But they had not been deficient – the trains just wouldn't go. In one case, whilst we were all (the traincrew, the technician and me) reviewing our options, the faulty equipment started to work again, for no apparent reason. I told the driver to get going and get to the train into the depot asap, but to immediately call for the following train to give a push (called a 'push-out'), if the fault recurred on the way. It didn't and we never found out what went wrong. LUL had a rule that, if a defect couldn't be cured in 6 minutes, the driver should call for the next train to push. In those days (no computer-aided analysis), few serious defects could be traced that quickly. Realistically, it often took at least 10-15 minutes, whilst the driver trolled up and down the train, changing fuses and so on. As a result, 'push-outs' tended to get over-looked; then, after 20 minutes or so, a serious situation could build up, with trains all held up behind and passengers stuck in tunnels.

It was similar with lifts. The staff was always told that, becoming aware of a defect involving passengers, they should tell the Controller immediately. I once went to a station to find that the staff had spent 30 minutes trying to get people out of a lift that had stalled between floors. They said they hadn't bothered the Controller because they had assumed they would get things sorted in a few minutes. Normally, this was true, but not this time. They could not believe they had been more than five minutes, they were so engrossed. I had to put them right, but I felt sympathetic. It just showed that following procedures IS important.

My next promotion came about after a conversation between a colleague (R) and our boss. The weaknesses of a number of his new appointees had come to light after some months. His own performance was coming under scrutiny; as a result, he wisely promoted R, a very competent manager, to help him out of the mess. One evening, over a drink, the boss confided to R: "I'm a bloody poor chooser of men." *In vino veritas*. R told me he "took a brave pill" and agreed with him. My boss realised things were not going well for him and he needed more help. R suggested that I would be an asset to the team and so it was arranged, at first on a temporary basis, which became permanent. This was the job for which I had been qualified months before and he had hindered me doing. My boss never had any genuine cause to regret promoting me, although' I knew it niggled him. Eventually, his own situation caught up with him and he left the company.

Just after this promotion, an interesting incident occurred. Our admin clerk failed to show up for work one Monday morning. We heard nothing until later in the day, when we were sworn to secrecy. It appeared that his brother had become one of the first millionaires in the new National Lottery. A complication was that the family belonged to a religious group that forbade gambling. Obviously, they wanted to keep the money AND still be in the sect. A few days later we received another 'phone call from a Far Eastern beach resort (we could actually hear the waves in the background). Not surprisingly, the admin clerk never returned to work for us. I think the religious 'problem' was cleared up by a suitable donation.

Dealing with staff was always interesting. It's amazing the problems some people have. One day, the police arrived at my office. They warned me that one of my staff was accused of carrying an imitation fire arm and masquerading as a police officer. But they couldn't make it "official", so my hands were somewhat tied. It must have died down, as he still works for LUL and has been promoted. There was recently a feature about him and his new appointment in the staff magazine.

Another group of police wanted to check the days off over the last few months of another of my guards, to see if they coincided with some incidents. It seems this guard had (amongst other things) been exposing himself to young women in his off-duty time. Five girls had made complaints, but the police only had two that they thought might be good witnesses in court. The guard was very matter-of-fact about it when I spoke to him, although he did not admit his guilt. I had to go to court, to see if the situation was such that he could be sent to a Disciplinary Hearing. LUL obviously have to prevent unsuitable staff from working with the public and this was a serious allegation. I went to the magistrate's court for the first appearance. The guard was there with his legal rep – but the Magistrate was not. We had all been given the wrong time. We were told to return that afternoon, but, when we did, we found the court room was being painted. We were given another date. I arrived and asked when and where the case would be heard. I was given the court details but told I would have to wait in the court until the case was heard; no time could be given. After a long wait, I asked the Usher. I was again told to wait, but the case would definitely be heard in that courtroom. After another long wait, I asked the Usher again. I was then told the case had been transferred to another court. I hurried over and just arrived in time to hear the evidence. This and other experiences with courts have left me with some serious doubts as to the efficiency of the British legal system.

One of my new accountabilities was to oversee a group of new managers. Some of the older managers had retired and we needed new blood. At that time, LUL was infatuated with a new method of job application, involving much paper-work. It was supposed to make applications fair, but it actually based success on presentation rather than proven ability. We thus lost potentially good managers and got some who could present well but just were not managers. We had a youngish driver, who I felt to be more than eligible. In the past, he had had a colourful life-style, but had recently married a very nice girl and – put simply – had made good and settled down. He wanted the job and I wanted him to do it. There was a problem, however. He had a learning difficulty. It would not have disrupted his practical ability to do the job, but it would have made a successful job application under the new rules almost impossible. I telephoned a lady I knew in the appropriate department. She said there was nothing she could do about the interview, but, if I sent him to her, she would see what could be done about the application form. That was all I wanted. I didn't ask what she did, but she got him an interview, he was accepted and he became one of our best managers at that level, which is what we both wanted.

This approach did not always work. I had another excellent driver. He frequently got commendations from managers and the public. When I heard or read the commendation about an un-named driver, I didn't have to check up who it was, he was so consistent. Anyway, I felt (still feel) he had potential as a manager, without fulfilling the Peter Principle[39]. I asked him what he thought about applying for the first level manager's job. He asked time to discuss with his wife (which shows the kind of chap he is). The next day he sought me out and thanked me but said "no thanks". The reasons he gave were that the rise in pay was minimal; he currently did his job and went home with it finished, whereas, as a manager, he would "take the job home". He paused for a moment, then added apologetically, "And let's face it, Mr Melville, 55 Broadway treat you managers like ****". Sadly, there was little I could say, as it was a fair assessment of the situation.

One day, I had an anonymous telephone call. The caller said he was a driver at another LUL depot. He wanted me to know that a driver, who had allegedly died whilst visiting a certain African country, was actually alive and well, having been seen walking around the east end of London. Whilst not condoning anonymous calls, I was not going to pass up the info, especially as it had the ring of truth about it. Interestingly, the caller was not concerned about any fraud in general, but was incensed because the driver's colleagues at my depot had taken up a collection of £120 and it had been collected by the driver's 'widow'. Further investigation revealed a doctor's certificate from a hospital in the African country, stating that the driver had crashed in a brand new car, having hit a tree, whereupon the car burst into fire. He had (allegedly) subsequently died in the hospital. I also found that the £120 had been collected by a rather stunning lady, according to those who saw her. I then telephoned the LT Pension department. After checking that I was whom I said I was, they revealed that they already had their own suspicions regarding the alleged death and, before shelling out a very large amount of money, a representative was going to the said country to make further

---

[39] *"The Peter Principal"* by Dr Laurence J Peter and Raymond Hull, Souvenir Press, 1969. *See* Appendix.

enquiries. They made it clear that they were not intending to pay out any money on the information to date. I later discussed the affair with friends of mine who had spent many years in those parts. They found the story quite believable and said that certificates like that could be obtained easily – for a price, of course.

One part of my work latterly was involvement in the selection of new staff. Many people realised that the pay was good and it was secure employment. Despite the draw-back of the unsocial working hours and other issues, LUL found itself with many potential employees and could afford to be choosier. By the time the interviews in which I was involved took place, many of the less likely candidates had been filtered out, but it was still interesting – to say the least – to listen to some of the applicants.

One particularly sticks in my mind. A young Scotsman entered the room. He immediately gave the impression of confidence and security. He stated that he had been a barman at a large pub in Glasgow. However, as we questioned him, it became obvious that he had undersold himself. He had trained new staff, organised the roster for bar staff and arranged cover for sickness; also, he had been responsible for checking that fire exits remained free and other safety items. After the standard questioning, we asked him to leave the room. It did not need a minute to confirm that we were both not only willing to accept him, but also to have him fast-tracked for the renamed Station Supervisor course. Scots will, I hope, forgive me for thinking that, if he could cope with a Glaswegian pub on a Friday or Saturday night, he should cope with anything he might face on the Underground.

Another revealing opportunity arose. LUL participated in a scheme where managers visited schools to assist students to think about their future employment. I went to some schools in what could only be described as the more deprived areas of the capital. I was surprised at the security precautions at the school entrance, which I would have thought more likely in New York. I remember one girl saying that she wanted to be a TV presenter. I thought she had no hope (but did not say so) until I later saw a presenter on one of the specialist channels and thought perhaps, after all, she would be ideal! One morning, at the first break time, a teacher approached me to ask if all was going well. I said I was concerned that one student took absolutely no part. The teacher apologised for not explaining that he spoke no English. She then pointed out the one of the boys had killed at least two people, having been a child soldier in Africa before coming to the UK. She also said that for many of the children, a visit to the shopping centre a couple of miles away was a big event. London was virtually an unknown quantity. I thought I was un-shockable, but learnt a few lessons that day. Interesting times.

One feature in which I became more involved latterly was in-depth investigation of incidents on the railway. This gave a manager scope to use various abilities. Something in which I would like to have been more involved and which became a feature of investigations was what was called 'human factors'. Essentially, this sought to appreciate underlying issues that could cause staff to do things that seemed inexplicable and out-of-character. For example, one driver, who seemed a sensible sort, drove his train backwards along the line until he met a train coming the opposite direction. We sought to understand why he did it and see how repeat incidents could be prevented. Simple carelessness seemed not to be the answer. Later, I heard a case of a US Air Force pilot, who led his flight to their deaths, despite his instrument readings and warnings from control. An investigator finally found the missing planes, many years later, miles off course. He found a series of geographical features that could lead a pilot to be convinced he was elsewhere than he actually was. Such quirks could explain many aberrations in performance by otherwise reliable staff. I would like to have developed this aspect more.

By now, LUL was trying to put the 'black mac' past behind it and be 'professional' – whatever that meant. To me, the black mac generation was professional in the true meaning of the word. As I said, many of the older-style managers couldn't cope and left. Some should probably not have been managers anyway, but many others were perfectly good at what was needed: the job description had changed and so had the emphasis. The problem was that often the results achieved were far short of desirable.

The consequence of all this was many managers who could "talk the talk" but not "walk the walk," as the new buzz-phrase put it.

I recall one of these managers who was advised one evening of a problem on the line. He sent G, who was more than capable of sorting the matter out, to the scene. He soon became fidgety, even though we assured him that G would do all that was needed. But he then became paranoid, thought we were keeping information from him and started blaming G for the delay in the matter being cleared up. It subsequently became almost unbearable to work with him, so, from then on; I stayed away from the control room when he was on duty, only going there when he'd gone home. This may seem childish, but I'm afraid I found it difficult to work with someone who was so incompetent - and then likely to blame others for his failures.

The tragedy in all of these changes was that higher management couldn't see why performance in many areas was slipping. They were so wedded to the new ideas, they searched elsewhere for answers. Which leads me to a later subject ...

9 – SEX, RACE AND RELATED ISSUES

I have kept referring to staff as males. This is partly because it is difficult to keep putting "s/he" and "him/her" and it is tedious for you to read. Also, when I joined LUL, the vast majority of the train staff was male. On the stations, of course, many were female, including Booking Clerks. But, to the best of my knowledge, at that time no operating managers were female.

A particular station was known as 'petticoat junction' (by the ladies there). As there was no mid-day Supervisor and the ladies did the 9 – 5 shifts, they were in charge in the middle of the day. The two regular ladies had been 'clippies'[40] at the nearby bus garage until conductors were dispensed with, when they chose to work on the station. One Sunday, when we arrived at a terminus and went to make tea, we found a full Sunday roast lunch being served in the staff room, for the lady member of staff's family and the other staff on the station, cooked in the staff cooker. But, why not? As long as they were doing their job, why not ease the situation for all concerned. Pity we hadn't got time to join them – it smelled good.

Just before I joined LUL, the first lady guard was appointed[41]. She qualified as a driver in 1978. During my career, more and more ladies joined the train staff grades. In general, I found no opposition to ladies working on the trains. There were isolated cases of opposition from individuals (one driver resigned from being a trainer, rather than "have a woman in [his] cab", but I think that reflected on his personal circumstances). I do think that some women had a difficult time, but that was due more to individual prejudice than institutionalised sexism.

Some of the ladies remained very feminine, whilst others became 'one of the boys'. I recall one of my young women drivers playing cards in the messroom. She wore a very loose-fitting tee-

---

[40] = female bus conductors
[41] This excluded those who worked as guards in wartime.

shirt and kept leaning over the table. I think she managed to distract her male opponent from his game ...

London Transport buses encouraged husband and wife bus crews, but I never knew this on the railway. We did have some married couples that were both on the railway, but not working together. One Area Manager was forced to change lines when it was found he had a live-in relationship with a lady Station Supervisor on his original line.

Little by little, more female staff went through the ranks. One day, just after the first lady at our depot had been qualified as a driver, I saw her on a train with a female guard. I don't know if this was a 'first', but I had never seen an all-female crew before. The driver's father was a manager and she subsequently married another driver, who then became a manager. I think one of their children also subsequently went to work for LUL.

At one depot, we had a very pleasant Asian lady driver/instructor. It was always a good experience to get in a cab after she had left it, as she wore very nice perfume ... a change from the stale tobacco smell left by others. She left LUL not long after to get married and live in the West Midlands.

Mentioning an Asian driver brings me to the race issue. Many Caribbean men and women came to work for the London Transport in the 50s and, later, more of other races.

One day I went into the Inspectors' office at Baker Street for some reason. Inside, I found I was surrounded by six Afro-Caribbean gentlemen. My face must have shown something, as the duty Inspector, normally a very serious and well-spoken man, caught the mood of the moment and quipped, in exaggerated *patois*: "It's aw-kee; de natives arr frien'-lee." I'd never heard him crack a joke before and he had the laugh on me. But it taught me what it must be like to be the one different person in a group.

I worked with many black drivers when I was a guard and never had any friction. One of them was highly amused when I pointed out that he put white sugar in his tea and I put brown in mine.

There were a number of miserable white drivers at one depot, but the Afro-Caribbean men were fine. Black people were welcome at my family home; that and my good relations with non-white staff at work made me very angry when, some years later, I was accused of racism, when I had to reprimand a black manager.

Quite a lot of non-white staff had become supervisors and Station Managers by the time I worked on trains. Later, some of the more senior managers who came from racial minority groups were not up to the job. It was similar with some female managers. (Note: I say SOME.) I sometimes wondered if particular staff from these groups were promoted just to 'make up the numbers' or even if there was a deliberate attempt to promote unsuitable people from certain groups so as to make a perverted point. Yet, at the same time, there were others in those groups who would have made excellent managers, but were overlooked. Indeed there were always excellent people from all groups. I must leave you to decide what lessons one can draw from this.

Many of the non-white staff were quite open about the race issue. Even when I 'overtook' some of them and was promoted over them, I found no acrimony from the vast majority. I remember one evening, when I saw a young (white) guard illegally walk cross the line. Afterwards, I spoke to him when the only person able to overhear was his (black) manager, Vince, who was senior in service to me, who had not seen the incident. The young guard became quite rude. I did not wish to make a greater issue of the matter, but Vince, who had diplomatically been pretending to doze in the corner, suddenly 'woke up' and remonstrated with the guard: "Why don't you shut up and listen? The Governor's just thinking of your safety". Vince was such a placid man; I'd never heard such an outburst from him before and never did again. Sadly, he died about a year later. We were invited to the funeral. It was the first Caribbean funeral I'd ever been to and was accompanied by a saxophonist.

I'm sure there was racism, but LT did not seem 'institutionally racist'. However, much later, there were accusations that some of the tests for promotion were skewed in such a way as to favour white, Anglo-Saxons. I understand a group of non-white managers sued LUL for unfair examination questions, allegedly causing certain groups to get poor results.

There were individual race issues from time to time. One crew at a depot I will not name consisted of a white driver and an Asian Guard. They would not speak to one another, other than when making the 'brake test'. At a terminus, the guard would get off the train, cross the lines illegally, walk along the other platform and then cross back again at the other end, so that he could swap ends of the train without passing the driver. When this was discovered, pressure was put on them the separate, as it was nonsense to continue like that. The friction was covert, so it was difficult to deal with as a disciplinary issue. It may well have been a case of 'six of one and half-a-dozen of the other' – I don't know.

There were many Indians and Pakistanis on the staff. In my experience, Indians seemed more willing to talk about racially-related issues. I remember one Indian driver telling me how, just as he was about to go to work early one morning, he received a telephone call from Heathrow Airport. A family who knew an uncle of his in India had arrived overnight without warning. They expected him to go to the airport, pick them up and arrange accommodation for their stay in the UK, because that's what his uncle had promised them. So he just couldn't come to work that day. He said he realised how English people would not understand such a situation, but he was duty-bound to drop everything and help these people he didn't know as a matter of family honour.

On another occasion, one of my colleagues went to sort out a vilent altercation between two West African ladies. One of them shouted: "It's not my fault: it's that f****ing African! They were of different tribes. Racism is not just a black/white matter.

On a different tack, I had as one of my staff an African man of about 40. He came to me one day to say he was about to be deported. He had come to the UK as an asylum-seeker 10 years previously, under an unfriendly *régime* in his home country. He had been allowed to work here while the UK government considered his asylum application. He had joined the

Underground and had been a train driver for some years. At that time, there was a national shortage of train drivers. This man was a decent, God-fearing man. He came to work regularly, did his job well and caused no trouble. From the UK's point of view he claimed no benefits, earned an honest living and paid his taxes, but suddenly the UK wanted to be rid of him. For some reason, LUL were unwilling to help me support his case and six days later he was put on a plane back to West Africa, despite the fact that other immigrants remained here, not working, not paying taxes and living off government hand-outs. Sounded daft to me.

We had quite a lot of homosexual people on the underground. We had a few lesbian ladies. I never encountered problems with this group apart from the incident I mention later.

On the Area Manager training course, we were given 'real life' incidents on which to comment, to see how we could handle such things. One of the incidents was when one of the trainers (an Area Manager himself) visited one of his stations and witnessed two members of staff having 'an intimate physical relationship' on a table whilst on duty. He frankly admitted he turned and left the station before they saw him and said no more. Another case was of a passenger who wrote and complained that he had seen the (male) Station Supervisor trying on a dress in his office. Yet another was when a manager appeared in a local newspaper report of a 'wife-swapping' party. We were assured all these were real incidents, but that would not be surprising in an industry of LUL's size.

On a lighter note, the last train on one of our lines was regularly seen away by the Foreman in 'long-johns' showing below his overcoat. He was obviously ready for a little shut-eye before rising for the first train. All human life was there on LUL.

One day, I was selecting a short-list of applicants for management posts. As I went through the applications, I found that two of the applicants claimed to have exactly the same experience in their lives, down to some quite specific details. Smelling a rat, I recounted what I had found to the others also vetting the applications. One of them then said that she had read a similar story in another of the applications. We checked it out and found it was indeed the same story, albeit that the third person had apparently tried to make the details slightly different. All three were from the same ethnic group. Coincidence? What is the fairest way of responding in such cases?

I once did a check of all my staff in a particular post I held. Of about 380, 51% were not white people of UK background. As well as black and Asian staff, there were Chinese, Cypriots, Greeks and Turks, as well as others, including the odd American. We had one American Station Foreman, known (including to himself) as "The Sheriff." He actually looked the TV image of one and it would not have been surprising to see him toting a Colt .45.

In such a situation, there were allegations of racial and other discrimination and they needed addressing. I mention elsewhere how I was blocked from promotion because of my religious beliefs. A young woman I knew had a rolled newspaper put up her skirt between her legs in a staff room, in front of other staff. Despite the fact that there were other women there who saw the incident, none would come forward as a witness, allegedly for fear of reprisals. Her (female) boss refused to follow the incident up (I don't know why) and yet that boss later became a 'Harassment Manager' (*see* below). These were but a few examples. I once heard a manager call a homosexual member of staff "scum". Such incidents do occur in a big organisation but were totally unacceptable.

Whilst steps should be taken to prevent such incidents, the later attempts by LUL to try and eradicate racism, sexism and so on went to the manic stage. The carrying out of the policy actually became more of a witch-hunt, with many casualties. PC ruled to an incredible degree. I'll elaborate.

When the new harassment policy was introduced to us, the 'positive' discrimination bias was clear. I asked the obvious question as to where white, middle-aged, heterosexual, male managers would stand and what about false claims. I was immediately pooh-poohed by the promoting senior manager. There might be a few frivolous cases, but no more, he assured me.

My experience was different. Within a few weeks, a particularly appalling case started. A member of staff put in a claim of harassment that involved nearly every manager he had ever had, plus numerous colleagues. The alleged incidents were said to have occurred before the policy was instituted. Despite the paranoid and neurotic way in which the claimant conducted himself, the matter was investigated to the nth degree. I suspect it was partly because it was one of the first claims and partly because the managers were inexperienced and afraid to be seen as unfair and possibly because the claimant was from an ethnic minority, whereas virtually all those he accused were white – but that does not excuse what happened. The man was interviewed time after time. He consistently failed to provide evidence that he said he had; he failed to turn up for meetings with his written reports on what he alleged happened; and most of what he said was unsubstantiated and insupportable. Yet a witch-hunt of nearly 20 managers and other staff ensued and one manager, whom I esteem to be one of the fairest LUL had, was eventually driven out of the company after 18 months of investigations without a shred of evidence against him. As he said, he didn't need the aggravation. Despite the behaviour of the claimant and the fact that he was off 'sick' for nearly two years, I don't think any evidence to back his claims was ever found. The cost in stress to those accused must have been enormous, apart from the financial costs. On one occasion, I witnessed a punch-up between the claimant and one of the staff he accused, such was the tension. I think the man who made the claim finally left LUL with the case never finished.

This was far from being a unique case. Managers whom I knew well were made the subject of harassment claims. They became so numerous that one could no longer believe they could all be true. Accused managers were sent on 'gardening leave' for months on end. Marriages were stressed; careers and health suffered. Yet, at the end, often nothing could be proved – yet neither could it be disproved. Some managers left LUL, rather than let it all drag on any longer, since they knew they could never cast off the slur on their characters. LUL lost a number of good managers over the issue. The injury to the company in the Stalinesque blood-letting must be enormous; not only to those directly concerned, but the consequent fear and consternation in others that made them loath to take reasonable actions, for fear of false accusations they, too, might not be able to disprove.

An element that showed itself was that people made claims of harassment as their performance-appraisal times approached. Since some of the claimants were poor performers, one is justified in wondering if their claim was a way of fending off a poor assessment by their manager.

I suspect that, in some cases, someone had said or done something unwise or silly - possibly after provocation - and the opportunity was taken to enlarge it out of all proportion.

I was accused of racial or sexual harassment on no fewer than four occasions. Twice I was challenged as being racist when I refused to consent to what a person wanted. On both those occasions, the person dropped the claim immediately they found I would not be blackmailed and insisted that they pursue the matter through the correct claim procedure. The third case was dropped after much investigation found no evidence. Yet another person claimed that my attitude toward her sexuality had influenced me to her detriment. The next day, she admitted she had accused me out of fear of an imminent transfer (which she had requested) to a place where she felt her sexuality would be unacceptable. She even thanked me for what I had done to help her. In each case, I had followed a course of action I would have done for anybody, claim or no claim. I was fortunate in that none of these accusations were pursued. As others have found, it is often difficult to prove a false accusation is false. I know the accusations against me were untrue. I find it hard to believe that this sort of thing only happened to me, so how many other accusations were false? These are serious issues.

Harassment Managers were especially appointed and trained to investigate these cases. I asked to become a Harassment Manager myself, as I believed my experience would have made me very good at the job. But I was told I could not be considered, because

I was white, middle aged and heterosexual. Homosexuals and people from ethnic and other minority groups were wanted. It was told that the reasoning behind this emphasis was that, unless you are lesbian, a single parent or black (as examples), one cannot appreciate the situation of lesbians, single parents or black people. I would have thought that the best person to make an objective assessment of any situation was a fair-minded person who was not biased. Using LUL's twisted 'logic', magistrates should be petty thieves and High Court judges should be hardened criminals, so as to fairly appreciate the cases they hear.

A number of Harassment Managers threw in the towel when they found cases that were expected to take a few weeks, part time, to investigate actually took many months and absorbed virtually their whole working life, as well as bringing much stress. Before the new system was instituted, I had been involved in a couple of similar cases and know what difficulties can arise in such hothouse situations.

After the policy had been in place 18 months or so, a Harassment Manager, whom I respected, told me that he reckoned at least 50% of the harassment claims were false. He was certainly not the kind of man to make wild claims. Whilst I can only accept that statement at face value, the fact that he told me in a low voice and would not dare have it repeated tells its own tale. It also accords with my gut feeling, based on things I heard and saw, although his estimate was even greater than I had feared.

I know of one manager who resigned from LUL because they were convinced that the PC criteria they were being forced to follow in choosing staff for promotion was intrinsically immoral and unfair, and they could not, in all conscience, continue in their job.

As LUL followed a path of trying to emphasise that all staff were equal, some thought others were more equal. Staff often feel aggrieved if someone gets promotions apparently because of a quota and not on ability. A (male) train driver recently said to a new (male) recruit who was seeking promotion: "If there's a woman in the queue, forget it; she'll get the job ahead of you". To a certain extent, it doesn't matter if it is true or not, the danger is in the perception. It does staff morale no good

With such a policy, it is not surprising if there are those who, if criticised for their standard of work, state it is because of sexual/racial/religious oppression.

There used to be (may still be) a senior manager responsible for representing the interests of female staff, which she did vociferously. LUL now has six Network Groups, charged with identifying common workplace issues for LUL to address, each providing a forum to share ideas and best practice, and give information about opportunities for personal development for a given group. Specifically, these groups are:

- A Women's Staff Network Group with three priorities: "improving workplace culture, encouraging flexible working practices and supporting personal and career development for women".
- A Faith Staff Network group, including provision of multi-faith quiet rooms, food products in the workplace appropriate to beliefs and seeking ethical investments for pension contributions.
- An Age Staff Network Group "to help all employees to realise their full potential no matter their age".
- A Lesbian, Gay, Bisexual and Transgender Network Group.
- A Black, Asian and Minority Ethnic Staff Network Group "to encourage equality and inclusion among staff".
- A Disabled Staff Network Group.

Should an organisation need such groups? The view of many managers, like me, was that all staff members are considered on an equal basis. It matters not their gender, sexual orientation, colour, politics, religious beliefs or race. The issue was essentially: can they do the job or not? And, if there is a case of promotion to a limited number of posts, the second question is: are they the best equipped person/s for it? Forget quotas, pressure groups and so on.

And whether or not all these make for a happier and more contented workforce is debatable, judging from grassroots comments which I hear. For example, a member of staff recently said to me "what about white, heterosexual males?" – *ie,* almost exactly the same query as I raised a decade previously!

I often wondered how many of the policies LUL introduced came as a result of the government using LUL to test out social engineering policies. Or is that too paranoid?

In any case, the foregoing shows something of the minefield in which managers had to work.

10 - MANAGEMENT ATTITUDES, REORGANISATIONS, THE "COMPANY PLAN" *etc*

Here we come to what must be the crux of LUL's problems. I have mentioned in passing, the attitude of LUL management. In most cases, by that I mean the approach of the higher management/directors, as many of LUL's Directors were working ones, acting as top managers.

One cannot but feel that LUL's management problems arose as a result of the political intervention following the 1948 nationalisation of LUL (then called London Transport (LT)) as part of the British Transport Commission. Indeed, probably, the amount of governmental 'interference' since that time will never be fully appreciated. I refer readers to books such as Christian Wolmar's *"Down the Tube"* and *"Broken Rails"* for a good overview[42]. Essentially, LUL had to fight for limited funds from the Treasury, which, as an arm of successive governments in the UK, has failed to fund transport adequately. The UK seems never to have fully appreciated the priority of transport and communication as part of a civilized society and for the success of Great Britain Ltd.

After the Second World War, Britain increasingly looked to the USA for patterns of behaviour, rather than Europe. In the US, rail passenger services diminished, being replaced by bus services or, often, discontinued with no replacement except private cars. Here some New Towns were laid out on a grid pattern, aping Los Angeles and similar US cities, on the assumption that the car was to be the mode of transport for all, consequently making them very difficult to serve by mass transit. Older towns and cities that still had them got rid of their trams. The bus was seen as tolerable for a time, as it could (it was thought) better mix with the car, which was king. Such writings as Colin Buchanan's Report[43], exposing the futility of such a policy, were largely unheeded, let alone acted

---

[42] Both Aurum Press
[43] *"Traffic in Towns"*, the Buchanan Report, HMSO, 1963. Shortened edition published by Penguin and HMSO in 1964.

upon. Public transport in general deteriorated and the London Underground system began to be neglected. The strikes of the 1950s did not help. By 1960, LUL (then LT), once leader of the world in urban transport, was on a downward slope.

The common choice to explain situations is usually between conspiracy and cock-up theories. In this case, it would seem to be a some of both. There were certainly cock-ups in LUL, both before and after the King's Cross fire[44]. But there also seems to be conspiracy.

There had been a less-than-happy coexistence between Conservative governments and nationalised industries, including LUL. The cold hand of the Treasury ruled and kept any management from managing in the full meaning of the word.

One example of the friction was the appointment of Dr Richard Beeching to oversee the reshaping of British Railways in the early 60s. He came from ICI at an unprecedented (on the railway) salary. When this price was queried, the government response was that, if you wanted good management, you had to pay. In other words, a version of the "if you pay peanuts, you get monkeys" concept. It also tacitly acknowledged that the normal BR management were not well paid. Not, mind you, that BR top management were monkeys. It is generally acknowledged now that any management who could achieve what BR's did with what they were given were miracle-workers. Compare that with their successors.

It was no good governments saying that private sector management was/is intrinsically superior to that of the public sector. Managers move from one to the other and, in any case, common sense shows that people are people and managers are managers wherever they work. I have a family connection with a large, well-known multi-national company and, when exchanging anecdotes, one finds that the same weaknesses and failings exist in

---

[44] This occurred on 18th November 1987. A small fire on an escalator suddenly erupted into a fireball. 31 people were killed, including a fire officer attending the incident. It had extensive ramifications in LUL.

both public and private sectors. Indeed, members of the armed services make the same complaints about their lords and masters.

No, the basic problem was the control by governments and specifically the Treasury, followed by the management they employed. Funding was a perennial problem.

Latterly, the situation became more vexed when a New Labour government took over. We subsequently had the additional complication of the newly-created post of London Mayor, who was to have control over the Underground, especially when it became clear whom the new mayor would be. I once tried to explain to some Continental friends the three-cornered situation that arose with Tony Blair and the Labour government; LUL management (largely influenced by their government masters); and the staff with their trade unions (at that time thinking that Ken Livingstone was their bosom friend and benefactor). It was not easy to comprehend, more difficult to explain and even harder to work under.

The conflict became more open as the mayoral election approached and even more so when Ken Livingstone took office. There were accusations that the LUL managers were 'dullards' and 'knuckleheads'. Such *badinage* hardly helped. I recall a meeting when a director came into the room brandishing a toilet brush, with the comment that it was seemingly all he was fit for. Ironically, he was one of the 'good guys'.

Against this political back-drop, a management grew up that, at best, 'held the fort' and was apparently incapable of serious development.

There was lack of vision. For example, a manager once bemoaned the fact that LUL had been offered a prime corner site for the entrance to the new Angel station, for £1. But, such was the indecision, that it was lost, with the result that the station entrance is now not so prominent. With the interference by politicians, it is hardly surprising that LUL management at the time had little vision – their expectations for the future had been severely curbed over the years. 'Just hold on and keep things ticking over for as long as you can keep the job with its perks' seems to have been the policy for many of those at the top of LUL. There were accusations that Freemasonry was rampant in LUL management - there was a Lodge at 55 Broadway - with the common rumours that membership was the key to progress in the company. What effects this may have had - if any - it is impossible to assess.

When I first joined LUL, many of those in higher positions had worked their way up from such lowly positions as 'box boy' (a lad who helped in a signalbox). They were proud of their career. In some respects that was beneficial, because they knew the company inside out – especially the operations side, which, after all, is what the system is all about. But it also meant that there was inertia and even stagnation. Others were 'officers', who, by and large, seem not to have appreciated developmental needs. But the dynamism of the Ashfield & Pick[45] era had gone. New blood was needed, but the aversion to 'college boys' that existed amongst some in LUL militated against such a transfusion. And complete organ transplants would have been rejected totally. Maybe, like Shakespeare's Julius Cæsar, they believed men who thought too much were dangerous. Or perhaps, in mitigation, Richard Bowker's recent description of British Railways senior management as

> "held back by the organisational and structural straightjacket, and the institutionalism that characterised all nationalised industries in some form[46]"

applies also to LUL.

There was even a rejection of the use of computers at one time. One Area Manager was taken to task for printing up reports on his new home PC. His boss stated that hand written documents remained the correct way to do things. Fortunately, that attitude was soon changed.

---

[45] Lord Ashfield and Frank Pick, who headed the Underground in the 30s. Herbert Morrison (later, Lord Morrison of Lambeth), the prominent Labour statesman, called them a *"formidable pair"*. They *"were not succeeded by anyone with comparable drive and ability to take London Transport forward."* Quoted in *"The Moving Metropolis"*, Ed Sheila Taylor, Laurence King Publishing, 2001.
[46] *"Modern Railways"*, April 2008.

Political pressure following the King's Cross fire was an incentive to get outsiders involved. Unfortunately, it is wrong to think in Orwellian terms that *post*-King's Cross management was the 'four legs good' and that *pre*-King's Cross management was the 'two legs bad'[47]. One kind of poor management was replaced by a different management with different failings.

During my time with LUL, virtually all the most senior positions came to be taken by outsiders, many of whom had little or no idea of how the railway 'ticked'. The correct solution was to have a cross-fertilisation within management, with insiders and outsiders balancing out. Unfortunately, the baby-thrown-out-with-the-bath-water situation applied, as it so often does.

About the time I entered the management grades, in the wake of the King's Cross disaster, the structure of LUL was being reorganised, particularly with regard to front-line management, which had been criticised in the Fennell Report[48] on the incident. This was continued by an initiative known as the 'Company Plan'.

The symbol used in association with the Company Plan was a rising sun; but many managers suggested, with good reason, it was actually the sun setting. I believe the Company Plan and what it brought was the beginning of a dreadful slide in LUL's fortunes. I hope I can explain this in what follows.

The incumbent MD, Denis Tunnicliffe, introduced monthly open meetings for managers, held in places like the Central Halls at Westminster, to allow as many as possible to attend. They were introduced to try and keep managers up-to-speed with what was happening in the company at a time of significant change. I think it was at the first forum that he asked managers to ask him any questions. He seemed genuinely taken aback - even shocked - at the anger and frustration then forcibly expressed by many managers from the floor. At the time, I watched him and

---

[47] George Orwell: *"Animal Farm"*.
[48] *"Investigation into the King's Cross Fire"*, Desmond Fennell QC, published by the Dept of Transport, 1988.

wondered if he really did not understand the legitimate points they were raising or if he were a darn good actor. I even felt sorry for the man, brickbats coming from all directions, but found it quite staggering that he should (apparently) have been so out of touch and unaware of the deep current of feeling at the time. He should have known. Possibly, his advisers sought to keep the truth from him. LUL always had its quota of yes-men and -women with their smiles and false *bonhomie*. My boss once stated that, if a certain MD had a problem with flatulence, his *coterie* would immediately comment on the nice smell (only he put it rather more crudely than that).

These meetings degenerated after Denis Tunnicliffe left. I complained to my manager that it seemed a waste of time going to a meeting that only told me more or less what I could read in the *Evening Standard.* Increasingly, we were just being told the Company Line – not the truth, the whole truth and certainly not nothing but the truth.

Various managers responded with their own ways of making it clear they were not being fooled. One used to look out of the window when some patent falsehood was promulgated. "Just watching the pigs fly by", he would say. At other times, he would give a quick burst of the theme tune from *"The Twilight Zone"*. My favourite was the one who carried a small set of wind-chimes in her handbag – shaking them gently when some other improbability was expressed. It was an insult to LUL's middle management that they were treated as if they were so gullible. One manager became notorious in his group for his exasperated "What ARE we doing?" It was a wonder morale was not much lower.

One of LUL's answers to the challenge of Fennell was to make many more managers. But this was done without checking to see if the right calibre of people was available in sufficient numbers and, secondly, without ensuring that throwing managers at the problem was the right answer. My experience is that less managers of a good quality serve better than more who are not up to it.

For example, on one pair of lines there had been team of about 24 managers. Everybody knew everybody and communication was fairly easy. The lines of communication between two people are two – one in each direction. Between three people, the lines of communication amount to six, and, between four people, 12: the rise is exponential. Almost overnight, the number of managers on the two lines rose to about <u>ten times</u> the original number.

Change in an organisation - especially a big one, with a long history, like LUL - is not easy and needs good, solid management. To increase the number of managers by such a proportion in a time of great change was a serious mountain to climb. I don't believe the huge communication task that had been created was ever done - it certainly wasn't done well.

At the time, it was reported that the MD had told some of the new middle managers to "enjoy themselves for two years". If true, it seems to imply that he envisaged a honeymoon period, when managers would be able to jog along in their new positions. It sounded a dangerous philosophy, as strong change-management was needed. The new system took a long time to bed down. Indeed, I don't think it ever worked well and almost immediately became the subject of tinkering and later numerous restructurings.

The manager making actually became farcical. At one station I know, each member of the staff was called a manager of something (*eg,* Heritage Manager, Community Relations Manager, Gardens Manager) until the concept was quashed. Somehow, being called a manager went to many people's heads. Managing is more than wearing a different uniform or badge. Many never appreciated that fact.

The case of one keen, newly promoted manager still amuses me. Although he was supposed to wear the manager's uniform, he always seemed to wear a new suit. He also put his new ID card in a transparent wallet, which hung in a very noticeable position on his chest. His whole demeanour shouted "Look at me: I'm a manager". He reminded me of a character played by Russ Abbott, the comedian. Abbott played a RAF officer in flying suit, wearing a white scarf. To give the impression of speed, the scarf was stiffened as if it was being forced back by the aircraft's slipstream. This new manager used to stride though the office, his ID forced back on tape as he went - as with Abbott's character - giving this great impression of speedy new management on its way to sweep clean!!

To compound this, LUL seemed to believe that one could make people managers simply by training them into the job. If they did not at first succeed, they trained them some more. The training course for the grade below that at which I entered management has now become a year, I believe.

LUL did not seem to realise that being a manager, like being an artist, is a mixture of instinct, skill and innate ability. One can take someone with the latent talent to be an artist and train them to bring out that talent; but, if artistic ability is not there to start with, a life-time of training will not produce an artist. One might create a painter, perhaps, but not an artist: there's a big difference. It's the same with being a manager. A promotion process was created, whereby anyone who could talk about being a manager was promoted. And what a mess they made, whilst there were frustrated well-qualified would-be managers, who were denied the chance, because they could not verbalise their ability in the designated way. If one commented on a new manager's failures, one was told they were on a learning-curve. But one often wondered which way the curve was going.

The fact was that many of these people were good supervisors, but not managers. I knew a number of excellent supervisors, who were never managers in action, although they were made managers by name. And that's no insult to them. They performed well at their original jobs and made the railway run like a well-oiled machine. I'd be glad to have my quiver full of them. But, no, dogma required they be called managers and put in a different uniform. The Peter Principle again. It is now recognised that such poor managers can seriously damage the health of a company by irritating the workforce and even provoking litigation

Some time after they were put in position, LUL tried to rectify things by ensuring that all those in the starter management grade did a work-based course of the National Vocational Qualification type. One *ex*-supervisor-become-manager stated he would not do it. His boss told him that, if he did not, he would be reduced in grade. He said he didn't care; he had reached the point in life where he didn't want the hassle and could afford any reduction in pay. Last I heard, he was still in his management job, because LUL changed their policy again and the *status quo* was maintained – after hundreds of managers had gone through the course.

We were all sent on another management course which took up an afternoon a week for many weeks. It was a 'sheep dip' – in that every manager was supposed to go, irrespective of whether they needed it or not. I suppose an argument was that it should produce consistency amongst the managers, which was certainly desirable. But there was no check that the course had been effective and the net result was that, in general, the good managers remained good, the not-so-good remained not-so-good and the poor ... It was yet another example of LUL throwing money at a 'problem', without proper analysis or checking on its effectiveness. I still have the 'prompt cards' we were given on the course, to guide us when interviewing people. Mostly, it was just common sense.

As all these changes hurried on, those members of staff who had remembered the 'good old days' and who dared to say the word "but" were considered dinosaurs and one felt that there was much rejoicing at their departure. Shades of Orwell's *"Animal Farm"*.

Many people, inadequate to their tasks, were put in places of authority. Peter's Principle applied with a vengeance. Don't get me wrong, LUL still had many staff and managers, who were good at what they did. But they became 'diluted' by the others. When we had the daily visits by the Fire Brigade (of which more *anon*) they came to distrust what they were told by these new appointees and soon they came to distrust almost everyone.

I mention in Chapter 8 how I managed to circumvent the system to get a potential manager placed. But that was a rare occurrence. Fortunately, the new system was not foolproof and good managers did still manage to get promoted. Eventually the weakness of the system became apparent – but not before the railway's performance declined drastically. Incidents that should have been cleared up in 10-15 minutes took over an hour, often due to the incompetence and lack of confidence of those overseeing the situation[49].

A great flaw in the changes at this time was the breakdown of the business into sectors. Station and train managements were now divorced. Until then, the two had been run closely, with local Area Managers managing both. When you know that LUL considers that the greatest place of risk in its operations is the interface between a platform and a train, to split the business at that very point seems madness. But so it was. The lowest grade at which both trains and stations were jointly managed was the Line General Manager, which was far too high for day-to-day, let alone minute-by-minute management. Later, the point of unity was raised still higher. No wonder fragmentation took hold. Melvilles's theorem applies: "That which you disintegrate administratively will soon disintegrate practically."

The break-up was a case of so-called 'business' considerations over-ruling operational common sense.

There had always been a sort of rivalry between train and station staff, but now it became antagonistic. If station staff were asked to assist in a situation involving trains, many just said that trains were nothing to do with them any more. The higher management decision to split the two activities gave force to that view and the concept soon filtered down. Whereas an Area Manager could view a potential conflict situation with equanimity, now it could escalate into a mutual blaming game.

At the time, many AM's said that re-integration would soon follow. It did not, but the General Manager of the Metropolitan Line, in an interview much later, stated that it was necessary to integrate station and trains' management teams, to aid efficiency, so they were being increasingly moved physically closer to one another[50]. What a shame it had taken so long to be appreciated.

---

[49] *See* comments later in Chapter 18 ,"How Good is the Underground"
[50] Interview with John Glover, quoted in "*Modern Railways*", December 2004

Why not have a single management team? But re-integration is always more difficult than disintegration[51] - that's Melville's follow-up theorem. How much time, money and effort do we waste on ill-thought-through management ideas?

It is often asked why other transport modes can have fragmentation, but it doesn't appear to work well on railways. For example, airlines and ship-owners do not own the sea and air ports their vehicles use; road-hauliers don't own the roads they run on. Why not fragment railways? The answer seems to be negative, as a consequence of being a fixed track system. It is like a production line and one divorces one part of it from another at one's peril. We have seen this widely in the UK.

There was an effort to recruit new managers with so-called 'business experience', as that was one of the things it was felt the earlier management lacked. But the 'business' ability seems to have been at the expense of understanding how our business worked, which seems madness to me.

Interestingly, the managers who oversaw stations were called Business Managers, whist the trains' managers were called Train Managers. It was as if the stations were the business and the trains a side-line. What a skewed perspective. Our business was a railway – and, as such, we ran trains. Yet it followed the thinking of government departments which always saw money-making activities as more important than money-spending ones, even if the latter were where the work was done. But most people only come to a station to catch a train, so that's what our business was (and is).

This, of course, parallels the process of national rail privatisation, where making money, became the business and providing a service secondary. The inevitable result was that operational issues became undervalued and thus neglected.

---

[51] This is no new concept! Virgil (70-19BC): *"Facil descensus Averni:/ [...] Sed revocare gradum superasque evadare ad auras,/ Hoc opus, hic labor est"*. Simply translated and paraphrased, it means it's much easier to go downhill than come back up!

How has this come about? It seems to stem from a traditional attitude in Britain, where practical people are considered lower in status than academics. This is a similar dichotomy to that propounded by CP Snow as "The Two Cultures". I think it's in his book *"The New Men"* that one of Snow's academic characters refers to nuclear physicists as "garage mechanics". Mrs Thatcher, when UK Prime Minister, allegedly stated that, if they were any good, BR management would be working elsewhere and that only losers travelled by public transport. Such an arrogant (and stupid) attitude was still alive and well at that time. Incredible damage that has been done to Britain's railways by this new style of management; LUL was not alone in being seriously affected by it.

Hands-on management is essential. One of our managers was asked on a visit to North America how he would get staff to get their trains away from termini in a timely fashion. Essentially, he said you have to watch them and chase up tardiness. On LUL, crew reliefs (when a train changes crews en route) have always been an irritating source of delay. The relieving crew is supposed to be there on the platform BEFORE the train arrives. An old-style manager, Dave, at the north end of one of our lines, kept up an old tradition by making it his business to be on the platform in person each morning rush hour – and woe betide the crew who delayed their train on his patch! Unfortunately, that was another feature of LUL operations that became lost as new management views took root.

Some time later, a General Manager was shifted from his post because of his line's poor performance. One of the first things his replacement did was to get his managers out and about in the old style, like Dave. Performance improved overnight.

Another of our managers paid a visit to a metro system in Canada, which had been modelled on LUL practice of the late 50s. He was given a copy of their Rule Book, which was a masterpiece of clarity. It consisted of punchy 'dos and don'ts' that left staff in no doubt as to their responsibilities – and also stressed that ignorance of the rules was not an acceptable excuse. LUL could have learned a lot from that.

One of the things that concerned me greatly was the way many very senior LUL managers simply failed to appreciate the way their railway worked.

We live in an age where people are increasingly aware of eco-systems; that if one tampers with one aspect of nature (such as a rain forest or a river) one can cause untold damage elsewhere. Yet we now had top managers who seemed unaware that a transport system such as a railway is an eco-system, not just like many other organisations. There seems to be a belief amongst those with MBAs that one can apply standard 'one size fits all'[52] management principles unchanged any- and every-where, in any situation, be it a hospital, a biscuit factory, a school, funeral company or a farm. They blunder in, applying their management concepts in the belief that they will work universally, failing to appreciate what they are doing. Britain's railways and LUL in particular show the folly of all this. We have the equivalent of rain forests chopped down or a river dammed, with surprise at the consequent disasters. Rather than a process of evolution, top management have tried revolution with its attendant bloodletting. Stalinism in miniature?

One example of management failure to understand basics was when a train derailed in a depot. A colleague was taken to one side by a Very Senior Person and asked to provide a report for the MD on how it had happened. He pointed out to the VSP that the MD already had the report in his hand. He was then asked for a report in simpler form, so that the MD could understand it. So he produced one side of A4 with pictures.

Another example: LUL had a group of staff called 'Operating Officials'. These were of Area Manager grade or above. They were able to instigate certain safety-critical actions, such as reversing a train in a single-track tunnel. As it goes totally against the signalling system, you will appreciate that such a movement can only done with great care and co-operation, to avoid a head-on collision. But one did not get to the grade of Area Manager without considerable experience and training (remember the 90+%

---

[52] It should be "one size fits nobody".

pass requirement?). Now, however, people were installed in the equivalent grades <u>without</u> any such training and experience, let alone an examination. Following a security alert, a new manager evacuated everybody from his very large station, including a train in one of the platforms. A train with passengers aboard was stuck in the tunnel behind the evacuated one. Now, when an experienced manager knows the railway has stopped for any reason, one of the first questions asked is "are any trains stuck in tunnels?" It is easy to concentrate on the epicentre of the 'incident' and forget such trains, which also need urgent attention, especially if they are full and/or the weather is hot. This man ignored the lot for about an hour. When I later remonstrated with him, he said he assumed that we would just reverse the train out of the tunnel. I asked him if he had any idea what that involved. He laughed: "Oh, I don't know anything about operating," he said, totally oblivious of the potentially dangerous situation he had caused. He saw only his station, not the railway as a whole. Yet he was an 'Operating Official', not by any experience or training but simply by being in the grade. Dangerous nonsense. Yet this was far from unique.

Today, one reads of railway companies "refocusing on operations" and "facing up to customer requirements." What twaddle. By what common sense or business goal were these twin basic needs ever lost sight of?

The latest concern about risk management accepts that operational management is one of the key elements in reducing risk – yet LUL senior management did not seem to grasp this.

Furthermore, LUL said it wanted to move from being what it termed 'Operationally Focused' to being 'Customer Focused'. Sounds impressive, but what does that mean in real English? I'll give you an example, as given by top LUL management to staff and managers. Operationally Focused concepts included:
> *"We expect our staff to follow laid down procedures."*

The Customer Focused equivalent of that was:
> *"We encourage and trust our people to do what they feel is best for the customer."*

Let's take that from theory, de-bunk it and try and put it into a real-life situation. We have a railway line, with stations and signals along it. Most sensible people, including those on the proverbial Clapham omnibus, would say that we want drivers to stop trains at the stations and obey all the signals. Does it really matter if they do so in fulfilment of the first or second statement above? Logically, one would think both would achieve the same result.

But no. I came across a significant number of drivers who had passed red signals and carried on because (they said) they were concerned about the delay to their train. That is what happens if you

> "trust our people to do what they feel is best for the customer"

and if you don't expect them to

> "follow laid down procedures".

If you have proper 'laid down procedures', they will achieve what is 'best for the customer'. Allowing the outcome to depend on what each person feels is right is a recipe for disaster.

Frankly, I see no reason why staff should not follow both of the above maxims!

Looking again at the document we were given at the time, propounding this new change to so-called Customer Focused attitudes, I find it as hard to believe now as I did then, that it (with a page of similar stuff) was a serious proposal. It is full of empty verbiage. And there was nothing about implementation. At best, all this Modern Management Gobbledegook was not taking us forward and, at worst, it opened the door to anarchy.

As a contrast, here a couple of quotes from Roger Ford[53] – a true professional in the railway business. He says we need

> "total commitment to running the railway by the book, all day, every day. It's called professionalism and it's very hard work. [54]"

---

[53] Roger Ford AInstRSE – see Appendix
[54] "Modern Railways", October 2000

But, he points out, it also delivers a better service:

> *"...[B]etter operational and engineering management can produce significant reductions in delay minutes without massive expenditure. Running the railway properly, with a relentless focus on minute by minute control, can save an awful lot of delay ...*[55]*"*

He's not alone. Gerard Fiennes'[56] view was the same:

> *"Running a railway safely and punctually is first good planning, second persistent attention to detail and third shouting the odds at the right time and at the right people."*[57]

No prizes for guessing which of these two approaches I plump for!

Notice in the above that LUL contrasted being focussed on railway operation as being inferior to being focussed on the customer/passenger, having failed to realise the vital link between the two. After a few years of all this in LUL, it seems the penny dropped. The lack of operating experience led to the recruitment of managers from other transport organisations, but not before immense harm had been caused. Indeed, only recently I read that LUL, had revived its apprenticeship scheme I mentioned in Chapter 2, as it is now seen as an ideal way of training people to positions of responsibility. Like other apprenticeships, staff joined from school and learned the various aspects of the railway before following their chosen path. A spokesperson said that the company was rediscovering the value and importance of apprentices as an investment for the future. The aim is to have, in 20 years, top managers who were apprentices[58]. I immediately think of one of the most practical managers LUL still has (there may well be more), who was once an apprentice. What a shame it has taken so long to come back to basics.

Following Denis Tunnicliffe, we had other MDs, who lacked even his transport experience.

---

[55] *"Modern Railways"*, January 2008
[56] The late GF Fiennes MBE, MInstT, MA, erstwhile General Manager of the Eastern Region of British Railways. *See* Appendix.
[57] *"Modern Railways"*, February 1968
[58] *"Railnews"*, March 2007

A classic statement was made by one MD after a fiasco over a timetable. Everybody who knew anything knew that what was being asked for in the timetable was doomed from the start, as it was totally impracticable. One of the basic faults was that it involved train drivers from half a dozen different depots changing crews on trains to a level of three changes in an hour at disparate places, sometimes with two crew reliefs within five minutes. And this kind of thing was to be repeated with scores of trains, running at 2-3 minute intervals, over the whole day for many weeks. Remember what I just said a few pages back about the potential for delays in crew reliefs. Of course, it never worked from the first morning and, after a few days, the rosters were completely rewritten, with the crews being given a bonus for their inconvenience in changing duty times. The highly experienced man who was forced to write the original rosters told me that he had kept copies of all his e-mails protesting at the scheme's impracticability, so as to be ready for when a PTB (person to blame) was needed as a scapegoat. In fact, the failure of the scheme led to an amazing announcement from the MD at a managers' forum. "We have found," he said, "that, if we push the railway too far, it will break." This was the equivalent of a head of a health authority standing up in front of a convention of nurses, doctors and surgeons and saying "We have found that, if we don't sterilise surgical instruments, disease will be spread."

On another occasion, when there was a driver shortage, this MD applauded the decision of one of the other directors to cancel off-peak and weekend trains rather than rush hour ones. "Isn't it good to have a director who's an economist?" he beamed from the stage. Rubbish – it was a perverse operating decision. With trains arriving every 90-120 seconds, the odd rush-hour train need not be missed. But, with a late evening 10-15 minute service in the suburbs (as on the east end of the District), with staff shortages and absenteeism, plus trains taken out of service due to vandalism, the controllers were hard-put to keep a half-hourly service or worse some evenings. The rush-hour person has paid his fare: what incentive is there to take the train at the weekend, paying extra fares into LUL's tills, if the service is unreliable? LUL has more than enough peak customers – it needs off-peak custom to boost the revenue and fill empty seats. Is it a wonder that managers lose confidence in their lords and masters with barmy decisions of that kind?

He also cancelled the annual 'Steam on the Met' event and he got rid of the excellent Flagstaff House Training Centre, to which I refer in Chapter 7. Steam on the Met was a great Public Relations Happening, where steam trains ran over a week-end or two (often in conjunction with a canal festival, carnival and classic bus operation). Included were special trains for school children, disabled people and staff. Flagstaff House, by then, was open to other companies as a conference centre. The MD said these things were not 'the core business' and must go. I got the impression he didn't really care.

This MD really showed his true colours when he came to leave LUL. When his new job was confirmed, he started making snide public comments about London Mayor Ken Livingstone and Transport Commissioner Bob Keily. If he had really felt that way, he'd have obtained more credibility by sharing his feelings before he had another job lined up. He hadn't lasted long - and neither did his successor.

That was another problem. The top management kept changing. It is impossible to run an organisation the size of LUL properly without adequate continuity. Toward the end of my time, we had an HR director who seemed to understand what was happening. But he only lasted a year. How can one get confidence, understand issues and deal with them in such a short time?

Sometimes, the evil that top management did lived after them and the rest of the management and the staff was left sorting out the results (I give an example below). A colleague referred to it as the pigeon-style of management. A pigeon flies into a room, does what pigeons do all over everybody, then flies out, leaving the mess to be cleared up by others. But that's not unusual in business, I suppose.

Another MD seemed to have even less touch with reality. He used to strut about the stage, telling us of all the lunches he was having with influential people in London. His ill-considered promises to Londoners of lavish cash-back compensation when the Central Line closed for weeks on end caused incredible pressure on staff. One felt he just loved being important. I think he eventually stopped the series of open meetings for managers. The story circulated that he left us to manage deck chairs at a south coast resort.

Both these later MDs joined and left LUL with no appreciable benefit to the company revealing itself. A colleague remarked that they passed "without trace"!

Reorganisations were also a feature of LUL. Gerard Fiennes[59] quoted the maxim
> "When we re-organise, we bleed."
His advice:
> "Don't reorganise; don't, don't, don't."

A reorganisation is only of use if the result benefits the re-organised company beyond the damage done by the reorganisation itself – otherwise it becomes the equivalent of the medical statement that "the operation was a complete success, but unfortunately the patient died".

But the railway has not got better.

A book was written in the 1920s on how the Underground was run then[60]. I have a feeling of *déjà vu*, when I read of ways the Underground conducted itself then and which we were now reintroducing as if they were new.

Just one example. The operators at that time believed 40 trains per hour on a line were possible, whereas, today, 30-33 seems the maximum achievable and we have had to cut back on those figures in some cases, after experimentation. It was recently announced that one line is to have an expensive new signalling system with

---

[59] *"I Tried to Run a Railway"*.
[60] *"Handling London's Underground Traffic"* by JP Thomas MIEE MInstT, then Operating Manager, Published by the Underground, 1928

automatic running of trains, but there will still be fewer trains than were actually run years ago using old-style signalling and manual driving. Some progress! In a number of cases, longer trains were run and/or trains that missed out certain stations, thus speeding the service. Why was it possible to do more in the 1920s (and the 50s) than we can do now with expensive equipment? The reason must surely be that the staff had experience, were disciplined and could be relied on to do their job to a very high standard and were better managed.

LUL loved projects and initiatives. It looked as if someone was DOING SOMETHING. Many times, it was using a steamroller to crack a nut. Often, LUL had a procedure already in place to tackle an issue. The problem was that the procedure wasn't being used. But instigation of new initiatives without ensuring people followed procedures was a waste of time. If staff were failing to follow the existing procedure, would they follow the new?

A strange effect was that these projects/initiatives were implemented with much trumpeting as if they were new, yet they often were not. One initiative was to have specific staff to deal with getting trains away from platforms in a timely fashion. This had essentially come about as a result of the division of trains and stations' management. Seemingly, the staff could not be said to be despatching trains for legal reasons. I went to a discussion group on the project and pointed out that we had had staff doing for years what was being haled as an innovation. I even brought some staff from one of our best stations and asked them to describe what they did. But the leader of the implementation team could not accept that what he had planned was not new.

A particular personal irony for me was that the planned system included a refinement (the use of a 'baton' like a small tennis racquet, which had been used on Continental European railways for decades). I had suggested this 15 years before. On LUL, many staff had previously waved a newspaper or their hat, to try and stand out from the seething crowds on the platform. When I had suggested batons, the idea was turned down because (I was told) passengers might be hit on the head with them! Now, with many more passengers on the platforms, that was not considered a danger. As often happens, it's not what you say but who you are that affects the outcome of an idea.

When implemented, a new project frequently failed in its effect because of lack of staff discipline. For example, I once saw one of the new train departure staff wave his baton whilst a family were caught in the train doors, only a few feet in front of him, separating a small child from its parents. I managed to stop the train and sort the matter out. Afterwards, when I asked him why he gave the signal to start, he said that the doors of the train were already closing. He seems to have totally forgotten any safety considerations. But, since the prime reason given by management to have these staff on the platforms was to despatch the trains in a prompt manner, his skewed vision was not so surprising. Despite protests to the contrary, time-keeping could take priority over safety. Frequently, the trains left without the 'right away' from the person with the baton, making the process a waste of energy.

Another initiative was concerned with ensuring that information was correctly passed around from station to station and to other interested parties at times of disruption. But we had a perfectly good system for years, which had fallen into disuse.

If a system is thought to be failing, the staff should be made to use it, then have it analysed to see if it has any flaws. It is no good inventing a new system and providing new kit if they are not going to be used either. This seems so basic.

Of course, it is desirable to give staff suitable equipment and systems, but it is just as vital – indeed, even more so – that everybody does their job correctly. Some do, of course, but consistency is needed. This was an aspect that LUL increasingly failed to ensure over the years I worked for them and performance inevitably suffered as a result. But much money was spent trying schemes to compensate for the poor staff performance, rather than tackling the root problem.

This highlights one of my pet themes: to get people to do their jobs properly. If you have committed staff with bad kit, you will normally get a better result than good kit with a staff that doesn't use it properly. Fortunately, LUL had many good staff at the lower levels and they worked hard to make things work, often despite the odds. For that reason, I am happy to reiterate that they were (and are) the heroes of the piece.

There is an argument in favour of engineering oneself out of a problem – *ie,* providing equipment that avoids a problem area. But if this is done to the extent that the staff thinks that it no longer matters if they do their job well or not, a bigger problem arises.

You may well have noticed in a number of these cases, the re-inventing-the-wheel syndrome that seemed to have got into LUL. Systems were abandoned for something new and then re-introduced months or years later. What a waste in the meantime – and very frustrating for those involved in the operation of the systems.

Sometimes, these initiatives were undocumented and conflicted with others, making things worse.

One very senior manager caused problems by his 'instant management', without considering the effects. As an example, the staff at one station was quite correctly collecting excess fares from passengers using that station, at which the passengers' tickets were not valid. This caused friction at times. When one of the staff mentioned this to this senior manager on one of his visits, he told them to stop collecting the fares as "good customer relations"! Not only did he thus undermine the local management (with whom he failed to consult), but common sense. On that basis, let's not charge anybody to travel: that would be good customer relations – and bad business! But that knee-jerk response is typical of him …

Licensed busking was something advocated for a long time by some of us, but LUL resisted until, one day, it was heralded as a great new idea. Until then, the staff had a wearying and time-wasting war of attrition with buskers, many of whom were very good. Presumably it was another case of who had suggested it that caused a change of policy.

Until about 12 years ago, LUL used the Question and Answer (Q&A) system of instruction for staff training. Essentially, this took the student from what he knew to understand how the railway worked. For example, a question as to what happened with a bicycle if the rider stops peddling, when the bike is going down-hill, introduced the point that an electric train will coast, like a free-wheeling cycle, if the electric current that drives it is switched off. This teaching method built up confidence and knowledge in the student and also enabled the instructor to know the understanding of each student was by the answers they gave. LUL abandoned this for more modern instruction methods like Computer Based Training that were used by the students. But many of these methods only taught without ensuring that lessons were learned. I recently read that LUL has just returned to the Q&A method, introducing as something radically new! They also had a model railway and imitation station, which were scrapped. They have also recently been re-introduced as an innovation!

LUL was very wobbly about pay rises and this caused middle managers problems. LUL negotiators would make an offer, then add a bit and then say it was their final offer. But after more haggling they would then offer even more. This farce became a yearly tradition. One year, managers were told to interview as many staff as they could and impress on them that the offer being made really was the absolute limit LUL would go. After all the previous annual vacillations, the managers naturally didn't want to look stupid and asked if this time it really was the final offer. They were assured it was. They went up the hill once more and did what they were asked. But (you guessed it!), after more pressure from the TUs, LUL again gave a bit more! – once more undermining their managers' standing with the staff. Yet another reason for managers not to trust the hierarchy at 55 Broadway.

Another time, managers were told to interview as many staff as they could on a one-to-one basis and record their intention or not to strike. The majority of staff said they would not strike but, when the day came, did so. Peer pressure was greater than management pressure.

I was part of a representative group formed by top management to advise negotiators on the 'grass roots' situation, just prior to a new pay offer. The idea was that we had more of a feel of what was meaningful to staff. We were asked to give an opinion on how the negotiations should proceed. The group agreed almost unanimously on 2 or 3 things that we felt would be positive and 2 or 3 things we must not do. The next week, we were told of the new agreement, which had been signed the day after we made our suggestions. We found that not one of our suggestions had been followed. Indeed, in two cases, the exact opposite of our advice was part of the deal. But I'll speak more on the vexed issue of staff relations later.

Mind you, this kind of thing was par for the course. Over the years, I participated on a number of brainstorming sessions – you know, where ideas are written on flip-charts all around the walls. At a number, I had a sense of *déjà vu* – indeed, repeated *déjà vu*[61]. At one of the sessions, I spoke to the American chap running it. "Look," I said, "we were both at a session like this two years ago, when you asked the same questions and got the same answers. What's the point?" He looked at me with a smile: "Your management want us to do it again." Why should he care? - he was getting good pay for what he did. A few years later, I went to yet another session, where again the same questions were asked, with much the same answers. Mac, a senior manager I had known and respected for years was there. At a tea break, I asked him if the Directors kept asking the same questions, as they did not like the answers they were getting, and hoped they'd one day get the 'right' answers. He looked at me, shrugged and gave one of his enigmatic smiles. We both knew it was all just a game ...

About this time, I got another new boss. He came to introduce himself and, within minutes, was telling me a confidence, which he said he would deny if I ever repeated it. None of my bosses had ever lost me so quickly! How can you trust someone who blatantly betrays a confidence and then says he'd lie to protect himself? I resolved to have as little to do with him as I could get away with.

---

[61] *déjà vu bis?*

Just before I moved on to my last job in LUL, we had yet another reorganisation. My then boss moved on. A colleague and I were also about to move. One Monday morning, a fellow manager said to me: "Do you realise its 10 o'clock and there's been no call from [the Line Management office] to ask about the train cancellations this morning?" True. This colleague had always got all the details as to how and why, ready for our previous boss' regular check-up. But it did not come. From then on, we received no enquiries as to why things had gone adrift. It was a precursor of the new way of managing and of the decline that followed.

My loyalty was always to 'the company' rather than to 'the management'. The latter came and went with dreadful frequency. One felt that many had little if any loyalty to the company themselves: LUL was just a stepping stone along their career path to bigger and better things. I did have personal loyalty to my immediate boss and my colleagues. And I knew that the railway would not have functioned at all, had it not been for the daily dedication of many staff, willing to keep their train or their station or their signal box or their office functioning to the best of their individual abilities. It is to those unsung heroes that the credit is due for the continued operation of LUL.

My personal feeling was that people like Keith Bright, Tony Ridley and their team probably did as well if not better than some later top managements – but they were sacrificed after King's Cross[62]. Frankly, unless the person concerned has really been guilty of serious wrong-doing, what is the point of them committing *hari-kari* or being made to walk the plank? They usually leave with no financial loss - even a gratuity - and end up with a better job. Surely, they should normally be forced to stay and get the organisation out of the mess they are accused of making. As I suggested earlier, a number left whatever cock-ups they had created for the regular managers and staff to cope with as best they could.

Let me give you a simple example of this.

---

[62] *See* Appendix

We had an agreement with the TUs over medical retirement. It was more than fair to staff overall, but it contained a very restrictive clause, that seriously hindered its management. I spoke to my Employee Relations Manager (ERM) about it. He said my interpretation was too legalistic. He said the clause meant something different. I pointed out that, whatever he liked to think it meant, what it said was what the TUs insisted on. And, if we interpreted it another way and the matter went to an Employment Tribunal (ET), they would interpret it the literal way as well. He felt I should act on his interpretation, but I knew that would be unwise. He was unhappy about my stance, but, shortly afterwards, he left the company. Some cases soon went to Tribunals and, as I anticipated, they decided that the literal interpretation was the one we must follow, not the ERM's version.

The main point I'm making is this: During my researches into what the restrictive words should mean, I finally managed to find a lady who was on the committee that drew up the document. She explained what had happened. The committee was chaired by a very senior manager, who was nearing retirement. The Trade Unions had wanted this restrictive clause in the document, but the management side didn't. The arguments continued and this senior manager's retirement got ever nearer. She admitted that the clause had finally been left in, as the chairman wanted the document to be agreed before he retired with the *kudos* and so he capitulated to meet the deadline. He left for another good job and we were left with the unsatisfactory agreement. I wonder how often that sort of thing happens.

Possibly the most dangerous philosophy in LUL - and probably in any business - was the "we are where we are" stance. It was said with such depth of feeling and assurance that no-one seemed able to speak against it. But I believe it to be not only one of the symptoms of the *malaise* into which LUL had fallen but one of its chief causes. As a simple, pragmatic statement about a given situation, which must be faced, it is fair comment. But the idea seemed to be to continually wind the clock back to a 'year zero' every time something went wrong and start again. I know that today is the first day of the rest of my life, but it's madness as a business policy. Its failings include not asking "how did we get here?" "why are we here?" and "where did we go wrong?" It considers these useless and a waste of time, besides which they might show up an error in management. But it is far worse than that. Refusal to ask diagnostic questions and dealing with every problem by throwing some 'new' idea at it is a flawed strategy which reveals profound arrogance. If we don't know where we went wrong last time, we are likely to do it again.

"We are where we are" takes its place along with "we must learn the lessons", "we must draw line under this affair" and "we must move on" as glib statements, not actually examining the causes of what has happened. But I've lost count of the times I have heard top managers trot out these slogans.

How can we really improve? As I said, I saw numerous initiatives with people trying to re-invent wheels. I'm all for seeing if there is a better way of doing something. But one should also ask if there is an old solution to what might not be a new problem. Much valuable time could be saved by re-visiting old ideas, dusting them off and finding that they may well work again. A blatant example of this is the hand-held whistle. A number of Train Operating Companies (TOCs)[63] and LUL have found that simply blowing a whistle has made significant effects on shortening station dwell-times and expediting the despatch of trains. One can't get much more basic than such a very low-tech tool. Would a 'blank sheet of paper' project, with a multi-discipline working party and umpteen international consultants (at huge fees), have come to that conclusion? I doubt it.

So the moral is to have a healthy look at our origins and development. To quote the well-worn statement of George Santayana: *"Those who cannot remember the past are condemned to repeat it."* At the very least, it would be wise to listen to those who do remember and indeed were part of it, not ignore them. LUL used to move on in the past by standing on its firm achievements and taking calculated steps forward. *Festina lente*

---

[63] *See* Appendix

(make haste slowly) is not a bad maxim. That is the safe way to
go.

11 - DISCIPLINARY BOARDS (DBs) AND THE DISCIPLINARY PROCESS

Having already mentioned the importance of staff discipline, we need to see what LUL's procedures were in this regard.

LUL's disciplinary process was in line with the ACAS[64] guidelines. Simply stated, if staff were repeatedly absent, committed an error/s or failed to act as they should, there was a process of advice and warnings. These generally started informally, with what is called "a word in the ear" and then continued through staged, formal, written warnings.

Unlike most shop- or office-based staff, many railway employees spent a lot of time on their own, not working in an office environment, so their performance was only generally known if seen by a manager or if a member of the public made a complaint. Self-discipline was therefore a vital part of railway staff's make-up and that is what made railwaymen, over the years, a responsible group, with pride in doing their job.

As I explained earlier, much of the day-to-day management was done by Area Managers. Whilst they had offices, they also spent much of their time out and about around the railway, conducting inspections and seeing the staff in action. Thus they were likely to detect particularly good or bad performance and could take suitable disciplinary or other action. With a small group of managers, each was aware of what others in the team may have experienced – and there was consistency. For example, one AM would say to others "Watch guard A. I saw him doing ... the other day." The Traffic Manager held a card index, so repeated offenders could be easily distinguished from those who made an occasional slip up. If an AM saw poor performance, he would consult the TM, to see if it was a 'one off' or habitual by the person concerned and take action as appropriate.

---

[64] The National Advisory, Conciliation and Arbitration Service.

But this disciplinary process was weakened by the managerial shake-up that followed the Company Plan. Now the out-and-about management was segregated from the office-based managers of the staff. It became very difficult for those monitoring staff to follow up and ensure bad practice was stopped. The poor performers soon realised they were more than likely to get away with their poor performance. This was aided by the introduction of amendments to the disciplinary system which were suited to an office or factory environment, with staff normally in one place, but not suited to a workforce that was continually moving about and thus not visible to their 'own' managers.

Assuming the disciplinary process was invoked, if a member of staff committed a grave error or repeated a series of lesser errors they could end up at a Disciplinary Hearing.

A Disciplinary Hearing was a simple sort of court with a Disciplinary Board (DB), who were actually the persons judging the case. It was formal, but the very formality of the DB gave weight to the seriousness of the situation and allowed all parties opportunity to review the matter in a cool and calm way. At least, that was the intent.

The board or panel consisted of two senior managers, who had no previous involvement with the matter in hand. They reviewed the whole case and decided on one of a range of possible outcomes, such as cancelling out the record to give a completely fresh start, reverting to a lower level of warning (a 'second chance'), an escalation of level of warning (eg, "you've now had two chances, another offence and ..."), a change of job or (most seriously) dismissal. Papers laying out the issues were prepared and distributed to the panel, the member of staff involved and a person he chose to accompany him (an advocate). The advocate was usually a TU rep, but could be a workplace colleague, who was not his manager. There was a supporting member of staff from the Employee Relations' Office, to take notes and give advice on procedures, but who otherwise took no part. Some of the TU reps were skilled at making a case to get their 'client' off. Often, they had very little to work on, the case was so tight.

Involvement in DBs gave an opportunity to use various aspects of managerial expertise in arriving at a solution and a fair outcome for all involved.

With DBs, as with investigations generally, I am a great believer in the OMF philosophy. OMF stands for 'One More Fact' and was introduced to me forty years or so ago by that old sage, Dan Archer of *"The Archers"* radio series. Dan and his son were discussing an Ambridge situation. Dan warned his son not to make up his mind in advance, telling him about OMF. One can decide, he said, and then - out of the blue - find out that new factor, the One More Fact, that changes one's whole perspective.

I experienced this often. After reviewing all the information that had been presented, the diagnosis seemed obvious. Then something new would emerge at the Hearing. It might not change the facts - perhaps a difficult domestic or health situation was revealed, or the involvement of another member of staff - but it might influence the action to be taken. For example, it might seem obvious that a Train Operator had made a serious error. Every piece of evidence would support such a conclusion. But then someone would say something like "But the Station Supervisor at X said/did ...." This had previously been unreported but, if found to be true, could change the disciplinary decision, if nothing else. By all means have a working hypothesis in an investigation, but always be ready for that new information. One can end up with egg on one's face, if one carries on without being open to that.

One problem was that staff often used ignorance of LUL rules, regulations, procedures and so on as excuses why they had done wrong. It is accepted generally that ignorance of the law is no excuse. It certainly shouldn't be in a safety-critical job. The Canadian metro rule book I mentioned earlier had a very clear rule that LUL should have had:

> *"All employees shall know, understand and obey all rules which apply to their work.*
> *Employees may be disciplined for breaking a rule. You may not say that you did not know the rule or did not understand it."*

Many times, I had staff in front of me, seemingly oblivious of the seriousness of what they had done. On more than one occasion, I went through their actions and pointed out what the outcome could have been – a dead colleague or passenger. On too many occasions, I saw their faces go white as the seriousness of their actions finally dawned on them for the first time. What made me angry was that they had not seen the problem themselves and neither had their TU rep pointed out the seriousness of what they had got into.

I recently saw an interesting TV programme on Indian Railways. Whilst the camera showed a poster announcing 'DICIPLINE MAKES A NATION GREAT', a railway official was talking about a disciplinary matter he was about to oversee. His statement was much as I would have said, to the effect that his aim was not primarily to punish but to get people to do their job properly. I often said to people who were before me on some charge, that I could do nothing to change what they had done – I could only do my best to ensure they never did it again. If they could persuade me they never would, all well and good. If not, then I could prevent them from repeating the error by removing them from the job where they could fail again.

All too often, I had no confidence that they would not do the same again and then I took their driving job away – either reducing them to a non-driving job or sacking them. Likewise, fraud in a Booking Office could often only be dealt with by dismissal. This may seem harsh, but it was the only way to definitely prevent a repetition of serious error or malpractice. It also sent a message to other staff that the matter was, indeed, serious. And if a manager allows a person to continue in a safety-critical job in such cases and they then cause another incident, is not the manager at least complicit?

If you think that's severe, how would you like to think, next time you travel by train, ship or plane, that the driver or person in charge did not know how to do his job safely nor what to do if things went wrong? - or cannot be relied on to act correctly in an emergency.

Unfortunately, over the years, the disciplinary system became so complicated and the process of writing a DB charge, with all the associated paper-work, so lengthy, that some managers just couldn't write one correctly and others found it not worth the effort. Numerous cases foundered as a result of poor preparation of documentation. I oversaw a case where I had to let off a habitual poor attendee because of a paper-work error three years before.

This was another example of 'back-room' staff formulating procedures they rarely if ever used. DBs in office environments were not as common as in the station and train grades. For example, a train manager saw a member of staff open a train door as it pulled out of a platform and into a tunnel. (The perpetrator had been a train driver, put to alternative employment for medical reasons, so he knew how to do it.) This was a serious incident that could have resulted in injury or loss of life and the colleague who witnessed the incident advised the man's new manager that a DB would be an appropriate forum to decide the case. She became very embarrassed and admitted she hadn't the faintest idea how to go about arranging one.

The DB papers were supposed to be checked for accuracy by the Employee Relations' Manager's (ERM's) Office, but errors still got through and staff often got off on a technicality, when any 'man in the street' would say they should have been sacked. I remember being asked by a lady in the ERM's office to have a quick look at a set of DB papers "for interest". She had not turned away before I said that "if I was the DB chairman and this was presented to me, I'd have to throw it out." She looked at me in amazement and I showed her a glaring error in the second paragraph on the first page that would, indeed, have blighted the whole case. She stammered: "But X and Y have already looked at it and said it's OK." But she agreed that the document was seriously wrong and hurriedly took it away to be corrected before it was distributed. That was far from a lone case. The ERM's office also often failed to pick up on a technical/operational issue because of their lack of expertise in certain areas. I'm all for fairness, but it was crazy to have a system that was so fragile. It actually prevented justice.

As an aside, I often despaired of our Employee Relations department. Many of the key staff there had no idea of how other staff actually behaved or what their work entailed. They were thus naïve in their judgements and this extended to their compiling of procedures and policies. From speaking to those in outside industry, this does not seem confined to LUL.

I recall one DB, before the system became so bound in red tape, when a colleague, R, and I were the panel. R had done his homework. "Mr M, he said, I've done some sums. You've worked with us for 8 years and, in that time, you've had two and a half years off sick." M was sacked. A few days later R heard his name called, as he was on an escalator. It was the same man, leaving for somewhere up north. R expected a stream of abuse, but the chap openly admitted he'd been shocked at the statistics that had pointed out. "No hard feelings, Guv." He accepted he'd played the system for years and finally been caught. But that case was by no means exceptional.

R was good at DBs. I once watched him lead a man to fully admit his errors, after he had confidently entered the room, certain he could bluff his way through as he had before. He left looking bewildered that he had lost his case. Justice had finally caught up with him, too. After he'd gone, I told R I had seen a master at work. "What do you mean?" he asked. "I saw the way your mind was working. You were thinking: 'If I was sitting in his chair, I would be working out how I could I fool this stupid manager' - and then you asked your question accordingly to prevent him." He roared with laughter. He had done exactly that.

At DBs, other staff, such as TU officials and managers, could 'sit in' for training purposes, taking no part in the proceedings. On one such occasion, the TU official entered the room and slumped into his chair. After the chairman had made the customary introductions and explained the procedure, the TU representative said he wished to make a statement of TU policy. The chairman said he was prepared to accept such a statement, if put in writing, but couldn't say if it would have any affect on the outcome of the Hearing. The rep wished to read it out, but the chairman gave a short adjournment for him to write it and hand it in. He came back with it written in pencil. The rep was told what he should have known, that anything in pencil would be valueless and he must re-write it indelibly and sign it, which he then did. It was just a political blast against LUL and its procedures. But an observer, from central Employee Relations, who was sitting in, was astounded at the TU rep's performance. The chairman was not sure if he was believed when he said the attitude was not unique, even if more extreme than some he had witnessed.

On another occasion, the TU advocate made some unsubstantiated statement, which the chairman easily repudiated. He then said to his 'client', "It's no use; they're going to sack you anyway" and began to pack up all his papers. The chairman ignored him and carried on with the Hearing. After a few minutes, the rep realised no-one was talking to him any more. So he un-packed his bag and joined in again. Such histrionics were all too frequent. And, all too often, the reps got away with it.

At another DB I was part of, the TU rep started shouting and threatening us with all sorts of dire repercussions in law and that he would take the matter up with the MD if we continued the case. The panel chairman decided to dismiss the case rather than become embroiled in any unpleasantness. The member of staff was obviously amazed that he had got off Scot free with his misdemeanour. I was livid, but the decision was not mine to make.

But many TU reps were much better than that and were let down by the few. They readily admitted their member had done wrong and, sometimes, that they were unfit for their job and a danger to themselves and others. I always tried to support such TU reps. Sometimes they made a good defence of their 'client', or make a reasoned case for leniency. If so, I would say so in my summing up.

As people realised that bullying by TU reps would work, those expert in such tactics became much in demand as advocates, whilst the 'reasonable' ones were ignored.

One TU rep I know left his union in disgust at the situation. He could still represent staff as a 'workplace colleague', as allowed in the rules, and he did so effectively.

But the relentlessness of the TUs in trying to make their members fireproof took its toll. Managers who gave a fair decision and suspended or sacked a serious offender were often not supported by higher management.

I cite later (in the chapter on SPADs) a case where a driver of an empty train passed a signal at danger, over-rode the safety device and carried on. The panel sacked him, but, on appeal, a more senior manager gave him his job back. At the time, another reorganisation was in process and I suspect he didn't want to hamper his chances of promotion.

On a similar occasion, a top manager overturned the DB decision, making an excuse that the panel had not taken a fact into account. It was pointed out that he was wrong; it had and their deliberations had been fully covered in the minutes and Chairman's Summary. "Well, I've made my decision now," he replied. Later, when I was discussing this with a colleague, he told me that this manager had recently said to him that "I'm not going to an Employment Tribunal at this stage in my career." His de-motivation was thus clear!

A driver was sacked for throwing a coffee machine at his manager. His case was taken up by the TU officials and LUL higher management gave him his job back. A few weeks later, this driver was promoted. A member of the panel that had sacked the driver tried to avoid ever taking another DB. That shows the insidiousness of such lack of support by management at the top: it permeated down and rotted the basic disciplinary system of LUL.

Another driver's train was derailed after he drove over wrongly-set points and ignored a stop signal. He admitted he had not looked at either the points or the signal. Yet he suffered no adverse action from his serious neglect. Indeed, shortly after, he, too, was promoted to a post where he trained other drivers.

Such lack of backbone in top management made the processes weak and ineffectual. It all had implications for safety, which I will deal with later.

12 - STAFF RELATIONS and TRADES UNIONS (TUs)

As you may have come to realise, this issue was a great weakness in LUL's set-up. I am a firm believer that good customer relations can never be achieved in an organisation unless it first has good staff relations (another of Melville's theorems). But 'good' does not mean weak[65].

In the 1920s, JP Thomas, the Operating Manager of the Underground at that time, wrote

> *"The company firmly believes [that] the fostering of the spirit of camaraderie [is essential] for success."*[66]

I'm afraid that was not true of LUL in the 1970s. There <u>was</u> *camaraderie* and *esprit des corps*, but it came from a sense of united purpose amongst many staff, not from above.

Every year or so, LUL surveyed its staff as to their attitude toward the company. There was usually a poor response, even when incentives to return the survey forms were offered. There were good points, but the survey frequently revealed general dissatisfaction. Interestingly, one repeated complaint was that good employees were not treated better than bad ones and there was a lot of truth in that.

Originally, LUL and its predecessors provided many facilities for their staff. There were football, cricket and shooting clubs, Sports Days, Institutes/Clubhouses and so on. Perhaps the day for those had passed, but I found many who still enjoyed them. One by one they were abandoned, including a good library, which was closed with about a week's notice "because the space was needed". I never discovered what happened to the books.

The company had a Staff Suggestions Scheme, but it seemed to be run half-heartedly and only when there was someone to sort the

---

[65] I came across this quote from TS Lin, Chairman of the Taiwanese Tatung Company: *"There is an English proverb that says 'there are no bad students, only bad teachers'. I believe this also applies to a company. There are no bad employees, only bad managers."*

[66] Quoted in *"Handling London's Underground Traffic"*, ibid

suggestions. I had a number of suggestions accepted and others turned down. It was amusing but irritating, over the years, to see a number that had been turned down subsequently implemented. One, regarding the re-scheduling of late night trains, was implemented six months after it had been shot down in flames for the most obtuse reasons. When I made a fuss, it was agreed that my suggestion had been the catalyst for the changes made. Again, it was not so much what the suggestion was as who made it that influenced its implementation. Many in higher management thought train drivers stupid, whereas that was far from the case. I once went to the Divisional Office to collect an award. After about half-an-hour, a lady I knew there came out and said she was very sorry, but there was no-one to see me. I said I bet there would have been if I had committed some error. She was embarrassed as she knew it was true. I still wish I had told her to tell the manager to leave the award until he had time to see me, but I did not wish to put her in that position.

One feature of the staff conditions that LUL needed to radically address was train staff toilets. One toilet I recall never had soap, hot water and toilet paper available at the same time. One (female) senior manager wrote a vitriolic paper on the poor toilet facilities for female staff – but she cited the worst stations as being some run by British Rail and not LUL. In fact, male staff had endured poor - and often worse - toilet facilities for years. LUL should have heeded the advice of Sir Peter Parker, when Chairman of British Rail:

> "Take the loos – I've always believed industrial democracy starts in the lavatory"

Very true.

Lord Sieff of Marks and Spence wrote in a similar vein:

> "Top management ... must eat in the employees' restaurants ... visit the washrooms and lavatories. If they are not good enough for those in charge, they are not good enough for anyone."

But that probably applies to much of UK industry.

The Directors of LUL were very keen on obtaining Investors in People (IIP) accreditation. A lot of time and effort was expended, but we failed (allegedly) over some paperwork short-fall. Nevertheless, we were assured that the IIP team thought LUL was wonderful. The manager responsible for the process was very excited at the compliments he received from them. A year later, LUL got the accreditation and the IIP logo went on the LUL notepaper. Every member of staff got an IIP badge to wear and large IIP plaques were delivered to display in each office. In fact, many managers and staff were furious, as they felt it was a merely a paper exercise, that the company wanted the status and that it was a travesty of LUL's true staff relations. Managers left the plaques lying tucked away somewhere, often still wrapped. One admitted he'd put his in a skip. Another did not put it up, so his boss sent a man with a screwdriver to do so. As soon as the man left, the manager took his own screwdriver out of his desk drawer, took the plaque down and screwed it back up, facing the wall. These were not the actions of stupid people. They were incensed at something which, in their view, had nothing in common with the real relationship between the top level of LUL and the staff. As to what all this says about the true value of IIP accreditation, I leave you to judge.

There always seemed a groundswell of discontent in the organisation.

In a large company like LUL, some sort of staff organisation like a Trade Union seems necessary. I am generally in favour of Trades Unions, having been a member of appropriate unions almost all my working life and held various offices in a TU branch that had over 1500 members. I think many managements would not treat their staff well if they could get away with it. A lot then depends on the relationship with the Trades Unions that represent the staff.

LUL's Operating Department – that which dealt with the running of the trains and stations – negotiated with three Trades Unions.
- ASLEF – The Associated Society of Locomotive Engineers and Firemen. This was essentially for those in the line of promotion to train crew. Since any station person (other than a Booking Clerk) could pass through the grades to train crew, at that time station staff could join ASLEF (I think that has now changed).

- RMT – The Rail, Maritime and Transport Union. The rail part was formerly the NUR – National Union of Railwaymen. All station and train staff could join.
- TSSA – The Transport Salaried Staff's Association. Then mainly for clerical, supervisory and management staff, but station staff may now join.

There was a degree of rivalry between these three, varying in intensity at various times. I understand that the notice board for one union had a picture of the Churchill Insurance nodding dog affixed, implying the union always said "yes" to anything management said!

LUL was generally far too soft with its Trade Unions and I wonder how much governmental interference influenced this.

As time passed, managing staff became more and more fraught. Managers were supposed to manage, but with greater and greater restrictions – like the Israelites having to make bricks without straw. One irritation was that, whereas in the past I would make a decision on whether a thing was practical and necessary, I would later need to know if such and such a decision was currently 'politically' acceptable or not for some reason.

One day, after a number of drivers had reported a signal not operating correctly, I went out with one of our TU reps. I drove the train over the section concerned and we agreed that something was not right. I said I would contact the Signals' Dept to try and progress the situation. About an hour after I got back in the office, I got a call from my boss. He said he had heard that I had driven a train. (I'd been driving trains for nearly 20 years by then and still had my certificate.) I said I had (I often did). He said LUL top management had agreed with the unions that managers would not drive trains. I pointed out why I had done it and that the TU rep, the rostered driver, was with me in the cab at all times. He said that made no difference. When you realise that part of a manager's rôle is qualifying new drivers and the yearly re-assessment of qualified drivers, this seems madness. Can you imagine Department for Transport Driving Examiners being banned from driving cars?

It was good for managers to know what their drivers were doing and good for the staff to see their managers understood. Sometimes, when giving a potential driver his practical test and I saw him making an error, I would drive the train to show him where he was going wrong. I recall another occasion, at a station with a steep approach, having a short drive with one of our more awkward drivers. I stopped the train correctly, using the Westinghouse brake. As we waited at the station for the guard to open and close the doors, the driver let out a deep breath, turned to me and admitted: "Oh Mr Melville, I had you down as one of those managers who just tell us what to do. But you can actually do it." I think that makes my point.

On another occasion, when a number of train drivers were on strike, a train full of passengers arrived at a station, *en route* to Heathrow Airport. No relief driver was available. Rather than leaving the train there or putting the train in the depot after making all the passengers get off, two managers (trained to drive trains) drove the train to the airport. Most people would think that the right thing to do. If drivers are free to strike if they wish, others should be free to take over if qualified. But, rather than being thanked for their initiative, these managers were censured for their action.

This was just another case of LUL management *kowtow*ing to the unions.

Managers should not be autocrats. But I do believe managers should manage. And that involves accepting accountability and taking responsibility. There would also seem to be a place for an enlightened management to involve the TUs and staff in some aspects of management. But that, too, involves them taking accountability. Sadly, they often wanted one without the other.

Often, a pragmatic approach to a situation was best. Normally, staff had a free pass for their own travel. They were also allowed facilities for their spouse, although this was amended to allow for a 'housekeeper' for those men with a less formal relationship with a lady. One of my guards changed the picture of his 'housekeeper' from his old girlfriend to that of her replacement. It was quite innocent: he had changed the lady, so he changed the pass accordingly. But he was breaking all the rules. One National Rail TOC had complaints from homosexual staff that they were discriminated against, as the facilities pre-supposed a partner of the opposite gender. This incident prompted me to suggest to our HR[67] director that we adopt a realistic stance and give the second pass to a nominated person, who could be the employee's parent, partner or whomsoever they wished. This should stop all the allegations of discrimination. In my view, it would take the wind out of a lot of sails and probably save an expensive legal wrangle sooner or later, such was the PC climate at the time. My idea was rejected, but I understand that one of the Train Operating Companies introduced a similar policy a year or so later and that it has since become common practice.

Staff would often unofficially modify their duties to suit their convenience. Normally, there was nothing unsafe about such practices, although they may sound so to the uninitiated. A work-study ('time and motion') expert knows that workers will always seek to change work-practices to what they perceive as their advantage. They then feel that they have 'scored' over their employer - 'bucked the system' or however you like to put it - and have a measure of control over their work. It can be good policy to allow some slack in systems of work to allow for this. The view is that it's preferable to allow latitude that one knew staff would take, rather than close every obvious loop-hole, with the possible consequence that workers would find another short-cut that might be unsafe or at least undesirable.

Staff Reps could well have been involved more in aspects like the allocation of duties and holidays, as the staff was considerably affected by such issues. An example: the decision as to who worked at Christmas and New Year was made by managers, although there were criteria agreed with the unions to try and ensure a fair distribution of work and time off. But, one year, the

---

[67] Human Resources. I use this term because it is a current convention, although I do not like people being referred to as merely a resource. At least 'Personnel Dept' begins to accept people as people.

local TU reps at a depot said they were not happy with the way the manager did the job and wished to do it themselves. In fact, I believe the manager who distributed the duties was very conscientious and fair. But, he allowed the reps to do it and gave them the job well in advance of the holidays. The weeks passed. Staff kept asking the manager when they would know what they were doing over the holiday period. He referred them to the staff reps. Disquiet grew. You will guess what happened. The reps brought the whole thing back, saying they couldn't handle it, as there was so much pressure and the job was far more difficult than they thought. So the manager did it after all.

I recall another fair-minded manager, who sought to take action against a new female member of his staff. Whilst working at his station, she became pregnant and everything possible was done to help her do her work. Despite all this, she had repeated altercations with managers, staff and passengers. He gave her a severe warning, pointing out that she had breached the conditions of her probation. He said he would give her a final chance and extended her probation by two months. She did not improve and so he tried to terminate her employment. He was then told he couldn't; if he had thought her behaviour so bad, he should never have given her a final chance. In fact, she did not improve and eventually she parted company with LUL. About two years later, we heard of a woman who had stabbed someone in a South London Job Centre and found it was this past member of staff who had wielded the knife.

Another issue, which must affect other industries too, was that management negotiators came from socio-economic groups B and C1, whilst many employees came from groups C2 and D. The management didn't seem to realise the differences in sub-cultural view-points and thus misunderstood expectations. Many years ago, I had an older friend, who was a Director of a company in the printing industry. He was repeatedly thwarted in trying to bring in a simplified pay-structure. He was a very fair man and assured me that it would not be to the detriment of his workers and would stabilise their income week by week. But their negotiators wished to keep the existing system, with various bonuses. They felt they were getting something extra that way. LUL eventually brought in a salaried system, with the same pay, whatever day or time of day or night the work took place. But many workers felt they should get enhancements for 'unsocial hours'. It's a question of viewpoint.

At one stage, one of the directors seemed to take pride in being 'one of the boys'. She even went about dressed in a station staff uniform. Another was spouting on about 'green shoots' of change from the TUs, when anyone with their ear to the ground knew otherwise. The same morning as this statement was made, I had found a case (one of a number) where TU reps were running rings around managers because there was no support from above for a challenge. Whilst on the one hand, we were buying back so-called restrictive practices at a high cost in increased salaries, directors were giving into TU requests for more restrictions on the amount of work staff - especially Train Operators - had to do.

I quite understand that TUs will try and protect their members, but there must be limits. Years ago, TU reps would admit to not wishing to represent their members in some cases, because they thought their behaviour unacceptable. One rep said to the manager in charge of the Disciplinary Hearing that he personally thought the member of staff appearing before the panel deserved to loose his job, but that he had to represent him, because he was in the union. But, later, the culture of 'them and us' seemed to lead the majority to the view that anything went if it attacked management and so they would defend anyone, whatever the rights and wrongs of the case were. Despite drivers claiming to be 'professional', the TUs seemed quite willing to accept unprofessional behaviour on the part of their members, even where it had threatened the well-being of colleagues.

One day, I was in the office of one of the LUL directors, whom I consider to have been one of the 'good guys'. He'd asked me to wait as he was trying to sort out some issue. After a few minutes, the senior HR manager entered. "Do we say 'no' or agree?" was the gist of his query. "What's the point?" the director replied. "If we say 'no', we'll be overturned when it gets to the end of the corridor [ie, the MD's suite]". When the HR manager left, the director just gave me that hopeless look, said nothing and we got on with our business. Not surprisingly, when an opportunity arose, he left LUL for a location as far away as possible. How could one truly manage under such control and with such a lack of a cohesive approach? Another experienced manager stated that directors were afraid to take firm steps on issues in case they lost their jobs. No wonder one could drive a coach and horses through LUL management. It explains much that happened.

Alan, a manager of great experience, was 'removed' from his job at an hour's notice because the TUs made strike threats. His 'crime'? Trying to get his staff to do their job efficiently and correctly. This sent shock-waves around LUL's middle management and a very angry meeting was convened by middle managers to vent their displeasure. To be sacked for failing to reach targets was one thing, but to be effectively disciplined for doing what one was supposed to do was another. At least two other managers reported that their TU reps asked them threateningly if they wanted the same treatment that Alan had got. The TUs had tasted blood, not for the first time.

This kind of thing undermined the will of many managers to manage. A new manager asked an old established colleague how he was handling his local TU reps. "I just give them what they ask for," he replied. "If I say 'no', they just go over my head and get someone to change the decision." The older manager retired on health grounds shortly after.

This attitude gave rise to a joke: "Do you know, LUL management are taking over the National Lottery. Now every week will be a roll-over week." And the top brass wondered why operational performance and attendance deteriorated.

On the other hand, the occasional maverick manager would try and 'take on' a Trade Union rep or official on his staff. I had one TU rep, with a very bad reputation, transferred to me. I was warned to "watch him". When he came, he requested a day's additional training. One of my managers said he thought the rep was 'trying it on'. I knew that he should be treated no differently from any other member of staff. When I asked exactly what he wanted and why, it did not seem unreasonable. It was difficult to contest his request and an extra day's training seemed not worth arguing about, so I gave the OK. The manager concerned seemed to think I was 'being soft'. But, after his training, the man settled into his job and I never heard another squeak from him.

I suppose the old axiom of 'give and take' applies. Sometimes, one gave a little, so that, when one needed to refuse something, the reps could not accuse one of "always saying 'no'". Unfortunately, there were TU reps whose idea of 'give and take' was that LUL always gave and they always took. Even more unfortunately, there were a number of managers, including those in senior positions, who went along with that.

The *naïveté* of some managers was amazing. A local TU rep once come to me, asking, "What kind of idiots do you have in senior management?". I did not answer him directly (I sometimes asked the question myself), but asked what had prompted his query. He had been on a working party, examining how staff lateness and absence should be dealt with. Now he knew – and anybody who had been at the front line of the railway knew – that at that time we had a stupid system in that, in one category of our disciplinary procedure, lateness was considered as the same as a day's absence. So, some staff, once they were (say) half-an-hour late, would 'phone their manager and ask if they had been 'booked' late and so lose some pay. If the answer was "yes", they would often decide to take the whole day off 'sick', for which they would get paid and still be no worse in the disciplinary system. But, when this scenario was suggested at the working party, someone on the management side said in horror: "Oh, I'm sure no-one would ever do anything like that."

I'll give another example, told me by a long-standing *ex*-officer of one of our TUs. His union had been negotiating with management over an issue for a few months. The LUL directors were being taken for a ride, but they didn't seem to realise it and were about to agree to what the TU wanted. However, at the meeting where it was to be ratified, an old-time staff Staff Manager, C, turned up for some reason or other. As soon as he saw C enter the room, this TU official turned to his colleagues and whispered "we've lost it".

Indeed they had. As soon as the subject came up, C saw through it and it was not conceded. If he had not been there ...

On another occasion, the TUs asked for something they could hardly dare expect. They were amazed at their luck, when the newly-promoted LUL negotiator (a very senior manager, now promoted to an even higher position) agreed. They were so surprised, that the rep tentatively pointed out what the agreement would entail for LUL. The negotiator still agreed. He just didn't seem to realise the implications, but it cost LUL a fortune in overtime, imposed a very restrictive working practice on the company and much disruption to passengers.

These were by no means isolated occurrences. The trouble was that management often sent reps for their side that had no experience of front-line management, whilst the TU reps were very aware of day-to-day issues and 'on the ball'.

In my experience, many local reps were more than ready to 'play fair'. But, as time passed, those who pushed for further concessions were more likely to get elected. As top management were seen to be more and more ready to concede things, the TUs milked the processes for all they could get. It was easy to see what was happening, but one was repeatedly counselled by the HR department and other senior managers to "wait until next time" before taking action. When the next time came, of course, the reps could always quote the precedent of the previous occasion, which had been allowed.

An experienced manager, S, was asked to manage a key group of TU reps. He found office accommodation for them on LUL premises and they were given full office equipment, mobile telephones and the like by LUL. They were supposed to drive trains normally for most of the time, but allowed so many days off each per month for TU duties.

From the outset, they sought to circumvent the agreed conditions, claiming all sorts of reasons why they needed more time off from train driving. Yet they claimed that S was wrong in asking them to account for their time (even though they were still LUL staff and paid by LUL). The situation became such that many of them were driving trains one or two days a month at the most. But LUL top management repeatedly refused to back S or curb the reps' excesses. They even stated that they hoped the TU reps would soon be able to fairly manage their time themselves.

On a visit to the TU reps' offices one day, S saw a notice on the wall:

> *"Rules:*
> *1 – Do whatever S says;*
> *2 – See Rule 1."*

Another manager complained that the TU reps were using the offices and all their facilities to wage a campaign against LUL management and had combative notices on the walls of their office.

One day, S received a telephone message from someone who said that he wanted to meet a certain Employee Relations Manager in a pub to discuss a forthcoming Disciplinary Hearing, with a view to getting it stopped. The caller said he would bring some papers with him. He obviously had not realised to whom he was speaking. Such interference with the disciplinary process was akin to trying to influence a judge.

On another occasion, S was told to allow the TU reps to take time to go and brief managers on a new LUL/TU agreement. S asked why management reps were not doing so, since the TU reps might be tempted to give their interpretation of the agreement to their advantage (as if!). He was told that the agreement had been largely written by a senior manager, who had just left the company, and there was no manager left in LUL who knew the agreement well enough to undertake the briefings. Incredible.

I once asked an Employee Relations Manager why LUL gave so much. His reply astounded me: "Well, we think that, if we do, sooner or later they'll respond." Of course they didn't; they just squeezed harder. It amazed me that someone, whose job entailed working so closely with people, could have such a naïve assessment of human nature. A line from John Le Carré's *"Tinker, Tailor, Soldier, Spy"* sticks in my mind:

"Like anyone who's got everything, he wants more."

Another problem was that TU relations were divided amongst so many different managers and directors. There was an overall laid-down system for negotiations, with appeals to higher authority in case of disagreements, but it was frequently circumvented. For example, local issues were supposed to be negotiated locally with the local manager. But, if the reps didn't like the answer they got, they would not only try the agreed appeal process, but wheel and deal until they could find anyone who would agree to what they wanted. Divide and rule applied. On one occasion, a manager (quite rightly) refused something. Over the next 24 hours, I answered the 'phone about half-a-dozen times. The calls were from different TU officials, asking for different top managers, who were all away at some day conference. Their calls had been diverted to someone near me, who had forgotten to switch his calls elsewhere. It was obvious that they were working their way up the LUL hierarchy, trying to get the decision overturned. That time they failed, but frequently they succeeded.

Whilst TUs were frequently getting around procedures and front line managers got no support from above when they complained, any alleged breach of procedures or agreements by LUL managers aroused howls of protest from the TUs.

The long-time TU officer I mentioned earlier stated that anarchy had taken over. He said that, in his day, they knew the rules. They knew how far they could 'push' an issue. They also knew when they got the steely look and the final "no" from LUL and they respected that. No longer. They laughed all the way to the bank. As a manager of long experience said to me, "I think they just love the agro".

When managers found drivers of trains on the Central Line were reading newspapers as their trains went along, the TUs had discipline against them stopped. "We're not having that", a TU rep told me; "it's one man's word against another." The Employee Relations Department capitulated (not for the first time). Such incidents understandably made managers wonder who was in charge of the shop ...

Then there was the saga of the Waterloo & City Line. This line was built by the London and South Western Railway to take their passengers to and from the City of London. It passed to the Southern Railway and then to BR. It was a curious hybrid, being much like another tube line, but built with some variations. It had third rail electrification and special trains. When new trains were proposed, BR ordered a follow-on clone of the Central Line stock as a cheaper option to a special train again. Subsequently, the line was transferred to LUL. Presumably because the trains were similar to the Central Line stock, LUL decided to use staff from Leytonstone Depot on the Central Line to operate it, but this meant them travelling miles to and from Leytonstone for each shift (at least theoretically) – quite a waste of time and money, as they were on full pay for the journeys. Then LUL decided it would staff it with crews from Elephant & Castle Depot on the Bakerloo Line, which was just a few hundred yards down the road. The TUs objected to this for some reason and the argument raged on for months. I think it even went to ACAS arbitration. I heard the complaints from managers at the time, but have not found any manager subsequently willing to explain the details. Why such a local issue should be so hotly contended is a bit of a mystery. The loss of paid travelling time to the crews was a possible motive, but shows how difficult seemingly simple negotiations could be.

Whilst the railway is a very safe place in general, it is potentially very dangerous, if it is not run properly. And that includes good staff discipline - my recurring theme - especially in the operating grades. This is one of the reasons I applauded the military approach. Of course, 'discipline' is a dirty word. A colleague used the term 'operating discipline' to make it more acceptable. I don't argue with him, as we agree as to the essential meaning.

LUL, like other similar organisations, has important Rules & Regulations, governing the conduct and working of staff. They are vital. The railway tracks have high-voltage current in them, which can kill. The trains themselves can be lethal if one is hit by them. If two collide or if a train hits a bridge or tunnel, again serious injury or death can follow. It is only reasonable to expect staff to do what they are told. Later, I deal in more detail with the SPAD[68] situation, which became a significant safety issue.

But, with more and more pressure from the TUs, a soft and cuddly 'pink cardigan' approach came about.

To give a flavour of the issues I mention, a Trades Union Journal reported on three then-current serious LUL disputes. Of these, one alleged 'rogue managers' and 'breaches of procedures' by managers. I do not support 'rogue managers' or 'breaches of procedures', but have to say that the procedures had become so complicated that breaches could be committed in haste or innocence. Another was an item about SPADs claiming

> *"unjust treatment [...], failure to implement action plans following SPADs* [note the plurals]*, the manner in which the case conference was held, an appeal taking place without the presence of the member or a TU rep and* [again] *errors of procedure".*

In each of the three cases, a strike was threatened and I believe two strikes actually took place. When you realise that these three items, concerning three large LUL traincrew depots, were in a magazine covering the whole of the UK rail industry - with no reported dispute/s for the rest of the UK - there must be cause for concern, as the number of incidents is quite disproportionate to LUL's size. Irrespective of the rights and wrongs of these individual cases, they are symptomatic of a very fraught industrial relations' situation within LUL that is endemic.

One has only to listen to or read the news media to know how frequently LUL industrial relations are in the news, often including a real or threatened strike. Sometimes, a strike is called off very late and many employees fail to turn up for work, thinking the strike is still 'on'. Thus disruption is still forced on the company and passengers.

Reading the lines – and between the lines – of reports of a recent spat between LUL and the unions, it seems that both sides behaved less than reasonably. As usual, Joe Public in the middle suffered

---

[68] Signal Passed at Danger – *see* Appendix and Chapter 15

as a complete fleet of trains was withdrawn from service at about an hour's notice, stopping the complete service on two lines and part of another.

There is also reason to believe that the unions use an agreement with LUL as a first step to obtain similar facilities elsewhere with other companies, if they can.

Gerrard Fiennes[69] wrote of his experience toward the end of his lengthy railway career:

> *"I am no longer 'the Guv'nor', to be argued with and obeyed, but the Chairmen of the Management side of the Consultation Procedure, to be resisted, circumvented, delayed ..."*

How true!

We are now approaching the Olympics. We have seen in the past how a key group of workers can hold others to ransom over an approaching deadline. Already, one TU negotiator (whose union had opposed long-term pay agreements) proposed a 5-year agreement to ensure industrial peace on LUL over the Olympic Games' period. What are we to read into that? Will the government go for peace at any price again to ensure the games' transport is not disrupted? Or will LUL have an MD who is prepared to face his political masters and say "thus far and no further – we have to face up to this challenge once and for all". Call me cynical, but I "hav m'doots". Time will tell.

---

[69] *See* previous chapter and Appendix

13 - WHAT'S IN A NAME?

A modern trend is that of calling passengers 'customers'. This may have had some validity some years ago as a 'shock tactic', awakening staff and the industry to a lax way of viewing those they purport to serve. But, even if true, that has now passed. Not only do the passengers themselves not like the term customer, it has long lost any usefulness. To take the point further, should hospitals call their patients customers? Or what about calling passengers 'clients', like lawyers - and prostitutes - do?

By all means, give facilities for passengers to buy a stamp or a newspaper or a cup of tea, but to make stations primarily a shopping mall is not our job.

Talk to passengers, both actual and prospective, and you will find their requirements simple: trains that are clean, safe and run to time. Yes, of course they want reasonable fares and good staff, but an efficient system is the priority.

The abandonment of the term 'passenger' has blinded the industry to the chief reason people come to us: *viz,* to travel. We need to concentrate on giving them what they want: safe, reliable, efficient and clean transport. By blurring our vision on those scores, we end up with the disarray we see today.

And what on earth do Vision/Mission Statements like "We aim to be the best railway in Britain" or "Getting people from here to there quicker than anyone else" mean in real terms? We should be doing those kinds of things anyway, so why waste time manufacturing forms of words? The LUL Northern Line currently has the bizarre catch phrase "Altogether Stronger". Sounds like an advert for toilet paper, not a railway!

Think that passengers want bistros, staff in fancy uniforms, Vision and Mission Statements or other peripheral items and we have lost our way. If that really is the best thing to do with our time, we might as well pack up and go home.

Of course change is needed from time to time – but continual change is time consuming, can divert attention from the job in hand and can be very wasteful.

One exasperated passenger said to me recently: "Just get the bloody trains to run properly." I think he speaks for millions of others. Perhaps the entire British rail industry could use his comment as their Mission Statement!

It is better to spend the time doing than saying what we intend to do. As those in the industry have found, if one dares to try and swim against the current tide, if one gets a railway that works well, other items that are desired by the passengers, but as a lower priority, happen as well. And I am convinced that a railway that works efficiently is safer than one that doesn't.

I recall a manager from Midland Mainline stating that they used to have problems after an upset in the service, because the guard and the driver of a train worked very different rosters. The staff rosters were changed, so that a driver and guard stayed together with the same train for as long as possible and for the same amount of time. This greatly aided recovery from delays. Ironically, LUL had done this for decades. This shows how a simple stratagem can produce great benefits.

Why do managements keep reorganising? Well, it's another opportunity to show they are 'DOING SOMETHING'. They consider running a railway is not 'doing something' – or at least it's secondary to 'the business'. Secondly, reorganising something they can actually do, whereas running a railway is something many of them haven't a clue about. Me? – I find reorganisations boring and debilitating.

The word 'professional' is now in vogue. The use of the term professional for staff would appear to signify some change or other. To call modern railwaymen, of any grade, professional in that way surely implies an insult on those who have gone before. Not only were the great engineers of the past professional, so were the staff. One has only to read of their exploits - including the hard graft done daily - to know that. I recall the way the supervisory staff I knew 40-50 years ago did their jobs. For example, the SM of a vital station (in his bowler hat) was there with his staff each morning, seeing the trains away. They had nothing to be ashamed of. The railway ran as well – and often much better – than it does today. I particularly remember how my train and another, starting from two destinations about 50 miles apart, used to arrive in London side by side, day after day. Yet they were controlled by semaphore signals and signal box to signal box working, without the centralised control and radios of today. It was because each person knew their job and did it, day after day, AND IT WORKED.

And just what is this new term 'defensive driving' – aimed at drivers supposedly driving safer and not passing red signals? Is that to imply that the drivers of the past (including such as Norman McKillop, Bill Hoole and Sam Gingell, that some may remember), were careless and paid no attention to such basic safety issues. It's nonsense and is actually a slur on railway staff.

Why do I make an issue of all this? Because it is a distraction from the real job. The danger is of icing a cake so that it looks great, but fails dismally when you bite into it.

Porters and Ticket Collectors on LUL became Railmen, Leading Railmen, Customer Service Assistants and so on as the mood took someone. Changing a name must be backed up with some good reason. Why are we doing it? Does just calling them a different name make the member of staff different? In a very few cases it may. But there is the opposite in that being called some fancy name can give a person a false sense of importance. I have certainly sensed that in some staff. And some managers!

The fact remains that, if a person is a good worker, they will do a good job; if they are not, they won't. By all means, give a good worker some enhanced title if they deserve it, but don't think that a change of name will, *ipso facto*, bring about some dramatic change in itself: that's really naïve. Rather, be more choosy in one's selection of staff and get ones that have the desired attitude and do a good job. Modern Risk Analysis includes the right attitude of staff as a vital element. As one of our General

Managers (one who had his feet firmly on the ground) used to say: "If you can't change the people, change the people." Sorry - it may not be original, but it's as basic as that.

You may say from the above that I am not fit to be a modern manager. Frankly, I think much of 'modern management' has failed dismally, so I might regard that assessment as a compliment.

14 - SAFETY

You may find it strange that I have put this so far down the list. But safety is one of those things we often take as given. We usually assume something will be safe, especially if it is related to a subject we know about. When we buy an electric kettle, for example, we don't expect it to explode as soon as we switch it on! If someone is asked what they want from a journey, they will speak of speed, reliability, cleanliness, comfort and economy, but they will rarely mention safety unless there has been a recent accident.

But a troubled future awaits anyone who actually does take safety for granted.

At both initiation into the Underground and at promotional training, safety used to be especially emphasised to staff.

On the railway - as elsewhere - safety isn't something solid like a locomotive or a signal. It starts as an attitude of mind and ends as an ethos; a compound of many things, often built up over a long period and through bitter experience. That is one reason why change can be so dangerous, if established practices are altered without due care. We have seen this repeatedly on the railways of Britain over the last few years. Yet, in spite of this, it often seemed that LUL thought it OK to ignore the past 150+ years of railways and just start again.

I may have bored you by my continual mention of discipline, but that and safety are intrinsically linked, because they are both behavioural. We appreciate that there are rules of the road and we realise what would happen if some drivers decided to drive the wrong way on a motorway or along a one-way street. On the railway, there are processes. If everybody can rely on everybody else doing what they should, all will normally be well.

People often refer to railway accidents. I prefer the word incident. This is not being pernickety. Rarely is an so-called accident really an 'accident', that is to say an *"event without apparent cause"*[70].

In most cases there has been a failure of some kind:

- Human – wilful or careless act, illness, forgetfulness, mis-understanding, human frailty;
- Equipment – *eg,* a wheel, axle, track, signal or other inanimate object breaks or otherwise fails for some reason;
- System – in that a laid-down process/method/ procedure/rule is wrong or inadequate for dealing with a situation.

LTC Rolt's book *"Red for Danger"*, that I mentioned in Chapter 2 (note [3]), provides ample evidence of what I have just said. Little by little, the dangers of railway operation were addressed in a professional way until the railway gained its enviable safety record. *"Red for Danger"* should be required reading for everybody working on a railway, as it shows how each member of staff has their part to play. It warns how easy it can be to fail - and how appalling can be the consequences of failure.

This is why all incidents were investigated carefully on the railway. Essentially, it was not just to find a PTB (person to blame) but to seek the direct and indirect cause/s and see how a repetition could be avoided. One of LUL's incident reporting forms used to have a Box 13 "Action taken to avoid repetition". That was the most important box on the sheet. Strangely, when the form was revised some years ago, that box was omitted.

I have spoken elsewhere of the importance of timekeeping on the railway. Unfortunately, there sometimes came a clash between that and safety. Members of staff were frequently taken to task by management when they insisted on following a safety rule that delayed a train. Yet, when they cut a corner and an incident occurred, they were censured for that. Such schizophrenic attitude by management must end in trouble.

Some people think that these two elements - timekeeping and safety - will inevitably cause tension. But, as I've said before, I

---

[70] Oxford English Dictionary definition

believe absolutely that a well-run railway is a safer one. It is for that reason more than any other that I am a passionate believer in operating discipline. Any of you who remember the old American 1950s black and white TV series *"Highway Patrol"* may recall actor Broderick Crawford's repeated words at the end of many episodes:

> *"Remember, however new* [of course, he pronounced it 'noo'], *the safest thing in your car is you".*

So it is with the railway. Whatever safety device is included, if the staff does not use it correctly, things will go wrong. In my days, LUL management never seemed to realise that their laxity on staff discipline was causing poor performance at best and potentially serious danger at worst.

My career spanned the period when there were social changes of attitude. There was growth of the litigious attitude, which sought to blame anyone one could find for a problem and try to make a claim for compensation. Parallel with this was a change of attitude amongst some staff, mirroring that in the world in general, which, instead of saying "how much can I do?" said "how little can I do – and get away with it?" - rights being more important than responsibilities. This attitude contrasts with an earlier sentiment, reflected in JF Kennedy's famous words: *"ask not what your country can do for you ..."*[71]

Reading how railway staff coped in World War 2 and later the appalling weather soon after, one sees them anxious to get a job done well. There was a sense of achievement - 'pride', if you will - in that. During my time at LUL, I encountered both attitudes. I'm glad to say I met many who took their work as a personal challenge to do their best; whilst others saw it as a skive, to do as little as possible. I know there have always been the two approaches, but the latter came to be seen as more and more acceptable.

---

[71] *"And so, my fellow Americans: ask not what your country can do for you – ask what you can do for your country..."* Inaugural Address on assuming the US Presidency, 20th January 1961.

An example was the situation following a PUT incident. Staff usually went back to work soon after – I suppose an equivalent of getting back into a car and driving soon after a crash. But it came to be seen as a chance to have six weeks or more off work whilst one saw therapists and counsellors and the like. That's fine for those who needed it, but it increasingly became something every one should do, because not doing so would undermine the position of those who wanted time off.

All this has been assisted by the lunatic health and safety set-up responsible for rail safety in the UK, whose staff could not distinguish between a locomotive and a baggage van.[72] They seem to think it is possible to create a risk-free railway, which is as stupid as thinking that one can have a risk-free life. The same attitudes are not applied to the roads, one notices.

One example was the instruction that LUL had to follow after a man fell out of a train when it went into a siding. From then on, staff had to search all trains that reversed by going into and out of a siding. Yet the train was 'searched' by the driver walking through from one end to the other, soon after it stopped in the siding. And there was the inconsistency that many passengers walked through trains from one car to the next whilst travelling along in normal service. A number were killed doing so. But no equivalent requirement was made. It would have been totally impractical.

The Trade Unions jumped on this 100% safety band-wagon. If there was anything they wanted, they would find some safety tag and shout that, if they didn't get it, it was because LUL didn't care about safety. I can think of a number of issues where they became increasingly nit-picking and the Health & Safety authorities went with them, a reasonable approach to risk management flying out of the window. At the time I wrote this, the RMT union was trying to stop the loss of 100 or more cleaning jobs on the basis that the rubbish that will be left un-cleaned will cause fires.

---

[72] *See* the official report on the crash at Hatfield.

This accusation that the TUs try to play the 'safety card' excessively is not just mine. In an interview with Paul Coleman, Terry Morgan the MD of the Tubelines Infraco, stated that, whilst there were ideological differences between the Infracos and the unions,

"[...] I only object when they use the safety ticket"[73].

Sometimes, the unions' position could be justified, but they become more and more like the boy who cried "wolf".

Yet, when it came to simply asking their members to drive their trains with care, the TUs demanded more and more back-up mechanisms to help ensure they made no mistakes. One example was the Trades Unions' insistence of a large increase on tripcock testers[74]. Yet I cannot recall in my career any serious outcome occurring as a result of a faulty tripcock[75]. Compare this with their attitude on SPADs, in the next chapter, which <u>did</u> cause serious incidents.

As an aside, I remember seeing in my cab one morning a notice saying that, if I passed a signal at danger, I must expect to find a train just ahead. Since one of the main reasons for having a red signal is to protect a train ahead from one approaching behind, I can think of nothing more obvious. I often wondered if I would one day find a notice saying "Pull the handle on the right to make the train go and the one on the left to make it stop."

Against this background, safety was bound to suffer. Which leads us on to the next subject .....

---

[73] *"Rail Professional"*, December 2007.

[74] These are pieces of equipment on the track, that check that train tripcocks (*see* Appendix) are in working order.

[75] A historian of London Underground believes the last such incident was in 1911!

15 - SPADs (SIGNALS PASSED AT DANGER)

Most people would agree that a train passing a signal at danger is something that should not happen. Indeed, it was treated as such over most of my career, as it had since railways first had signals.

When I joined LUL, if a driver could not drive safely, he could be demoted for a period. In particular, passing signals at danger was regarded as a serious breach of driving standards. If he repeatedly offended or was involved in a serious incident, he could lose his job – or be "promoted to customer" as one manager called it! This does not seem unreasonable. But the Trades Unions had consistently pressed for a softer management approach to SPADs, despite also advocating a Professional Train Drivers' Agreement with LUL – which would surely hint at a raising of driving standards.

By the time I left the company, LUL had a very weak SPAD policy, which allowed drivers to have about four SPADs in a couple of years with little danger of losing their job. This policy was actually featured on a peak-time TV programme. One driver, who had previously been a bus driver, referred to a SPAD incident as being an "occupational hazard … like crashing into a car", as she put it.

I understand that an average UK train driver can be expected to have a SPAD no more than once in 15 years. A significant number of LUL drivers were exceeding this figure by a large margin.

All that happened latterly was that the driver who passed a red signal would be 'counseled', 'advised' and given an 'Action Plan' to do better in future. These Action Plans were, in fact, very weak. Train Operators were shown a video as part of the Action Plans. A manager once admitted on peak-time television that some drivers had seen the video six times. Obviously, its remedial power was limited.

A retired manager heard recently that drivers who have numerous SPADs now get taken off driving and given a job on a station as a Customer Service Assistant (CSA) for a few months. But they don't lose pay, so they are earning about £15,000 per year more than those with whom they are working and with much less responsibility than the drivers still driving. A strange form of punishment. But, then, when we hear of captains of industry and cabinet ministers losing their jobs and keeping their salaries, I suppose it's a question of 'sauce for the gander'. One further problem is that some of those so demoted work with ill-grace, as if they are being hard done by, causing ill-feeling among their temporary colleagues, who have a blameless record, but who are being paid far less.

A driver came before me, having passed four signals at danger in three months. On the last occasion, leaving a depot, he passed a line of 12 red signals and proceeded toward a tunnel in which a train was stationary. Fortunately, another member of staff saw him and managed to attract his attention over the radio and he stopped before hitting the train ahead. But because of the LUL SPAD policy, I could not stop him from driving. At the Disciplinary Hearing I advised him and his TU rep to seriously consider if he should not cease to be a train driver. Yet this driver just could not accept he had a problem, as he had not yet actually hit another train ...

Arguments adduced by a number of drivers as excuses for SPADs include that they were "distracted momentarily", that they "never saw the signal", that "drivers never see green signals" and that "I was concerned about the delay". None of these is satisfactory. The fact is that drivers should see every signal and, if they do not see a clear signal to proceed, they should not continue. To a non-train driver, this may seem harsh. But drivers are trained to know the whereabouts of every signal on their route. I have lost count of drivers who have passed a danger signal, derailed their train or something like that and said that they didn't see a stop signal and so moved forward. This is nonsense. They should have known by where they were that there should be a signal relating to their train and they should have checked what information it was giving. It's simple. What are signals for, otherwise? Safety is paramount.

One excuse given by some drivers and TU reps that I found particularly irritating and irresponsible was that a particular signal had previously been passed at danger a number of times, as if that excused the latest incident. When I was trained as a driver, I was told of those signals that had caught drivers out in the past. "Watch that one especially" older drivers would warn. There are now "Much SPADed Signals" around on LUL and the National Rail system. Posters and other warning devices are posted in the crew depots to advise them. Certainly, such signals should be investigated to see why and how the situation can be ameliorated. BUT, in the meantime, drivers know which signals have caught other drivers out and so they should be extra vigilant when driving toward them.

One signal I recall well was not only infamous as a much SPADed signal, but, despite the imposition of a speed restriction and a yellow caution light approaching it, drivers still passed it at red with alarming frequency, causing lengthy hold-ups.

A theory that was suggested was that drivers passed some signals because they were distracted by their mobile 'phone ringing as they exited tunnels. I don't know if that has been followed through and, if so, if it has been verified. Some police officers travelling on a District Line train arrested the driver after his train over-ran a station. They said they had heard him chatting on his mobile 'phone for some minutes before the incident. And I have read that train drivers in a number of other Train Operating Companies have been disciplined for using their mobile 'phones whilst driving.

The LUL SPAD situation has thus become critical over the last few years. For some months, the rate on LUL rose dramatically, whilst that on the National Rail system went down, until, in a four-week period, LUL incredibly had three or more times as many SPADs as the whole National Rail (ie, the old BR) network. Indeed, for a number of months, one line of LUL had more SPADs than the whole National Rail system.

This was nonsense. What on earth had caused such a decline in performance in this safety-critical area?

One of the key reasons for this lies in the attitude of senior managers. My General Manager was heard to wonder why passing signals at danger need be a problem, since LUL had the trainstop/tripcock system, which should stop all trains. Indeed, this attitude was followed in the LUL web-site. But it is not as simple as that.

- Firstly, the basis of all conventional signalling, including on LUL, is the driver reacting to the signal and stopping BEFORE it is passed. The the tripcock/trainstop mechanism only operates AFTER a train has passed a red signal.
- Secondly, tripcock/trainstop mechanism was designed to be and remains to this day a back-up, in case of driver error, incapacity or such-like.
- Thirdly, no system is 100% foolproof. It is dangerous to rely completely on a back-up system.
- Fourthly, SPADs cause significant delays to other trains, whilst the matter is being dealt with safely. These delays trap many passengers in tunnels and can be a source of danger in themselves
- Moreover, some signals in depots do not have trainstops and thus not the usual back-up (the LUL SPAD Policy seemed to have overlooked that loop-hole).

But there is an even more serious feature. It is often said that no driver ever passes a signal at danger deliberately, but the fact is that LUL had numerous cases of drivers passing signals at danger, being stopped by the trainstop/tripcock apparatus, <u>cancelling it and carrying on</u>. Is this not as bad - or worse - as deliberately passing the signal in the first place?

For example, I know a driver who over-ran a signal and the train was stopped by the tripcock/trainstop mechanism. The driver re-set the mechanism, released the brakes and drove his train into the path of another (passenger) train in a tube tunnel. Fortunately, this second train had not passed the protecting signal, which was correctly showing green, but which returned to danger when the signalling system detected the conflicting movement of the first train, and the second train was stopped in time. This driver's actions were the equivalent of <u>deliberately</u> doing what the Thames Trains' driver at Ladbroke Grove (near London's Paddington station)[76] did accidentally. The LUL driver had also lied to the Controller, when the latter called him on the radio, suspecting something was wrong. When he appeared before a Disciplinary Hearing, he was unrepentant, would not admit he had done anything wrong and was most aggrieved when sacked. However, he appealed and, once again, a more senior manager gave him his job back. He was demoted for a while, but continued to grumble at the unfairness of his sentence. To add insult to injury, this man was an official trainer of new drivers.

This incident also shows the inadequacy of letting the police deal with these matters. A year or so before this incident, the driver of a passenger train did something very similar, driving his train into the path of an empty train. He was summonsed and sent to Court for what he did. But, on the occasion I have just mentioned, the driver was not prosecuted, seemingly because he was driving an empty train. Yet, common sense (and what happened at Watford Junction a few years ago[77]) shows that the consequences of a passenger-carrying train hitting an empty train are much the same as an empty train hitting a passenger train.

There must be a system to over-ride the tripcock, in case of a failure, but it should only be used in very restricted circumstances, which the driver must report at the earliest opportunity and only when driving very slowly 'on sight'. But a few drivers thought they could escape detection from having had a SPAD by over-riding the system in an unauthorised way. The potential danger in this is horrific.

---

[76] This terrible accident occurred on 5th October 1999. The driver of the Thames train allowed his train to pass a signal at danger and it continued into the path of a correctly approaching train, hitting it head on at a combined speed of about 120mph. As the Thames train driver died, the reason for this SPAD can only be conjectured.
[77] A passenger train over-ran a red signal and collided with an empty train just south of Watford Junction on 8th August 1996.

Is the situation getting better? Alas, it seems not. LUL admitted that there had been an 18% rise in SPADs during the year ending 31st March 2007. A more recent news report stated that 20% of tube drivers were "unsafe" on the basis of having had SPADs[78].

LUL stated that a survey of Train Operators concluded that they blamed their own fatigue and boredom more than other causes of SPADs. Is the job more arduous today, with a 35 hour week, than 30 or so years ago, when drivers often worked a 13-day fortnight? Or is it that LUL have lost the ability to control a significant minority of their drivers? – or possibly that they are nor recruiting suitable drivers.

I have highlighted SPADs, but the general attitude to operational discipline augers badly for LUL's future performance as a railway. A large element in bringing about this decline was a failure of top management to get a handle on the situation years ago and support those managers who could have done more, had they been allowed to do so.

And, beyond that, once a serious matter like SPADs is treated lightly, other serious dangers rear their heads. This is not just my own opinion. LUL commissioned Arthur D Little Ltd to undertake an Independent Safety Audit, in which they state

> "a poor SPAD performance may potentially have a negative impact on the safety culture in other areas"

The only disagreement I have with this statement is when they say "may potentially". That is not strong enough in that context: I don't think there can be any doubt that it does have a negative impact, which permeates the perception of safety.

Risk analysis and risk avoidance tactics include having a staff whose attitudes to their jobs will tend to keep an organisation as far from risk as possible. The SPAD trend is not commensurate with that.

Train drivers on LUL have become quite pampered. Of course, their job is key to operating the railway (currently, no drivers = no

---

trains). They even boast about their power. But they have charged more and more for their services and are asking for more and more systems to ensure they do the job they are already paid to do. To their basic salary must be added their pension payments, uniform, training costs and so on. (It can take up to six months to train a driver.)

I look back over what I know of train drivers of the past. As a responsible and respected profession, I think many of them would shake their heads in disbelief at the current situation.

The cost-gap between a continually-monitored driver and an automatically-operated train becomes less and less. Even more so when the cost of the errors they commit is factored in. Train drivers are in danger of pricing themselves out of the market on LUL and the saving to LUL by having a cheaper member of staff - or no staff at all - on the train would be considerable

Is the sensible way forward for LUL now to be like other metros in the world and introduce driverless trains as soon as possible[79]? For many years, I was opposed to such a move and, as an *ex*-train driver, it would be a bitter pill to swallow. A member of staff on the train should be provided as a regular feature, but the absence of such staff should not entail the train being cancelled because the on-train staff is not essential for it to operate. With new-style trains, the member of staff can easily patrol the train, providing a 'presence' for passenger reassurance, security and assistance. Such a change would greatly reduce the effects of the twin curses of train staff absenteeism and SPADs – both issues that continually ail LUL and disrupt the service to passengers. With platforms carefully monitored, the platform:train interface, seen as the most dangerous part of the railway, could also be better covered than at present.

However, LUL's stated claim is to have automated running whilst retaining a driver, which seems very inefficient and is the most expensive way of tackling the issue.

---

[79] LUL had plans for this, which they called RTO – Remote Train Operation.

I must emphasise that most drivers are conscientious, competent and do their jobs in the best traditions of the Underground; but what I have just written is an appalling catalogue of the situation. It does the majority of staff a disservice and, I maintain, gives an indication of the indiscipline of some (I repeat: SOME) train staff and of the senior management that have allowed it. One cannot but wonder what the consequences of such a lax attitude will be, sooner or later.

16 - OTHER EMERGENCIES

Fire Brigade Matters

The terrible fire that occurred at King's Cross LUL station on 18th November 1987 is one of those railway incidents like the crash at Moorgate and, much earlier, the Tay Bridge disaster, that remain in popular memory. At Kings Cross, a small fire started under an escalator and could probably been easily extinguished. However, it was not and passengers were evacuated though the fire area. Complications caused a fireball to occur and 31 people were killed.

One of the great changes that occurred *post*-King's Cross was the demand on LUL that the London Fire Brigade (LFB) (later the London Fire and Civil Defence Authority (LFCDA)) be called to every reported possible fire, whether it was confirmed or not. Previously, a call the Fire Brigade was rarely needed and LUL were generally left to attend to matters themselves – which normally they did adequately. This change of policy seems to have come at a good time for the LFB. They were being pressurised to reduce the number of fire stations in the inner London area. The LUL requirement created extra demands on them and, as far as I know, no fire stations were shut for some years afterwards, although I believe some have more recently.

It is easy to become emotive about fire on the Underground. Many of the station platforms were originally made of wood. And remember that, from its opening in 1863, there had been portable fires in many of the tunnels, as trains on two major lines were drawn by steam locomotives. In fact, London Transport retained steam locomotives for non-passenger service longer than British Rail, so steam locomotives ran on parts of the Underground until the early '70s. And smoking was permitted.

With the predilection for passengers to drop litter, rubbish would accumulate around the system, despite cleaning. Often such debris would get caught under sleepers and pieces of lineside equipment. Latterly, it's true that cleaning was not as rigorous as formerly and the inevitable sparks and arcing caused by the movement of the train shoes along the current rails frequently caused rubbish to ignite. In the main, these were small fires and caused little real trouble. Two or three times, whilst driving, I found fires on the track. Where practical, I would stop the train, extinguish the fire and report the incident as soon after as possible. Other drivers and station staff did the same. 99.9% of these incidents were harmless. Some were not, but King's Cross was an exceptional case, caused by factors far more serious than the original fire.

The LFB was an autocratic organisation. They were used to 'taking over' a situation and doing what they liked. I do not doubt that most of the officers knew their stuff. But they didn't seem to think that anybody else knew their stuff. They also did not understand how the railway operated and some of their officers didn't seem to want to know. They would turn up at many of these incidents and concentrate on what they thought the issue was - which, to them, was just a possible fire. They generally insisted that the railway stop immediately and tended to ignore any trains that were stuck in tunnels. On hot days, such trains were an actual problem, whilst the alleged fire, which was probably a bit of paper that had gone out by the time they arrived on the scene, was not. Once, when one of our managers insisted that he move a train a few feet to let passengers out of the train stuck behind, the Fire Brigade made such a fuss the police nearly arrested the manager. All that had been needed was to move the train in the platform slightly, so that the first doors of the following train could get alongside the platform, when it would be possible to release its passengers. But, no, they would not budge. This scenario was enacted on numerous occasions, due to their ignorance and intransigence.

One aspect of investigations that caused considerable delay was when the Fire Brigade could find no fire, they would want to look for 'hot spots'[80] with an infrared camera. This would often take a long time, whilst one was obtained. We were told that, at that

---

[80] Places where the temperature was such that it indicated where a fire had been and/or – more ominously – could (re-)start.

191

time, the LFB only had two in the whole of London. LUL bought about a dozen and placed them strategically on the system. Usually the fire crew would accept our camera and this reduced this particular frustration and concomitant delays, but on occasion they insisted on waiting for one of their own cameras.

Another problematic aspect of LFB operations was that, whoever was the senior officer on site automatically became 'in charge'. Often, an officer of junior rank turned up at first and the LUL staff would deal with him; but, suddenly, they would find that a more senior officer had arrived at the surface, whilst they were down in the tunnel. The officer down below would then no longer be able to make a final decision without referring to the senior officer, who was nowhere near. An even more senior officer could then arrive and the deference be repeated upward. What could be worse was that the incident could be found to be a false alarm and the junior officer at the scene refuse to give the "all clear," believing a more senior officer to be in charge, only to then find out that that officer had left the scene and therefore returned the ultimate authority to the junior officer without having made that clear. London Underground was then left 'chasing' the more senior officer for his OK - not easy, if he had gone back to the fire station, or, worse, on to another incident. Sometimes, getting the 'all clear' took longer than dealing with the 'fire'! And all the time the railway remained stationary, with people often detained in tunnels and the service degenerating.

The Fire Brigade and LUL radios (when they appeared) were not compatible and the LFB ones did not operate underground.

Add to all this that some senior Fire Officers were especially officious and seemed to squeeze the greatest drama out of a minor incident (there was one who was particularly good at that) and you will see that with many 'shouts' (LFB terminology for a call-out) each day, the scene was set for chaos. Fortunately, not all the Fire Officers were difficult and, bit by bit, a *modus vivendi* came about, especially after individuals from both parties built up a *rapport* with one another. This could still be ruffled if, for some reason, officers from a far-off station attended. I once dealt with a watch (squad of firemen) from New Addington – a place miles from any underground line. This came about, it seems, because, if the force in inner London is stretched, others come in from outlying stations to cover, using a centripetal (reverse ripple) effect. (As it happened, the New Addington firecrew were professional and co-operative.)

Despite the fact that the incidents gave them work, the LFB probably got fed up with attending so many calls that were tedious 'non events'.

One can say that LUL's house-keeping should have been better and that these little fires should not have occurred. Also, one can say that one could not rely on LUL after what had happened at King's Cross. These are understandable reactions, but a less draconian plan of action could have been instituted from the start, which is what evolved eventually, but not until after a lot of expensive pain – and much disruption to passengers. One thing done was for certain managers to be given an authorisation to show they were considered competent to advise the LFB. For example, sometimes smoke occurred because a brake-shoe was rubbing on a wheel. This caused a strong smell and smoke-like dust-clouds, but was not a fire. Those of us with the right card could inform the LFB that a fire was not involved and cut the delay to a minimum. This was another repercussion of the make-more-managers policy, as many of them just did not yet have the competence. In the short-term, LUL had to accept that some of their managers had much more experience than others in managing these incidents.

The ultimate 'cure' for all this was a belt, braces and piece of string plan, enforced by the Fennell Report on the King's Cross fire. Wooden escalators were replaced by metal. But, with the total ban on smoking and other *régimes*, the chance of any similar incident recurring was much diminished. It was all part of the 'gold plating' culture of trying to stop all risks, which is actually impractical.

Modern underground stations have to be built with dual exits and other like features, possibly pricing underground railways out of the UK market for decades. LUL always had a procedure for removing passengers from a danger area by train, but it was rarely used. Ironically, had this been implemented instead of trying to send all the members of the public to the exit at King's Cross, things could have been very different. But we will never know.

LUL hierarchy were probably shocked at their mis-placed confidence in the *pre*-Kings Cross situation. But I cannot help feeling that LUL panicked in the aftermath of the fire and did not just ensure that people did what they had been trained to do. By all means fine-tune procedures with experience, which LUL had always done in the past, but again the baby got thrown out with the bathwater. But, by then, no-one seemed to have any faith in LUL management, so their measured reactions probably wouldn't have been heeded. For whatever reasons, revolutionary fervour meant tumbrels replaced the chauffeur-driven cars and the heads of the top managers rolled.

Terrorism

The foregoing sets the scene for the consideration of terrorist alerts on the underground. Whilst it is true that there were at least two actual bombs found on trains (and one on a bus) before 2005, greater 'damage' was caused by the false alarms and gross inconvenience caused during the political unrest in Northern Ireland. Matters were not helped by passengers leaving baggage all over the system, which often had to be treated as a potential bomb. The leaving of baggage was, of course, nothing new, but the repercussions were.

One way and another, an incredible amount of disruption was caused. One cannot help comparing the amount of dislocation to that caused during the *Blitz* and the later V1 and V2 attacks on London. Of course, the ethos was very different then. During the war, the public were determined not to let the enemy get to them – to show that "Britain can take it" and that we would "carry on". With the IRA and subsequent threats from other groups, there was very much a "play safe" approach. It was not helped by some people, both staff and members of the public, reporting innocuous items as "suspicious" and setting in motion the security system. I was once called to a security alert, which was a single packet of

Quickbrew tea bags – which could easily be seen as such through the polybag. On another occasion, it was a melted ice-cream, which also could be clearly seen.

Cases, some of which were locked, were more difficult and often a bomb-disposal team had to be called. On occasions, it would appear that deliberate hoax devices, with wires sticking out and so on, were planted – probably by mischief-makers.

On one occasion, a train stopped at Oxford Circus and a passenger told the driver that there was an unaccompanied brief-case in the first car. The driver came back and reported the item to the Controller. The evacuation process was about to start and the driver was heard on the radio to report that "the bag was on the train." A moment later, it flew out of the train and hit the station wall. "Not any more, it's not", came a shout – "now let's get moving." Drastic, but it shows the pent-up emotion in passengers caused by all these daily false alarms.

If the suspicious object was in a place where it could be seen as a threat to passing trains, then any possible passing trains were stopped. This frequently stopped movement on a line in the centre of London, the repercussions soon extending far back into the suburbs. Although one can turn trains short of their intended destination and send them back the other way, this often only puts off the evil moment, when the service is greatly disrupted by trains and staff out of position. The Wisdom of Solomon is needed to know how drastic are the steps required – to take either too great steps or too little, too soon or too late can easily be adversely criticised afterwards, with the great 'wisdom' of hindsight (a virtue enjoyed by journalists, politicians, the public ... and the most senior of managers). By and large, I think the Control Room staff handled matters very well.

Possibly the most disruptive incident was when <u>every</u> train in service on the underground was stopped at the next station and all passengers sent to the surface, following a warning from a terrorist organisation, stating that there was a bomb or bombs on unspecified trains. This was just before Christmas 1991 and was managed in (I believe) about 15-20 minutes. Each train had to be searched where it was before the 'all clear' was given and the railway put back into service. After that, all seats were sealed shut. They were normally accessible, as equipment was installed underneath many of them. From then on, any seal found broken meant the seat had to be lifted and checked before being resealed. All this was time-consuming and wasteful, as well as being tiresome. Presumably, this was all grist to the mill for the terrorists. Even the darkest days of the *Blitz* had never approached such total disruption.

Later, after the IRA threat diminished, there were the warnings about other extremists to be coped with.

When terrorism from other factions began to appear in western European countries, I asked what we were doing about the possibility of dealing with young radicals who might wish to undertake a suicide bombing on our system. I was particularly concerned about the 'flood gates' that had been installed during the war, to prevent water, especially from the Thames, flooding vast parts of the system[81]. At that time, it was feared that a bomb might pierce the system in a location where the water could enter. I can still recall the special lighting that was placed in the tunnels under the river, to assist drivers in seeing any abnormal ingress of water. The flood gates had been de-commissioned as deemed no longer necessary with the commissioning of the Thames Flood barrier. I queried this policy with senior management. There may no longer be a threat from bombs from above ground, but there could well be from beneath. I was told the risk had been assessed and the policy was sound.

Since then, of course, the events of July 2005 have passed. But, terrible as 7th July was, to me the parallel events that occurred two weeks later were more frightening in their implications. Two weeks after the explosions that killed and injured many people, four more bombs were set off but providentially only the detonators exploded. At the recent trial of the bombers, film was shown of what could happen if the bombs themselves had exploded. Yet the fact that those attempts were made quite easily

---

[81] In some locations, the top of the tunnel is close to the bed of the river.

when London was supposedly on the highest possible state of alert shows how vulnerable an open, democratic society is to such activity by those who wish it harm. The impracticality of subjecting every passenger entering the underground to airport-type security precautions is obvious.

A new era has arrived and London will have to come to terms with it, as it did with Hitler.

17 - PPP = THE PUBLIC PRIVATE PARTNERSHIP[82]

Following the rejection of outright privatisation of the Underground, after the problems with privatising British Rail (BR), politicians sought an alternative way of injecting private capital into the system. There had been Private Financing Initiatives (PFIs) for schools, hospitals and other normally government-sponsored areas of investment. A version of this was considered. The operation of the stations and trains would remain with LUL, but the maintenance and rebuilding of the system, which was seen as a horrific financial mountain to climb, would be opened to privately owned consortia of financiers, engineers and so-forth. The idea was that the infrastructure would be handed over to these consortia, who would take the agreed necessary actions (initially) at their expense and they would be paid back over a 30 year period.

With the considerable public concern engendered by the BR privatisation, much was made of the differences there would be between the BR pattern and that to be used for the Underground. John Prescott in particular tried to stem the concern. Much play was made of LUL's overall responsibilities and the protection of its 'Safety Case' document[83], which was supposed to cover everything, as safety had been the main concern raised by the BR privatisation. It was also emphasised that the system would be a partnership – a partnership between the public and private sectors, hence the name of the system.

However, whatever were the <u>differences</u> between the BR and LUL systems, the fact is that the greatest problem areas remained as <u>similarities</u> – finance and the segregation of different parts of a system that really needed to be kept together. The most vital break would be at the interface between operations and

---

[82] See Christian Woolmar's book *"Down the Tube"*, Aurum Press, 2002, for a detailed discussion of this issue, especially the higher politics

[83] This is a document, subject to independent review by the UK Health and Safety authorities, stating in great detail how safety and allied systems will be managed. It has to be approved before the set-up can be implemented.

infrastructure. This had been a great weakness of BR privatisation and remains a serious flaw in the PPP set-up.

Essentially, the idea was that LUL would continue to run the railway operations, more-or-less as before, whilst private Infrastructure companies (called Infracos, for short) would look after the maintenance and improvements to the system for 30 years. The private companies (actually, they were consortia of engineering sector firms financed by banks) would provide the money for their work 'up front' and then charge LUL a fee every year, which, over the 30 years, would recoup the money, plus interest and profit. The Treasury preferred this, as it was supposed to use private, rather than public, money. As we soon saw, events determined otherwise.

Originally, it was hoped the Infracos would take on the risks in all this, but that idea was soon seen as unsellable!

As a first stage, the split was made, but with LUL running both parts. This was called 'shadow running'. This was supposed to ensure 'bugs' could be got out of the system and any teething problems overcome. I think that lasted about two years, after which the private consortia (potentially three, but actually two, as one consortium gained two of the three contracts) took over the infrastructure elements.

I only ever heard one manager below the top management/director level saying he thought PPP a good idea. And that manager was making such a public play, in front of the MD and others, of how good a thing he thought it was, that even die-hard cynics found his fawning sickening. A colleague put his finger mockingly down his throat after listening to him. Apart from him, I never found a manager, among those who would give an opinion, who thought PPP was a good idea. So I was in the majority for once.

Most people don't like change. But, some people like change for change's sake; and I'm afraid that some like change because, whilst change is going on, all sorts of inefficiencies and inadequacies can be explained away by blaming the change itself. "You can't make omelettes without breaking eggs" is the cry, without questioning if omelettes were required in the first place – or if the eggs could have been broken carefully, rather than smashed to smithereens.

I recall a meeting where a man with a diagram of a plumbing system gave us a fascinating talk, seeking to explain the principles of PPP. There was a tank called X and a tank called Y, with a number of interconnecting pipes and pink- and blue-tinted water. He explained that if tank X overflowed, the water would flow into Y. If Y overflowed, it would do so into X. Thus he explained that, if an Infraco did well, it got extra cash and, if it did badly, it would pay LUL. Apart from the extreme *naïveté* of that presentation, there was a great deal of the 'smoke and mirrors' about the PPP process; it was far too complex for it to be so easily understood.

To try and explain the practicalities of the situation as it affected the day-to-day operation of the railway and of our management of it, I need to give an outline of how LUL and its predecessors had organised the twin needs of running trains and maintaining the infrastructure.

On a 'normal' railway, one can see groups of men (and women, nowadays) standing alongside the line as trains pass. Indeed, ignorant passengers often comment that these people are standing there, "doing nothing". Apart from watching the train passing over the track (often at reduced speed) and seeing if its progress shows any potential defects, there is often little that they can do whilst the train passes without the risk of being mown down. But, the point is that they can work, wait a while whilst a train goes by and then carry on again. There is normally plenty of room beside the line on which the train is running for them to stand safely. And the intervals between trains are such that work can be done effectively between times. For many years, work was done in a similar way in tunnels. There were refuges in the walls for the workers and/or they could stand on one track, whilst a train passed on the other[84].

---

[84] Sometimes this went tragically wrong. A serious accident occurred in Knightswood tunnel, Scottish Region, when track workers heard a train

Two things militate against such a practice on the underground. For one thing, trains are generally much more frequent – often 90 – 120 seconds apart. Also, in the single-track tube tunnels, there is only approximately nine inches between the tunnel wall and the sides of the passing train – far too close to stand clear. Emergency work in LUL double-track tunnels was occasionally done by staff whilst trains were running, but trains had to be stopped in the deep-level, single-track tube tunnels if a job could not wait. Of course, much of the underground is in the open and the 'main line' system of maintenance can be followed, but generally the underground used a different system.

(On the National Rail system, much is now done by large machinery, but, in the confines of LUL's tunnels, a lot of the work is still done manually.)

On LUL, essentially, the 24 hours of the day were divided into two periods:
- The 'Traffic Day', which started just before the first train was <u>due</u> to run and ended after the last train had <u>actually</u> run (in case it was delayed for any reason).
- 'Engineering Hours', which was the period of time from when the last train <u>actually</u> ran until the first train was <u>due</u> to run the next morning.

Staff were told the number of the last train and had to wait until they had actually seen it pass before venturing onto the track. When they reported in at night, they gave a contact name and the trains would not run again until that contact alone had confirmed that staff and equipment were all clear and the line safe. This system worked well for years, with all workers LUL employees or under LUL supervision.

As an aside, one must point out that there is often only about four hours at night to do work. This is based on the time between the last train at night (usually after midnight) and the first train later in the morning – from which must be deducted the time taken for

---

coming in one direction, stood on the other line and were run down by another train that they had not heard approaching in the opposite direction.

personnel and equipment accessing the site and setting up and then the reverse. This is why some jobs take so long overall and why it is not practical to run all-night underground services[85] as a matter of course.

I've mentioned fragmentation changes within LUL earlier, when talking about the management structure. PPP thus continued the fragmentation process on the railway much further. And, despite what was claimed, it left important things outside of LUL control.

Essentially, under PPP, LUL employs train, station and ancillary administrative staff, and runs the stations and trains. The Infracos, repair, maintain and improve the infrastructure, signalling and rolling stock (the trains). So LUL 'hires in' their work, but at arm's length. This involves more liaison, contracts and inevitable conflicts of interest.

The split between infrastructure and operations was called 'logical' by one of the movers in the creation of the form of PPP[86]. Theoretically, perhaps; but it was not a practical logic.

A consequence of the break-up was that the logical pairings of lines I mention at the beginning of chapter 2 were dissolved. On the Met and Jubilee, one has Met trains running on lines maintained by a Jubilee line Infraco but controlled by Met signalling staff, also with equipment maintained by another Infraco. A potentially serious incident arose after confusion between those in charge of the two lines where they were side by side and current was switched back on. Until recent events stopped it, we were faced with having two different automatic signalling systems to get trains in and out of Neasden depot, because the two Infracos were imposing different signalling systems on their respective lines and the two lines intermingle at that point. And we are supposed to be heading toward a single standard signalling system across Western Europe!

---

[85] There are ways around this, but they are expensive and the Night Bus service is now excellent.
[86] Statement on the House of Commons, 27 June 2002 (*Hansard*)

Moreover, the division of the railway day into the two periods I have just mentioned meant that, in effect, the whole railway - lock, stock and barrel - is handed over to the Infracos every night after the last train and back again every morning. One can imagine the potential for something going wrong.

An example of how this can bristle with danger is a railway depot that was being refurbished. This refurbishment involved the relaying of track, laying of new track and the alteration and installation of 630-volt electric cables to the track. For the depot, as for all the underground tracks, there is a source-diagram, with copies held by those who need access. These are essential guides to anybody who needs to go into the area, to know which cables feed which pieces of track, how and where to isolate the tracks and cables, and thus how to work without getting a high-voltage shock. But, every night over a period of months, the workers were changing the cabling, so the vital diagrams were never up-to-date, as the process of cross checking and publication of the revisions took some weeks. Imagine an electrician coming into your home and rewiring it, so that every day the fuses were feeding different plugs and lights - and you didn't know which, because the labels were not being changed quickly enough. This is how it was in the depot – but far more dangerous, due to the far higher voltages involved. And the depot was in use 24 hours a day. The LUL local manager, who was *de jure* but not *de facto* master of the situation, could only issue an edict that, if any incident occurred in the depot, ALL the cables and track must be considered live until ALL had been switched off. This was a comparatively easy situation to solve, provided only his staff was involved, as they knew the problem and it was a confined area. But imagine this happening all over the Underground, affecting thousands of staff. You can see how fraught this is. A manager colleague of mine spent a very unhappy holiday after a worker at a site he was overseeing received a powerful 630-volt shock because the diagram the manager was using was actually out of date. Thankfully, the worker fully recovered and the manager was later rightly cleared of all blame, but that was little comfort to him. The real fault had been somewhere in the recording system, as a vital change had not been registered correctly. The potential of this happening under this new system was enormous.

Then there were the complicated contractual ins and outs, plus the cost of actually designing and running the system, aside from the cost of doing the actual work. It was like a machine that used much of its power in working itself, leaving little for actual output.

And what if LUL don't like the service provided by an Infraco? If an airline doesn't like an airport, it can often use another in the same region (as the 'no-frills' airlines do). If a shipping company don't like a port, there is often an alternative. If the M1 motorway had to be shut for months, it would inconvenience road-hauliers, but Eddie Stobart could still run his business. But LUL can't move their trains elsewhere – a problem shared with the Channel Tunnel and, since privatisation, more and more with the National Rail system.

I was involved in a number of PPP-like projects. Some went quite smoothly, due to their simplicity and to those overseeing them adopting 'old railway' approaches. Out of the cupboard came my 'black mac'. Others involved even more meetings. One meeting I had was for a precursor of PPP. I went to a site, which had recently become part of my accountability. I was told what was being done for staff access to the site. I said it was not acceptable (for good reasons). There was stunned silence, followed by total consternation. It was quite obvious that the contractors had never heard the word "no" from LUL. They explained to me why I could not say no and I explained why I must. They then told me of plans that could not be changed. I explained that they should have seen the problem themselves. They bewailed the difficulties that it would cause them and I explained the impracticality of what they proposed. They really just expected me to rubber-stamp their proposals. In the end I got 75% of what I wanted, but had to make a compromise, as to have drastically redesigned something at that stage would have set back other parts of the project. And, despite their alleged computer assisted and co-ordinated design, they still planted a huge lighting mast a couple of feet from a tall tree that obscured most of the light and planted another mast so that it totally blocked an access footpath.

Another item: I found the layer of ash on some pathways was too thin[87]. I was told triumphantly that it "met LUL Standards". I later contacted the engineer who wrote the Standard. On checking, he found the Standard read "mms" instead of "cms", reducing the depth of ash ten-fold. He said that, one Tuesday, he had been told to write a sheaf of Standards by Thursday lunchtime and admitted that, in his haste to meet the deadline, his proof-reading had slipped. By then, similar stories were abroad and I could only sympathise. But it was too late to get an alteration without LUL paying for the extra ash. I believe the pathways were later paved – presumably at more cost to LUL.

The other major difference is that the Infracos saw their responsibility as providing contractual service to LUL, whereas LUL saw their obligation to provide a service to their passengers. The 'once removed' position of the Infracos, to my mind, led to them not focusing on the end user – the passenger. The contract didn't help. Infracos would let week-end work stretch on into a Monday morning (say), delaying many trains, rather than stop work on time and finish the job later. It seems that the penalties for late finish of work were smaller than the cost of doing the job later. But the public suffered, being in a 'pig-in-the-middle' situation – and they blamed LUL.

As with the national rail network, much of the work was done over weekends, seemingly on the basis that the Monday to Friday service was far more important. Well, LUL is supposed to provide a service to all every day (except Christmas Day) and the 'service' at many week-ends – as on the national rail network – leaves a lot to be desired. True, there has been the major catch-up of work needed, not only to keep the railway as it is but improve it for the vastly greater number of passengers now travelling. But one feels that week-end travel is no longer regarded as important by those in power. On the day of the Lord Mayor's Show, when far more people than usual might reasonably be expected to use the Waterloo & City line (normally fairly quiet at the week-end), it was shut for maintenance (shortly after reopening after another

---

[87] If laid correctly, the paths are self-draining, also meaning the paths are less likely to be slippery in cold/icy weather.

long shut-down for renovation). Would this sort of thing have happened so often if the directly responsible organisation had a more passenger-focused ethos?

This fundamental difference of view-point or mind-set is well summed up in the words of an LUL manager in an interview with Christian Wolmar:

> *"[... the Infraco's] decisions will be made on the basis of seeking profit, rather than what is best for passenger"*[88].

Succinctly put. Compare this with the view of Terry Morgan, the MD of the Tubelines Infraco, in his interview with Paul Coleman,

> *"I am here to provide a service to the public but I'm also in business to make money for delivering that service."*[89]

One direct consequence was the unprecedented shut-down of the Central Line for weeks on end, because motors began to literally fall off the trains, causing at least one serious derailment. It seems impossible to believe that such a situation could have arisen had LUL held the reins of maintenance. More recently, there has been a series of collisions and derailments of trains running into things stored but not adequately secured in tunnels. So a query as to the real ability of these Infracos arises.

You may recall that the infamous Railtrack, just before its fall from grace, was announced as likely to be one of the Infracos. Railtrack was the (apparent) instigator of an incredible 'Econo-Crossrail' scheme. This envisaged saving lots of money building a new railway from Paddington to Whitechapel by running Crossrail trains from the eastern to western suburbs along the north side of the Circle Line. How anyone with an ounce of *nous* could have considered this as practical is beyond me. Spending a few rush-hour minutes on the Baker St – Moorgate section in particular will show how impossible the scheme was. One can only imagine that someone, with no practical knowledge, had looked at a map of London's railways, seen that there already was a line between the two points and thought "Ah! – we'll use that". Nonetheless, a senior LUL manager was taken off his day job to

---

[88] *"Broken Rails"*, ibid.
[89] *"Rail Professional"*, December 2007.

prepare a refutation of the plan, which could have been done in 10 minutes on the back of an envelope!

I accept the scheme was just about feasible, if - a huge IF - LUL had withdrawn services for some years between High Street Kensington, Westbourne Park and Finchley Road to the west and Aldgate or even Whitechapel in the east and totally re-built the route with four running lines, grade-separated junctions and four-platform stations. We have experienced the disruption caused by the re-building of King's Cross station. Can you imagine the cost (possibly more than building a totally new line), the daily disruption and the mega-closure of much of the Euston Road, along which, one assumes, a replacement bus service would need to be run? The scheme was abandoned when the realities were appreciated. It really beggars belief and makes one wonder what other wild schemes such organisations might have come up with.

Of course, if Crossrail had been built first, lines like the north and south side of the Circle and the central section of the Central Line could have been closed for periods for refurbishment, with passengers using the new line. Disruptive - yes - but surely no more than the disruption that is currently caused by the repeated closures of lines, with no alternative rail service. This also shows how desperately London needs a cohesive transport plan implemented urgently.

The very fact that Railtrack was still being considered as a possible PPP partner, after its disgraceful record managing the national system shows how ignorant or indifferent the powers-that-be were. Only when the scandal became public was Railtrack politically stated to be a non-contender.

A serious incident occurred one Sunday morning. A train became derailed allegedly as a result of the Infraco staff (allegedly) mishandling some track work. Seven passengers were injured, including one with a broken leg. Fortunately, no-one was in the crush-zone of the sixth car ... The track, the train, the tunnel and a lot of cabling were badly damaged. The LUL MD came on site, with an LUL senior engineer in tow. A colleague told me how the MD left the engineer and had a pow-wow with the Infraco rep. He then returned to the LUL engineer. "He tells me he can have things up and running by Tuesday", he said. The LUL engineer let out an expletive that sounded like an order for seafood. "Tell you what", he continued, "I guarantee you the line back in service by Monday week – and a day or so earlier if all goes well." There just wasn't the experience in the new set-up. Again, it did not fill one with confidence.

The separation of the train driver provision (LUL) from that of the trains (Infracos) brings another inefficient fracture. With the re-equipping of the Victoria Line in the near future, LUL has the great opportunity to introduce a number of new concepts – fully automatic working, the introduction of the 'space train' (a train combining low-floor technology and other innovations to give more room inside the tube train loading gauge) and the elimination of the fourth (electric) rail[90]. It now seems none of these will be attempted. The Vic Line is almost fully underground (only tracks to and in the depot are above ground) and it does not inter-work with any other lines. With virtually all platforms straight, platform edge doors could be installed. Being underground, the low risk of outside influences should allow fully automatic working to be tried and tested before being extended to the older lines, which would, admittedly, be more problematic. There could be a saving (to LUL) on train staff salaries, but that would be offset by extra costs (to the Infraco) for the trains. Thus the division upsets a fair cost evaluation. Another simple solution would be for the Infracos to employ the drivers and supply both drivers and trains to LUL as a package, which would help the comparison.

A mystery is that, under PPP, I saw a timetable for replacements for the (then) 40-year-old Met line trains, which were scheduled to be for the same year as for the (then) 5-year-old Northern Line trains. A strange sort of prioritisation. But, then, the two replacements would be by different Infracos. And the designs I have seen of some of the trains seem ill-matched to passenger needs.

---

[90] Removing the fourth rail, which lies between the running rails, would allow an escape route for passengers, with far less risk of tripping, when detrainment (evacuation) is necessary in tunnels.

Such practical issues do not begin to tackle the issue of whether PPP is economic sense. I have listened to numerous comments, including some from one of the UK's leading economists, Stephen Glaister[91], who certainly should know what he is talking about. He stated that PPP was financially hopeless at best. Setting up the contracts alone cost £500 million, vastly more than a whole year's LUL subsidy for many previous years. What could have been done with that money? Only if it saved that amount – and much, much more – could the concept be justified. Having broken the close link between trains and stations, now the link between the trains, the stations and their staffing was broken as well. And, of course, who, in 30 years time, will ever be called to account if things do go wrong? 30 years puts anyone who set the thing up well out of the way of any accountability repercussions. (I once asked one of the constructors of the Medway viaduct for the Channel Tunnel Rail Link what the life expectancy of it was. He replied that it was 250 years. I commented that no-one was likely to worry about accounting for it failing to last that long.)

I said most managers were not in favour of the PPP, although many took jobs offered in the Infracos. But since their jobs in LUL were disappearing and they had offers of promotion and better salaries in the Infracos, who can blame them? One who did so admitted he had far less pressure and more money in his new post. Another said he'd been in his new job for nearly a year and had not been asked what he was doing.

So why, you may well ask, did we get PPP? Politics, politics, politics is the answer. And not necessarily party politics, because the PPP was pursued with the backing of none other than John Prescott – hardly a true blue Conservative – so Prescott, Prescott, Prescott would be another possible interpretation. The Treasury,

---

[91] Stephen Glaister CBE is Professor of Transport and Infrastructure at Imperial College London. His area of expertise is the economics of transport. Amongst many appointments, Prof Glaister was a non-executive director of London Regional Transport Board from 1984 to 1993 and later became a member of the Board of Transport *for* London

supported by Gordon Brown, was strongly in favour. Need I say more ... ?

Another reason is that there is a belief, strongly imbedded in the Treasury (and the wider civil service) psyche, that publicly-owned organisations are intrinsically inefficient and private industry the opposite. This is an unproved theory. When private concerns have paid their shareholders and others, their 'efficiency' is reduced. With PPP, all the participants will want a slice of the cake and, as we have already seen with the privatised National Rail system, some of the slices going to individuals are enormous.

I can only give a brief outline here. A number of books have been written on the subject and that written by Christian Wolmar, which I referred to at the beginning of this chapter, is a readable survey of a somewhat complex story, which I recommend.

The government had shown its lack of faith in the older style LUL management after the King's Cross fire, which was deemed to be symptomatic of LUL management incompetence – especially that which the government perceived to have occurred over the Jubilee Line Extension (JLE) project. Despite further changes at the top, ministers still failed to have confidence in the management (which, I imagine, had been largely foisted on LUL by the government, anyway). How much of the problem was poor management and how much was a governmental strait-jacket, it is difficult to assess. The stop:go financing that had applied to British Rail had applied to LUL, with devastating damage to firm forward planning. The 'down-sizing' policies of the early 1980s didn't help – but whose were they in origin? No-one with any appreciation of how these things work can believe that PPP was anything other than an example of the dead hand of the Treasury on the tiller, demanding something that accords with their doctrines - and to blazes with any practicalities.

Politicians are loath to admit they are wrong and the Labour government - particularly John Prescot - had invested a lot of credibility in PPP. The whole concept was continually changing. Another scene from the George Smiley Trilogy of John Le Carré comes to mind. Smiley is discussing fraudulent artwork with

Esterhase. He says, perceptively, that it becomes more difficult to admit you have been caught out with a fake work of art the more you have paid for it[92]. It must be so with political concepts.

Chris Bolt, the Arbiter for London Underground PPP Agreements, published his first review of the two Metronet Infracos in 2007. His report was adversely critical of weaknesses in the areas of stations, trains, track, maintenance, renewals, asset and risk management and a cost over-run of £750 million (which left little for praise.). His conclusion was that neither of the two Infracos had reached a required standard efficiently, economically or in conformance with Good Industry Practice. He said discussions with LUL were on-going over how the cost over-run could be filled (Metronet wanted LUL to pay). All pretty devastating stuff. And these were the consortia chosen to include established civil engineering companies and so on AND chosen from the competition as being the best. But possibly they, too, are still on a learning curve.

Only a few weeks later, Metronet called in Receivers, because it was financially unable to continue to function, after it had been refused (correctly, in my view) the right to claim the financial shortfall from T/L. Whether the failure of Metronet was due to essential failings in the PPP system, failings within Metronet management, or some of both is still unclear. The third is most likely.

In that respect, the seemingly better performance of the third Infraco, Tubelines, must be viewed, because, of course, they work to the same basic system, though with a different structure. To quote Chris Bolt again

> *"Because of the problems at Metronet, there is a tendency to think that Tubelines is perfect: they are not. But they are delivering broadly in line with the contract ..."*[93]

I sense there is a lot unsaid in that statement. Stephen Hall of Metronet believed that some work on stations had been too loosely

---

[92] *"Smiley's People"*, John Le Carré

[93] *"Modern Railways"*, August 2007.

specified in the PPP[94]. It all sounds rather shaky to me and again fails to inspire confidence.

This collapse of Metronet has shown the great weaknesses of the PPP system: its financial frailty and the lack of transfer of risk. The Infracos can walk away and the government - sorry, I should say the tax-payer and thus the passenger - picks up the bill which he thought he had already paid.

The Treasury, with Pound-signs in their eyes, Gordon Brown and John Prescott, as the chief proponents of the scheme, seem untouched by it all – not a rare occurrence with politicians. Mind you, the Conservatives must take their fair share of the blame. Their stop:go policies and erratic financial support hindered BR and LUL operating consistently and successfully. The resultant climate encouraged the privatisation ethos. The Department for Transport's (DfT's) attitude toward recent rail franchise awards seems to indicate that they are still carrying on the same policies.

There is now the expectation that large parts of the PPP projects will have to be deferred or 'scaled back', since Transport for London (TfL) haven taken over much of the *ex*-Metronet work. But we're told it's too late to go back on PPP, although the T*f*L take-over is far from the original concept.

I'm sure many people have said "I told you so" and it's difficult not to join in.

As to the grass-roots view of PPP, a member of station staff recently commented to me on the repeated failure of their Infraco to take successful action on repairs. The things they are supposed to have repaired fail again and they have to be called back to do the job again. Interestingly, I'm told that eastern European workers in the Infracos are some of the best workers and are far more reliable than others!

Despite the bad record of PPP, already myths are beginning to arise as to its (alleged) superiority compared with the 'old ways'.

---

[94] *ibid.*

For example, in an interview with a journalist, the MD of the Tubeline Infraco stated that an Infraco would be prepared to delay the start of the train service in the morning by 10 minutes, so as to finish a job, whereas LUL management would have been afraid to take such a decision and would run the service with a speed restriction. A former LUL manager quite rightly issued a refutation of that statement. LUL managers were more than willing (and were expected) to make decisions like that, taking a number of factors into consideration, to give the best service to passengers.[95]

Secondly, not long after the Metronet *débâcle*, Tim O'Toole, the then MD of LUL, wrote a reply to a member of staff who had complained about LUL management support of PPP. He replied that

> "*TfL fought hard to resist PPP prior to its imposition by the Government in 2003*[96]*.*"

Notice, he specifically mentions TfL's opposition. What he fails to mention is that the management of LUL at the time were all for PPP. The two factions had not agreed, but the truth was that LUL management had been in favour and showed no evidence of resistance. It appears that he used a politician's ploy – *ie,* he answered a different question to that asked! Another attempt to re-write history???

During those years of Treasury restriction over Underground finances, one could go around London seeing stations with tiles off the wall, cables hanging from ceilings and remedial work started but left unfinished. A general manager (one of the better ones) stated that one success marker of his tenure would be if the tiles that had been off the wall at a certain station when he had been an Area Manager would finally be replaced whilst he was GM. I think they were, but we are now facing the same situation again.

---

[95] Interview with Paul Coleman, quoted in *"Rail Professional"*, December 2007. The letter of refutation appeared the following month.
[96] Letter and response published in *"On the Move"*, the LUL staff magazine, March 2008

I have recently become interested in 18th Century Europe, especially the comparison between developments in Britain (political <u>evolution</u>) and our close neighbour, France (political <u>revolution</u>). Essentially, the PPP is a revolution. Like the Russian and French Revolutions before it – and many in the Third World since – it has involved the imposition of political dogma over naturally evolved situations, which have been suppressed. There has been and will be much blood-letting, but, hopefully, sanity will return once those who should be accountable have passed on. There will be a high price, not just monetary, and I doubt if it will be worth it. We can only wait and see how it all pans out in the end. As someone once responded to a question as to whether the French revolution was a success or not: "It's too soon to say". But, at present, it's not looking good[97].

---

[97] A recent assessment by Dr Mark J Gannon CMILT, *"Has Labour's Public Private Partnership funding policy for London Underground finally come to a halt?" in* CILT's *"Focus"* magazine, February 2010, has a very sceptical view.

18 - HOW GOOD IS THE UNDERGROUND?

Popular thought often places London's Underground as the biggest such network in the world. This is not true. Nowadays, there are quite a few larger systems worldwide and that in New York has been much bigger and more complex for decades.

However, the London Underground was probably the leading example of such systems until the 1950s. Indeed, a number of lines in other countries (*eg,* Canada, Venezuela) were modelled on the London system. The Second World War had taken its toll, although it could have recovered. But, after 1948, nationalisation, the post-war spate of strikes and increasing governmental interference took over and spoilt the undertaking.

The London Transport of the Ashfield/Pick-led 1930s was noted for its excellent design. Mind you, not all was wonderful, even then. The 1930s architecture of many of the stations was excellent in appearance, but there was a fascination with long flights of stairs. The designer of Harrow-on-the-Hill and Rayners Lane stations (as examples) should have been made to walk up and down the staircases until he came up with a more passenger-friendly design. Rayners Lane is known for its interchange between the Metropolitan and Piccadilly lines. But instead of an island platform to enable this to take place easily, passengers have to toil up and down two long staircases, frequently missing their train in the process. Now it is a listed building, so it presumably can't be changed. Harrow is next to a great shopping centre as well as being an important interchange station. Again, passengers face long up and down flights of stairs, frequently carrying shopping and/or children[98].

One of the things LUL became saddled with on the 1980s was a set of Key Performance Indicators (KPIs). These were supposed to be indications of how good the railway operated and were applied as were similar tests to other institutions like schools and hospitals. I don't know where they came from, but they appeared

---

[98] There is a subway at Harrow, to change platforms, but that also has stairs.

to be invented by someone who wanted statistics, but didn't know how to correctly measure how the railway operated.

Two examples spring to mind. One evening, I saw 6 fast trains to Amersham leave Baker Street within 10-15 minutes. The first was full, but the rest nearly empty. The service was running late, but one KPI was based on the mileage run, so 5 trains ran to fill the quota of mileage, even though their operation was virtually useless and probably delayed getting the service back on time. On another occasion, my immediate boss was harangued by his boss, because four trains went to one branch, whilst he waited for a train to the other. "Why didn't the Controller divert one of the four trains to the other branch?" (That's what used to be done in such circumstances.) My boss, who was also the Controller's boss, had to explain that the KPIs militated against such a sensible move and that the Controller's performance was measured by KPIs, not common sense! And so it went on, whilst the public did not get the better service the KPIs were supposed to ensure.

Once again, it's an example of a need to choose the right people to manage the railway and just let them do it, rather than tying them up in knots. The middle management LUL had at the time were more than capable of doing the job and this sort of thing just hindered them.

My time with LUL covered the period when vandalism increased, especially the scourge of graffiti. I got the distinct impression that LUL did not take it seriously for some time, perhaps thinking that it would just go away. This was despite the experience in the United States, where it was shown that only firm and sustained attention to the matter would turn things around[99]. The graffiti gangs came 'tooled up' with weaponry in some cases. Trains needed to be cleaned immediately, even if that meant being taken out of service – as had been done in New York. LUL were very reluctant to do that, unless the graffiti included particularly offensive language. What was done was far too little and far too late to avoid it becoming endemic and heavily graffitied trains were seen all over the system, especially on the Circle and

---

[99] See Malcolm Gladwell, "The Tipping Point", Abacus, 2001

Hammersmith lines. It must have deterred custom and given passengers the impression of a problem out of control – which it was.

Some trains had the whole sides of cars covered, including windows. Belatedly, LUL made their depots into stockades, with very high fences, cctv and alarm systems. The damage was reduced, but tagging[100] remained rampant, as this could be done whilst trains were in service. Stations were attacked and the Christmas closure of the system allowed gangs to get further into tunnels to increase their damage.

One station I knew was given a beautiful repaint, with all the Victorian artwork picked out carefully. It took a few weeks and looked splendid. Three days after it was finished, undercoat appeared all over the brand new paintwork and within a few days the station was covered in drab, anti-graffiti paint. The irony was that that particular station had very little graffiti and LUL didn't wait for it to happen to apply the standard drabness. Why the station had been given its magnificent paint job I never discovered and it seems it was obliterated before any pictures were taken. I've certainly never seen any. It was another 'one size fits all' approach and was a crying shame.

LUL was not helped by the legal system which also reacted too slowly and softly. Magistrates and so on were often weak in their responses. I recall one parent I had to deal with who just did not want to know what filth her young son had written on the train, lack of parental control being another problem. When perpetrators got killed or injured whilst carrying out their crimes, LUL was blamed for that too.

The police allocated seemed insufficient. The team was headed by a sergeant. It seems the graffiti criminals knew who he was and taunted him by writing messages to him on the railway, making jibes and so on. Sadly, I heard he eventually had some kind of breakdown, although I cannot be certain that rumour was correct.

---

[100] 'Tagging' or 'Tags' refers to the smaller but still irritating graffiti, usually with marker pens in the form of a name or word.

This reminds me of a problem that arose over the LUL section of the British Transport Police. There were only a limited number of officers in the force. After much pressure, we were told that more officers had been authorised (I can't recall the exact number, but it was about 40, I think). After some months with no apparent change, I heard that the officers had indeed been agreed by one committee, but then the cash support for them had been vetoed by another. So they did not materialise. How much of the blame lies at LUL's door, I don't know, but it shows how its performance can be affected by outside influences.

The recession around 1980 brought different problems, especially when numbers of travellers burgeoned afterwards, as it caught LUL on the hop.

Downsizing had been expected. For example, a number of stations such as Mornington Crescent, Edgware Road (Bakerloo) and Regents Park were expected to close. New signals were put in, to slow trains through the platforms rather than stopping. But, apart from Mornington Crescent, which re-opened later, the stations never closed.

Signalling was an area in which things went badly adrift. Between the 20s and the 50s, the Underground had refined its signalling to give a smooth throughput for its service, which is what should happen. One feature was the placing of up to 6 signals at the approach to busy platforms. Simply stated, the principle was that a train could make a full-speed approach to a platform with a train already standing there. If the approaching train did not stop at the first signal, which showed red as protection, it would be halted when it passed that signal by the trip-cock/trainstop mechanism. If the train slowed down correctly, as of course it should, the signal would change to green before the train stopped and the train would pass the signal, now at a reduced speed. If the second train continued at reduced or reducing speed, it would pass successive signals, each changing to green if the required speed was detected, getting nearer to the platform and the train in front, but always a safe braking distance away. Thus, trains could get closer together and increase line capacity, the second train running into the platform as the first left. This was with manually-driven trains and good operating discipline by the drivers.

Under the resignalling schemes, many of such systems were taken out and signalling simplified, as fewer trains were deemed necessary with reduced patronage. Ironically, LUL are now seeking such things as automatic running at great expense to achieve the same (and, in some cases, inferior) results as the Underground achieved years ago.

Unexpectedly, the economy revived, patronage of the underground soared and a reversal occurred, but now with reduced carrying capacity on some lines. LUL is now carrying more passengers than ever before. Bar Aldwych and the Epping – Ongar section, none of the station closures went ahead and the reduced signalling became a problem. For example, following the introduction of a new timetable, the Divisional General Manager of the Met wrote a great complaint to staff about the delays, which he blamed on the train crews. In the morning, some trains were regularly taking 15-20 minutes to get from Finchley Road to Baker Street, instead of about 6-7 minutes. But the new signalling of the north side of the Circle, into which many of these trains were funnelled, had reduced capacity of the line from 33 trains per hour (tph) or more to only 28 tph or less. In fact, under the new timetable, 28 trains were due to pass in the critical morning peak hour (actually, 29 trains in 61 minutes). So the line was at full capacity, even if all trains were bang on time to the second, which they were not.

Approaching trains now had to wait further away from platforms than before.

Also, many more signals were now programmed to show red as trains approached, even when there was no train in front, so drivers shut off power and even applied the brakes before the signals went green. A signal computer programmer travelled with me one day and I asked him about this. He said another train might need to use a junction, so the signal remained red until the last minute. I pointed out that one particular junction was normally used only once a day; why delay all trains? A few weeks later that signal was altered to normally show green.

But this brings us to a basic principle of signalling. Popular belief is that signals are primarily there to stop trains. They are not. The main reason for signals is to get trains along a piece of track as efficiently and safely as possible – in other words to maximise throughput. Stopping a train should only occur to prevent an accident or to regulate the service. If trains all ran as they should, stopping of trains would be minimised and that should always be the aim, if not (of course) always being achieved. But that basic concept seemed to have been lost on LUL at that time. No wonder trains were being held up.

Escalators have also been a continuing problem. They are used very intensively - often for 18 or more hours a day - far more than those in shops. In many locations, the number of escalators has been insufficient for many years. In general, where there are two escalators, there should be three and where there are three there should be four. I'm told that in the 'good old days', any station with an escalator had its own mechanic, who tended his charges continually. They were kept clean and well-functioning. But this was replaced with on-call mechanics and standards dropped. This was probably a contributory cause of the fire at King's Cross. The delays and inconvenience to passengers by escalators being out of service is evident. With so much of the London Underground being at deep level, the time taken to get to and from the surface is a large proportion of the journey and thus critical.

The Jubilee Line Extension (JLE) was heralded as a marvel. True, the service is usually quick once you are on the train and the stations are spacious. But many of the managers complained that grandiose station plans had been implemented at the expense of practicalities such as ease of cleaning and vast amounts of glass. Canary Wharf station had supplementary hoardings and home-made notices for months, because of poor attention to design detail. Compare the accessibility of the Jubilee Line extension from other Lines with the same-level, cross-platform access to and from the Victoria Line at many stations. The latter was built with ease of changing in mind, which the JLE was not (shades of Rayners Lane again). It is fair to compare the Jubilee Line Extension with the new Line 14 of the Paris Metro. To me the

French line is better in a number of ways. The fact that the JLE Project was virtually run as a separate entity is reflected in its lack of practical and passenger-friendly integration with the rest of the system.

The signalling for the Jubilee was another major embarrassment. Up until nearly the last minute, a new kind of system was expected, that would use new technology to improve on the kind of system that I mentioned a few paragraphs ago (allowing trains to get closer together), to increase line capacity. Belatedly, the company due to install the system admitted they could not deliver the goods and a conventional signalling system was hurriedly put in. There were subsequently numerous SPADs, partly due to the siting of some signals, but also, I suspect, due to the numerous newly-qualified drivers and the haste in some stages of implementation.

Another problem on LUL was the lack of follow-through of projects or abandonment of a subsequent phase of a project. Because of a desire to help disabled persons, the new Northern Line trains provide over 750 wheel-chair spaces per hour between Kennington and Morden, but there is only one station thereabouts where the platforms are accessible from ground level without stairs or escalators. Indeed, only two other stations on the Northern Line are wheel-chair accessible – both are north of London and accessible in one direction of travel only. I wonder how many unaccompanied wheel-chair users will ever travel on the trains.

This touches an area of improvement that LUL is repeatedly censured for, namely, access for disabled people. I feel that this is somewhat unfair. The system is very old and many of the stations are far below ground level. LUL are working through a plan to make a number of platforms step-free accessible from ground level, but there is still the problem of getting on and off the trains. This normally involves a step up or down, often with a gap because the platforms are not straight, and some platforms are served by trains with differing floor heights. There is technology to cover all these features, but the cost would be phenomenal. An articulated train, with short vehicles (like the new Parisian trains), would serve LUL better in this respect, as the straight sides of the cars would match far more closely the curved edges of the platforms. The cost of making the network as accessible as some modern systems is probably prohibitive. How much is society prepared to pay to make the system 80 or 90 or 98 or even 100% accessible? I have also heard that, with the PPP *fiasco*, the platform access program is being cut back or slowed.

Another area in which I believe LUL is unfairly pilloried is the continual request for 24 hour Underground service. This is not really feasible. Running trains all night would greatly impede maintenance. It is also not necessary. As long as London is provided with a good all-night bus service, all-night Underground service should normally only be needed for special events, such as Royal weddings, the Olympics and New Year.

LUL introduced a new fleet of trains on the Northern Line in 1996. For years after they were built they could not run at their designed speed as the second part of the project, for new signalling, was never even started. New signalling is still awaited.

This is typical of politically-inspired projects on a railway. New trains and, to a lesser extent, new and refurbished stations, are 'sexy'. But new signalling and track is not. The public see the first two, but little of the other two and really only notice when they fail. But new trains bring limited improvement if the signalling and track can't allow them to function properly. A similar truth applies to power supplies. Recently, there was the farce on the National Rail system when a new fleet of trains could not run as designed because the power supply was inadequate. A bit like getting a new toy for Christmas, but having no batteries for it.

Frequently, projects are hindered by political ham-stringing. The great new King's Cross transport interchange was stifled by unfinished platforms and a non-existent booking hall area until the approach of the Olympics gave it a fillip. Madness. Spoiling the multi-million pound ship for a few hundred thousand pounds of tar was normal.

Another small example remains in my mind. On a management trip once, we were shown a new 'electronic notice board' at a vital central London station. (This was long before such things became common-place.) It was not working because it had broken down. The Station Inspector said that LUL had bought the thing but there was no money for a maintenance contract, so it remained unmended and useless, whilst still standing in its prime location on the station, mute testimony to bad management.

On another occasion, we were shown a piece of equipment from a station. LUL had specified that it have a metal cover of a certain thickness (I can't recall the exact measurements). This meant extra cost, as the metal normally came in thicknesses of .5mm more or less than specified, so LUL's production had to be specially made. One has to ask if the difference of half a millimetre, which cost LUL a lot of money in obtaining a comparatively small order of specially milled metal, was really necessary.

Some LUL trains have selective door opening, some not and the policies on different lines differed. Standardisation now means that all doors open at every station. As a result, at many stations, trains stand for ages with the doors wide open, freezing or soaking the passengers in inclement weather, because the doors cannot be closed. The doors-closing tones differ from train to train – and even the lifts have different tones. If you want to be deafened, go and hear the lifts at Goodge Street. Quite why there is so much noise in these tones, I do not know. People with poor sight can often hear clearly; whilst those who are deaf can usually see reasonably well. I'm all for assisting disabled people and for making public transport easily accessible to all – but do we need all this noise (this complaint also applies to London's buses)? Many other metro lines have quite pleasing tones, why not London?

The handrails on some refurbished trains were in dedicated line colour; others in a special colour that those with sight problems could see more easily. Another case of inconsistency.

Lack of practical attention to details like the above show great weakness in thought processes, which one feels would not have been so likely in the pre-War LT, which was very detail-conscious.

Have you ever tried to sit on a platform seat at a station and found that your knees are just under your chin? You'll probably see that the platform is paved. In one of those rushed LUL projects, a number of station platform surfaces were paved with slabs that are at least an inch-and-a-half thick. They were laid without removing the seats, so that the seats are now effectively 2 ins or more 'lower' than before[101]. There are some at Harrow-on-the-Hill and, when I pass through, I like to make a little pilgrimage and sit on them (with difficulty). They remain as testimony to a sad era in LUL's history. Pick and his team would either weep or go ballistic.

Once, a pair of lifts were electrically and otherwise renovated. They were triumphantly returned to service and then kept failing. LUL called the contractor to account, but it was found that the contractors had done what was asked for; it was the spec, written by LUL, which was wrong.

When one station was to be renovated, the manager (whom I know well) said that, whatever happened, a certain make of escalator must not be used. He had had experience of the type elsewhere and they were always troublesome. Guess which type was installed at this flagship station?

You may think some of this is nit-picking. But they are just a very few examples of inefficiencies that just should not occur with good management.

A feature that was included at the end of a series of meetings for a project was the 'Lessons Learned Meeting'. At that, the good, bad and ugly aspects of the project were discussed and recorded for posterity, particularly so that those involved in a following project could learn from the errors and good points of this one. Well, that

---

[101] Of course, the seats have not moved; the ground has moved upwards!

was the idea. At one that I attended, one of the participants (who had joined the project late) pointed out that this project had made an error that had been made in a project he had been involved in some time previously. The Project Leader said it was a pity that they hadn't known about it before. It then transpired that the error had been recorded at the Lessons Learned Meeting for the earlier project – but no-one from this later project had been aware of it. There seemed to be no method for passing on the lessons learned.

This brings to mind an anecdote told by an engineer/historian. He was talking to a civil engineer who was finding problems in the geology of a part of the Midlands, whilst he was building the M1 motorway. The historian pointed out that the builder of the Grand Union Canal in the 18th Century and later the engineer for the London to Birmingham Railway in the 19th had encountered exactly the same problem before him. The historian had read of the problem, but not the 20th Century civil engineer.

The Circle line has now been operating more or less in its current form for well over 100 years, yet, over the last decade or so, LUL have repeatedly said they want to kill it off. The public like it as it is and they would be greatly disadvantaged by the latest proposals. It seems management find it difficult to operate. I worked on the Circle line in various capacities over ten years or more and have travelled on it for 50 years. It should have no more difficulties than any other line, if managed properly. True, it runs partly over the Metropolitan and partly over the District, but even when it was jointly managed for a while (when the Met and District were both part of the Sub Surface Lines management) there were moves to change it. At one time, LUL proposed a 'pan-handle' operation. Trains would start at Hammersmith, go all around the Circle and then terminate at Whitechapel or somewhere east thereof (and *vice versa*). The latest idea is a 'teacup' route. The trains would start at Hammersmith, go through Edgware Road, then all around the Circle and terminate at Edgware Road the second time they got there and go back the same way. Passengers to and from the western end of the Circle to and from the north side will thus always have to change at Edgware Road, which often means changing platforms and missing a train. I find it very difficult to understand how something possible in 1909 is not considered practical in 2009. Any 'problems' of operation just need firm management but seem to have been put in the 'too difficult' box.

LUL has stopped being innovative to any large extent.

I was involved – albeit in a very small way – with the choice of a new train for one of the lines. When I saw the choice, I was surprised at the lack of innovation. What was on offer was just a modernised version of the 1962 Tube Stock, which, in itself was a (then) modern version of the 1938 stock.

Why? Well, the story was a repeat of the situation in 1960, when new stock was wanted for the Central Line. Cravens had provided some prototype new trains, but it was decided that the re-stocking was too urgent and so a version of the trains already on the Piccadilly Line was ordered. This meant that many innovations were excluded. Prominent amongst these were the non-handedness (or non-ambidextrousness.) of the Cravens' trains[102]. In fact, the introduction of new trains was probably only provoked by the propensity of the 30-40-year-old trains then in service to catch fire, with some horrifying results.

Ironically, the "A" stock on the Metropolitan was reversible until they were modernised, when the ability was lost.

The 'rush job' approach has occurred on many other occasions, because of the stop:go government financing of LUL. Unlike most people, LUL could not hold un-spent cash over until the following year. If you have saved up for a new garage or house extension and the builder can't arrive for a month, you don't lose your money – you save it. LUL could not do this, so it either got the job done quickly or saw the money lost for ever. Since the money was often not allocated to them until a month or two before the end of the financial year, it was often impossible to get a

---

[102] Most LUL stock of the time had different couplings at extreme ends of the trains and one could only couple front to back, left to right or however you like to put it. As the Central Line included a loop, trains got turned around and so often could not couple up. The Cravens' trains would couple front to front or any combination and so would have been a great advantage.

decent project up, running and completed in time, so the money was squandered. This was the fault of the intransigence of government and especially the Treasury.

A simple example: One week-end, without my being told, my office was painted. The dirt on the walls still showed through afterwards. When I asked when the second coat would be applied, I was told there was to be no second coat. I told the man in charge not to pay for the shoddy job, but he said it was too late; it had been paid for already.

I know the world is always changing: it has always been so, if not always at the current rate. But LUL seems to be infatuated with change.

At a 'stir up the troops' meeting in 2007, a leading member of LUL's top management team told Duty Managers that, to face the challenge of the 2012 Olympics, LUL would have to change their way of working. This is an extraordinary statement. This man has been a top manager during more than a decade of changes: was he admitting they still hadn't got it right? And, anyway, no organisation should need to radically change its method of working to cope with an event lasting less than a month. Would it change back afterwards? A railway should have a good, robust system of working that can be adapted to meet temporary features. LUL have for long handled such traffic varying from evening dog racing at White City to large Wembley events, State Funerals, Coronations, the Olympics in 1948 and the Millennium. It handled the evacuation of thousands of children from London at a few days' notice during the last World War. Certainly, the 2012 Olympics is a big event, but, with the additional infrastructure being built and a judicious training and movement of staff, a well-organised company should cope and then get back to the normal day job of moving Londoners with no crises.

It's not that LUL needs radical change all the time. As I said before, one of the bases of LUL's earlier success was that they made haste slowly, not rushing into things but testing them out.

What should be happening is that LUL should have a few innovative items of rolling stock (for example) on trial much of the time, to be ready at a developed stage when re-stocking with new trains is possible. The RATP in Paris has done this with their automated, pneumatic-tyred and articulated trains. They have a train running on a quiet shuttle line that can be easily closed to the public if the tests have a hitch, since there are alternative routes available. London Transport used to do it and could use a line like the (currently closed) Aldwych – Holborn shuttle for experiments. The planned LUL 'Space Train', alternative types of current collection and fully automated running could be trialled there. By now, if successful, the experiments could have been extended to the Waterloo & City Line, ready to be introduced on the Victoria Line, as it receives new trains. But, because the management are always at the behest of their political lords and masters, a predicament made worse with PPP, such common sense measures are stifled and chances lost for decades.

At the other end of the scale, simple improvements get overlooked. Euston Square station actually starts below the ground very near Euston Square (*ie,* near Euston Main Line station), but the entrance is at the far end of the platforms, making its name a misnomer and misleading many. The resultant walk from Euston Main Line station is a long trek for passengers, often with luggage. A very simple thing would be to have a second entrance at the Euston Square end of the platforms, greatly reducing the walk. Even better, a covered walkway to the main line station could be provided. And Euston Square could be linked to nearby Warren Street station. These would surely feature in Paris; why not here? One feels that the answer is that such minor things don't set LUL MDs' blood racing – nor that of their political overlords – nor even, possibly, the Mayor. But a nice big project, costing umpteen millions, <u>does</u> get them excited. Compare with the public excitement when Thameslink up-grade or Crossrail was on the agenda for the umpteenth time, without actually getting built.

This inability of our political masters to see what is happening must cost billions and stifle good things. I remember being lectured by one of the senior managers who started up the

Docklands Light Railway system (DLR). He explained that the DLR appeared to be a white elephant, being grossly over engineered for the area's transport needs and its 11 trains more than sufficient for the traffic on offer. Obviously, he could not foresee the vast development of Canary Wharf and so on that was imminent. Within a year or so, the first of the mega-rebuildings of the DLR began, because it was far too small; all those 11 trains got sent to a tramway in Germany, being replaced by a new and much larger fleet.

About 15 years ago, LUL decided to get rid of its pocket-size Rule Book that staff were expected to have with them at all times when on duty. It was replaced by a Procedures Manual that grew to fill eight or more lever-arch files. It was fine for task analysis, but not for easy reference and memorisation. I suspect this is a large element in the decline of rule adherence amongst staff. It was just too unwieldy. But - guess what? - LUL has just introduced ... yes ... a Rule Book! - although it's nothing like as comprehensive or succinct as the old one. Round and round we go.

So - are things getting better since the new *régime* and PPP were introduced??

Not long ago, when talking about the number of passengers delayed checking in for Eurostar, Ian Brown, the MD of London Rail (part of Transport *for* London) stated that they try and make allowances for passengers delayed by connecting public transport. He admitted that the Underground was the worst offender in this respect[103].

A survey quoted by the Institute of Logistics and Transport in the spring of 2007 stated that the delays on the underground were worse than 10 years before. For example, the number of delays lasting 15 minutes or more was higher than in 1996-7. The figure then was 2656 delays, but it had increased to 2740. The District, Met, Northern and Victoria lines all showed a decline in performance since 1996-7. Services on the Piccadilly and Victoria lines had also worsened. Individual journeys were calculated to be

---

[103] *"Modern Railways"*, March 2007

taking, on average, five minutes longer than expected. At the same time, many fares had risen by 250%. It seems that the generation of new managers that have replaced those of us who have left has not effected an improvement. Or is it the way they are now expected to work? Either way, I'm not in the least surprised.

Here are three examples from my own recent experiences on a brief visit to the London area. Firstly, I made a short trip on the Bakerloo Line which had no hitch. A week later, I travelled on the simple two-station (Metronet maintained) Waterloo & City line, which had just re-opened after a second shut-down of many months. We had to wait some time for a train in the rush hour. At Bank, three train-loads of passengers awaited the one train. The waiting queue stretched way back to the circulating area. After I took 5 minutes to get through it, I heard a loudspeaker apology that the service was suspended due to a signal defect. The service was still suspended three hours later. On the Metropolitan Line, about a week later, Chiltern Line trains were cancelled and Met trains had to run on the local lines, due to "an obstruction on the track" – just after the shamed Metronet had supposedly finished a week-end shutdown of the line for engineering works. Not a happy record, but all-too-common for regular passengers.

I was very optimistic when 'the Americans' came to take over at the top of LUL. Good things were said of Bob Keily and his success in the US. Surely, I thought, he and Tim O'Toole would make a good team. But, in fact, I sensed little appreciable improvement. True, we often saw Tim O'Toole on TV, in a hard hat, telling us that the Underground would be going through an upheaval, which would disrupt passengers for years – but that there would be 'jam tomorrow' or more likely the day after the day after tomorrow. As I suspected, he left the scene long before the promised jam appeared! As for Bob Keily, it seems he was 'nobbled' from the day he arrived and was never allowed to do the job he came to do. Maybe we'll never know the truth about their era.

LUL is now carrying more passengers than ever before. That must be good. But compare that with a generation or so ago. They now have two completely new lines (the Jubilee extensions and Victoria) that did not exist in the 30s and 50s on which to carry the increase. In various places, in those days, the Underground ran a mix of 3-, 4-, 7- and 9-car trains, where it now runs 6-car trains; it operated a mix of 5-, 6- and 8-car trains where they now also only run 6-car trains; with all-stations and limited-stop trains on the same tracks; and more trains at more frequent intervals. These demanded a high level of staff discipline to handle them. Most of this is no longer done. .

I'm not saying that all these features of the past are necessarily needed now, but LUL just doesn't seem to be able to reach these previously-attained performances. As I have hinted, even with the promised expensive new kit, in many cases the result will not be better than in the past. One has to ask why and the answer seems to be that the management is just not up to it.

19 - FINALE – The Way Out

One last quote from John Le Carré's Smiley trilogy seems apposite as I came to my final chapter:

> *"In my time [says Smiley], ... I have seen Whitehall skirts go up and come down again ... I've watched people hop up and down and call it progress. I've seen good men go to the wall and the idiots promoted with a dazzling regularity ..."*

Sadly, I can see similarities with London Underground – certainly with regard to some of the alleged progress and good men and women being pushed aside.

In my various bosses, I looked for someone I could respect; who didn't give orders like a dictator, but was willing to be reasoned or even argued with if I thought he was wrong; who was big enough to change his mind if I had a good argument; and was able to give me confidence in his decision if he insisted on his original idea. Too much to ask? But, as they also say: "The boss may not always be right, but he's always the boss". So we soldier on ...

What lies behind the poor performance of railway (and, I suspect, many other) managements?

If you believe in creation rather than evolution, if you don't believe human-originated CO_2 emissions are the main cause of global warming, or if you fail to believe any other doctrine that happens to be in vogue, then you are treated much like Galileo, who dared to believe the earth went around the sun. Likewise, if you are not PC, if you think practical management is more important than just finance and so on, and if you fail to embrace the culture of 'modern management', you are rejected from the current business world as a heretic.

A friend of mine put it that a whole generation of managers who dared to state a contrary view to that propounded by those at the top has been labelled 'dinosaurs' - ridiculed, removed or bribed (by redundancy or other pay-offs) to get out. It's not a happy story

I was able to retire. But I sometimes wonder what might have happened if I had continued my career for longer. The whole ethos of management was changing. So-called performance issues came more and more to the fore. An able manager I greatly respected, with longer experience than me, was removed from his job as he had allegedly 'failed to perform' to some standard or other. He was replaced by a 'minority' person, who is still not performing to anything like his standard. Fortunately, he now has a less-stressful job in the company. Like others of the old school, I would probably have been side-tracked on some pretence, as I came in the dinosaur category.

I accept that one weakness I have is that I am not always able to prove my case on an issue with explicit data. I remember my boss discussing an important signalling issue with me. He gave me a couple of timings and then began to work out the third on his calculator. "It must be about 13.5", I said. About 20 seconds later he said it was 13.4-something. L was a great help to me on this. Like me, L had come from being train staff to being a manager. He was very good at what he did and the last I heard was being fast-tracked to a higher position, which he well deserved. He was then doing an analytical job. I would go to him from time to time and say something like: "Look, L, I've been thinking. At the moment we are doing X. If we change to Y, surely, such and such will happen. He'd grin; start tapping on his PC and quickly produce a spread-sheet that proved my point to two or three decimal places. I wished I had that talent. But at least I knew my instincts weren't off the wall. We just can't all be wiz-kids at data processing!

I have often been asked if the work was difficult. Frankly, I don't think so. On occasions, it was impossible; normally it was satisfying; rarely if ever tedious. But there was also the frustration of experiencing the influence of politics and the way such elements could hinder the operations of the railway.

On one of our training courses we were told that few people will destroy something they have created. But we often felt we were seeing others destroy it. Not exactly motivating.

Years ago, the late Gerard Fiennes (whom I've quoted earlier), the then General Manager of the BR Eastern Region, wrote *"I Tried to Run a Railway"* about his career[104], which led to his being sacked.

Having written much of the above, I re-read *"I Tried ... "* and found how many times I was in agreement with Fiennes' thinking. I have already quoted his wisdom in this book. He said of railway management in general and of operations particularly:

> *"There are many people who think they must Maintain Their Positions, all in capitals. There is probably less need for this self-importance on railways than in any other walk of life. [The railway starts] with the enormous advantage of a sublime discipline which we build into all the key grades through the rule book [...] the time-table [...] the men's workings, the rosters [...]"[105]*

I think that supports much of what I have said repeatedly. Along with many other railway managers, I respect Fiennes greatly, as a man who knew what he was talking about. Together with Rolt's *"Red for Danger"*, Fiennes' book should be required reading for all railway managers.

Roger Ford[106], whom I have also quoted earlier, recently said of a current senior railway manager

> *"[he] is one of those who regards "I Tried to Run a Railway" as a manual for the 21st century rather than a nostalgic memoir":*

Oh for many more like him!

By now you may have come to an opinion as to my suitability to manage. But at least I feel that, whatever your assessment, I was in good company

Fiennes said of his own life on the railway:

> *"[...] this book and my career are nothing to do with how to run a railway but everything to do with what fun it is to be a railwayman"[107].*

---

104 *"I Tried to Run a Railway"*, Ian Allan, 1967.
105 *Ibid.*
106 *"Modern Railways"*, January 2008
107 *"I Tried to Run a Railway"*, Ian Allan, 1967.

He undersold himself – he gave us some excellent pointers as to how to run a railway as well.

Compliments were rare in LUL, but, just before my departure, I did receive one that amused me. I had gone to see the chief of what had been the Rules & Regulations section, to discuss a new Procedure that had been published. I felt it had a wrong emphasis as to the way an important situation should be handled and gave my reasons. After having an "open and frank exchange of views" on the subject, he told me they would revise the Procedure to cover the points I had made. Then he said: "You know, Andy, you're a real pain in the butt. The problem is that you're usually right." Only "usually"? Ah, well, I can live with that! Perfection would be boring!!

Somebody who read this MS asked how I and those like me could continue in an organisation like LUL. Well, like Fiennes, I 'tried to run a railway' and had fun, albeit I never reached Fiennes' level of management. There was the enjoyment of seeing things happen as a result of my efforts. Apart from self-interest (*ie,* the job and the money), there was the genuine sense of serving a purpose, even if the public and my boss didn't always appreciate it. I was often able to go home feeling I had made a difference. I certainly felt much of that satisfaction during my career. Not a bad review.

Despite what I have written, LUL was a great organisation for which to work, regardless of its many failings at the top. There was the diversity of rôles, with different, able people meshing their expertise to make the whole thing work like the huge machine it was. As I said earlier, there was great *camaraderie* and *esprit de corps* amongst the staff and that compensated for much of the negative side. And there was the sense of achievement in helping make London tick.

I have few regrets as to my time with LUL. I met some great people, whom I liked, whose company I enjoyed and whom I respected for their abilities. To them I say a sincere 'thank you' for their support, for their contributions to this volume – and for a good time.

APPENDIX - Glossary, List of Acronyms etc

55 Broadway
See Broadway, 55, below.

1938, 1955/6/9 *etc* Tube Stock
Rolling stock (trains) operating on the real tube lines *(qv)* (the smaller trains) are known by the year of design/introduction into service.

A, B, C *etc* Stock
Designations of LUL rolling stock (trains) of the larger varieties, operating on the sub-surface lines *(qv)*. Strictly, in many cases, the letter is followed by the last two figures of the year of design or introduction into service (*eg,* A60, A62, C69, C77, Q27, Q38, R49), which can distinguish modifications of a type between different batches.

A1A-A1A and so on
Describes the arrangement of wheels under certain locomotives. If you don't know exactly what it means, believe me, you don't really need to. If you must know, ask a real 'anorak' or rail professional, who will happily spend hours explaining the minutiae to you.

ACAS = The Advisory, Conciliation and Arbitration Service.
An organisation set up by the government to act as independent intermediary ('honest broker') between employers and employees in disputes over terms of employment, salaries and such-like.

AM = Area Manager
See Ch 2

ASLEF = Associated Society of Locomotive Engineers and Firemen
One of the Trades Unions representing Train Drivers/Train Operators.

ATO = Automatic Train Operator or Automatic Train Operation.
Automatic Train Operator was a term used when there was a
separate grade for the 'drivers' of the (partly) automated Victoria
Line trains.

ATOC
Association of Train Operating Companies (*see* TOC below)

'Black Macs'
Term used to describe supervisory staff such as Inspectors, as they
frequently wore black Macintosh raincoats (and often Trilby
hats!). They were very much out-and-about, hands-on and get-
stuck-in types, rather than the "I'll-tell-you-how-it-should-be-done
(but had never done it)" sort. To my mind, the black mac gents
were true professionals. Roger Ford *(qv)*, the respected railway
journalist, refers to them as
> *"the warrant officers of the old railway who made things*
> *happen through a combination of knowledge and authority*
> *based on hard won experience"[108].*
An excellent description. The type is greatly needed today!

Booking Office
Original term for Ticket (selling) Office. (The transactions were
originally written in a book – hence the name.)

BR = British Rail (previously British Railways)
The name of the British national railway system following
nationalisation in 1948.

Broadway, 55
The Headquarters of LUL are in an Art-Deco building at 55
Broadway, London SW1 (almost opposite the latest New Scotland
Yard headquarters of London's Metropolitan Police), with famous
Epstein statuary on it. It is variously referred to as '55 Broadway',
'Broadway' or just '55'.

---

108 *"Modern Railways"*, April 2008

BTP = British Transport Police
A special police force that covers rail transport in the UK. The 'L' division covers LUL.

Car = carriage
Americans were much involved in some of London's earlier underground lines and so US railway terms came to apply in some cases.

Clip and Scotch
See Scotch and Clip

Company Plan
Part of a radical restructuring of LUL, which came about after the Kings Cross fire (*(qv)*. It is referred to in Chapter 10.

Current Rails
Rails provided to carry current to and from electric trains. *See* under "Track"

Customer Service Assistant
Latest title of a member of staff who works at the basic level on a station.

DfT = Department for Transport
Government Department - part of the Civil Service

Disciplinary Board (DB)/Disciplinary Hearing
A high-level event where repeated failure to work correctly or a first serious breach is dealt with by a small court. *See* the chapter concerned.

Division
The various lines of the Underground were previously grouped in two sets of 4 and later four pairs, known as Divisions, each with Divisional Head Offices and management. *See* Chapter 2 under 'Area Managers'.

DI = Divisional Inspectors ('Dee-eyes')
See Chapter 2 under 'Area Managers'.

Dmu/DMU = Diesel Multiple Unit.
A diesel-powered train that has the motors in or under the coaches rather than in a separate locomotive.

EP (often EPB on main line railways) = Electro-pneumatic brake.
A brake using a combination of electricity and air. Some earlier versions were not fail-safe and so trains with such also had a straight air brake system (*see* under Westinghouse).

ETMS = European Train Management System(s)
A modern *pan*-European railway signaling project, designed to bring a staged standardized signaling system to European railways, simplifying cross-border operation.

Fiennes, Gerard MBE, MInstT, MA
The late GF Fiennes (I understand it's actually Twistleton-Wykeham-Fiennes, although I've not discovered what the middle initial F stood for), then General Manager of the Eastern Region of British Railways, author and commentator. Surely a railwayman's – at least a railway manager's – guru.

Ford, Roger AMInstSE
Experienced engineer, journalist and commentator on the past and modern railway scene.

GM = General Manager

Guard
Railway employee who rode on and was in charge of the running of a train, including operation of or oversight of the passenger doors. Now not normally found on British rail lines except preserved lines.

HR = Human Resource/s
The staff of a company. A term I detest, as people are not a mere resource like bricks or a machine. Staff, employees, personnel or even people are better terms, with suitable related titles for the responsible department.

HST = High Speed Train(s) (Sometimes called 'Inter-City 125')
A great achievement of British Rail of the 70s, who created one of
the most successful Inter-City trains ever built. Essentially, they
have a locomotive at each end of a number of coaches. Being
refurbished, they are still in front-line service at up to 125mph (I
believe one reached 141mph on a trial run).

Infracos
Short-hand term for Infrastructure Company. This refers to the
companies that were set up to renew and maintain the
infrastructure of LUL. They are parallel organisations to Network
Rail although legally different.

King's Cross
A London main line railway station, the site of King's Cross St
Pancras LUL station, which was the scene of a serious fire in
1987. The tragedy was the catalyst for many changes in LUL and
the name 'King's Cross' is used as a shorthand term for that
incident, in comments such as "Before/After King's Cross …".

LFB = London Fire Brigade
Later part of the LFCDA = London Fire and Civil Defence
Authority.

LUL = London Underground Limited
This was the company set up by the government to run the London
Underground when it was separated from the bus service, although
both are under the control of Transport *for* London (the "for" is
italicized for some reason), the buses being operated by London
Buses Ltd.
When the buses, underground railways and trams in London were
amalgamated in the 1930s, they were known as London Transport,
although the Underground was still often referred to as 'the
UNDERGROUND', continuing a style of signage favoured by one of
the constituent companies. After nationalisation in 1948, the
organisation became the London Passenger Transport Board and
has subsequently been known by various other legal titles.
The buses and trains are still popularly known collectively as
London Transport and the Underground as 'the Tube', even tho'

the latter term strictly only applies to the deep part of the system in pipe-like tunnels (*see* 'The Tube' and 'Tube lines').

M25
The motorway that almost surrounds the London area.

'Mafia(s)'
See under "Syndicates".

MD = Managing Director

Met = Metropolitan Line or Railway

Metro
A generic term to describe frequent-interval urban railways, especially those that run (at least partially) underground. Dennis Tunicliffe (an earlier LUL MD) said he wanted LUL to be a *"thoroughly modern Metro"*, but generally LUL is never called a metro (nor by the North American term 'Subway').

Metronet
The name of two of the Infracos *(qv)*.

Metropolitan Railway
One of the railways that later formed part of LUL. Roughly the equivalent of the present Metropolitan Line, although the Metropolitan Railway was much bigger.

Moorgate
A street in London and the name of a station on LUL, which was the site of a horrific accident, in which a train hit a wall in a tunnel at about 40mph, killing and maiming many people. The cause is still a mystery. Like King's Cross, the name is used as shorthand for the accident and the preventative measures that were adopted in consequence.

Motorman
Description often used for a driver of an electric train as opposed to a locomotive.

Network Rail
The company that now maintains and renews the infrastructure of the National Rail system, having replaced Railtrack *(qv)*.

Off Peak (Hours)
Times when fewer people are traveling.

'One Under'
See PUT.

OPO = One Person Operation (formerly OMO, One Man Operation).
The system of staffing a train, whereby one person performs the functions of a previously larger crew – normally the driver and guard. In fact, sometimes, there are other members of the crew on board who undertake duties (*eg,* checking tickets), but the basic operation of the train (driving, opening and closing the doors) is performed by one person. On some railways, this system is called DOO – Driver Only Operation.

PA = Public Address system

"Parkinson's Law"
C Northcote Parkinson wrote a satirical essay, later included in a book (pub: John Murray, London, 1958), exposing the ways of the Civil Service. Its main contention or 'law' was that *"work expands to fill the time allotted"* to it. Thus, if a job can be completed in five minutes, but is allocated ten minutes, the worker will make the job last twice as long, so as not to have to do more work. Organisations thus tend to inefficiency, since people will do no more work than they have already, even if they have the time to do so. *See also 'Peter Principle (The)'*, below.

PC
Either Personal Computer or Politically Correct, depending on the context.

Peak Hour(s)
See Rush Hour.

"Peter Principle (The)"
A concept and the title of a book (Souvenir Press, 1969 and subsequent editions, incl Pan Books, 1970). Dr Laurence J Peter and Raymond Hull wrote a parallel book to *"Parkinson's Law" (qv)*. The basic Peter Principle is that *"a person is promoted to their level of incompetency"*. Most organisations reward good workers with promotion. If a person is good at a first level job, they are promoted to the second level; if good at the second level, they are promoted to the third; and so on. But, sooner or later, each reaches a level at which they cannot function successfully. Organisations are thus full of people failing to function adequately at their jobs. Organisations tend to use inefficient ways to dealing with these people, other than for them to revert to the jobs where they functioned well. The book elaborates on this scourge of business.

Points
A child once described these as places *"where the railway lines are joined together"*, which is true. They include moving pieces of rail to divert trains appropriately from one piece of track to another.

Porter/Porteress
Porter was the term used to describe a general worker on the platforms at stations, as much of their time was spent carrying or moving things. Porteress was sometimes used unofficially for women who did a similar job.

PPP = Public Private Partnership
See Chapter 19

PUT = Person Under Train incident.
See Chapter 5

qv = quod vide
Latin expression – literally "which see"; in this context meaning "refer to that item in this Appendix".

Railperson
One of the many names given over the years for a person
undertaking duties about a station (PC replacement for Railman).

Railtrack
A company set up under the privatisation of British Rail to
maintain and renew the track and other infrastructure assets. After
a number of huge problems, it was replaced by Network Rail *(qv)*.

Ramp
Slope down from platform to track level.

Resistors
Part of the electrical equipment on a train that operates when the
train is not moving at full speed. (Similar to a dimmer switch in a
home.)

Rheostat/ic Brake
A brake that retards the train through the electric motors.

RMT = Rail, Maritime, Transport Union
One of the rail Trades Unions on LUL. The former NUR
(National Union of Railwaymen) became part of the RMT.

RTC = Railway Training Centre
Known irreverently (and to the annoyance its staff!) as 'the
School'. This was the establishment in Wood Lane, Shepherds
Bush that undertook most of the classroom and some other
training of LUL staff for many years. It replaced the earlier
facility at Lambeth North. It no longer exists, but a lot of training
is now carried on at a site in West Kensington.

RTO = Remote Train Operation
A term used by LUL for fully automatic (*ie,* no conventional
driver) train operation. The term is used because the train is, in
fact, controlled, but from a central point, normally by machine
with human oversight. The trains so operated may well have a
member of staff on board, but who would not control the normal
running of the train. In fact, varying degrees of control might be
used, such as the one used on the Docklands Light Railway

system, where an on-board member of staff initiates departure from stations, under instructions from the central point.

Running Rails.
Strips of metal on which a train's wheels run. *See* under "Track".

Rush Hour(s)
Time(s) when most people travel. (Opposite of 'Off Peak' *(qv)*.)

Scotch and Clip
Tools consisting of a lump of wood and a G-clamp used to physically secure points *(qv)* in case of a breakdown of the normal mechanical or electrical locking system.

Shift (work)
System of work/period of time during 24 hours a member of staff is due to work, generally applying to those who do not just work '9 till 5' (09.00 -17.00 or thereabouts) on Mondays to Fridays. Often a method of working where a member of staff works at different times in different weeks or even on different days by rotation. Fixed shifts are when the times are more stable, say 10.00 – 18.00 each day, but still not 09.00 – 17.00. Staff often refer to them as "early/late/middle turns" and so on.

Shoes
These are pieces of metal, attached to the lower part of the train, near the wheels, that rub along the Current Rails *(qv)* to take the electric power to and from the track *(qv)*.

Shuttle
Term applied to branch line and other trains that "shuttled" to and fro on short sections of route. At various times, these included the South Acton, Chesham, Aldwych, Stanmore, Mill Hill East and Ongar lines, as well as others.

Sic
Latin expression, put after something that seems strange or wrong to confirm it is what the writer meant to say or that a quotation is correct.

Siding
A piece of track where a train can be put out of the way of other trains.

Signalman
See Chapter 2

SM = Station Master, later Station Manager *(qv)*

SPAD = Signal Passed at Danger.
See chapter on the subject.

Spare (Staff or Train)
A member of staff on duty who is available on call to work as required to cover absence, emergencies, etc.
Similarly, a stand-by train available to cover a breakdown or such-like.

Split Turn
A shift *(qv)* where staff work a few hours, have an intervening period not working and then finish the shift later (usually covering both the 'rush hours' *(qv)*).

'Star Guard'
Unofficial term for a guard *(qv)* who was qualified to drive and thus cover a driver vacancy. Officially a Guard/Motorman.

Station Foreman, Station Inspector, Station Manager, Station Master
Various supervisory staff.

'Suicide'
Term not in official favour but sometimes used by staff for a PUT *(qv)*.

Surface Line/ Surface Stock
The Metropolitan, District, Circle, Hammersmith & City and East London Lines and the trains that run on those lines. (The East London Line is now part of London Overground, not LUL.)

Syndicate
System where staff pool their allocated work and share it out again, so they get jobs nearer to the hours/days they wish to work. The groups who do this are sometimes called "Mafias".

Tannoy
A trade name of a loudspeaker system manufacturer and their product.

TfL = Transport *for* London   (I don't know why the *for* is italicized.)
TfL is the overseeing body for all transport media in London. After the Mayor of London was appointed, it took over LUL.

TM = Traffic Manager
See Chapter 2

TOC or Toc = Train Operating Company, otherwise called a Train Operator *(qv)*.
Companies set up to run trains after British Rail was privatised. (Although LUL is not legally a TOC, it fulfils a parallel function.)

Track
Track on LUL consists of two lengths of rail (the Running Rails, on which the train wheels run) usually fixed to pieces of concrete or wood called sleepers. Normally, they are to be found with other lengths of rail (the Current Rails), carrying the powerful electric current to drive the trains. The latter are insulated from the rest of the track and the ground by pieces of porcelain called pots.

Train Operator
Generic term as replacement for Train Driver, Motorman *(qv)* and ATO *(qv)*. This is LUL's and my usage, although I have tended to use the term driver throughout.
The term Train Operator is also used in the UK in reference to the National Rail system for a company (TOC *(qv)*) that runs trains.

Trainstop
A piece of equipment by the side of the track, provided at some signals and at other strategic locations. In the raised position, *eg,*

when the signal is red, it should hit the tripcock *(qv)* of a passing train, causing the brakes to apply. (The combination of trainstop and tripcock provide an effective and robust means of stopping a train and thus a simple means of automatic control over a train's progress.)

Tripcock
Equipment on a train (and some locomotives) near the wheels that can apply the brakes in an emergency, normally when striking a raised trainstop *(qv)*. (The combination of trainstop and tripcock provide an effective and robust means of stopping a train and thus a simple means of automatic control over a train's progress.)

Tripcock Tester
Piece of equipment by the track that tests that a tripcock *(qv)* is in working order whilst the train is going along.

Tube', 'The
A generic term popularly given to the whole London Underground railway system, but technically only applicable to those lines running through pipe-like tunnels (*see* Tube Line). *'The Tube'* is also the name of a docusoap about the Underground.

Tube Lines (with capital 'L')
This is the name of one of the Infracos *(qv)*. I have seen it printed as Tubelines.

Tube line (small 'l')(/Tube Stock
These terms refer to the pipe-like lines (Bakerloo, Central, Jubilee, Northern, Piccadilly and Waterloo & City) and the trains running on them, as distinguished from Surface Stock *(qv)* running on the Surface Lines *(qv)*.

Underground, The
Another name by which the London Underground system is commonly known. One of the earlier constituent companies used the logo 'UNDERGROUND' and this is still used in places.

Vacuum Brake(s)
As compared with the Westinghouse Brake *(qv)*, this brake relies on a vacuum (*ie,* negative pressure of air) in a pipe and cylinders keeping the brakes off. If air enters the system either deliberately or accidentally, the brakes apply. It is, therefore, fail-safe.

Vic = Victoria Line.

WCML = West Coast Main Line
The National Rail line from London (Euston) to Glasgow (Central) and other cities.

Westinghouse (Brake)
The Westinghouse Brake and Signal Company made, as you would expect, brakes and signals. When used by railway staff, the term 'Westinghouse' usually referred to that company's straight air brake, as opposed to the more modern electro-pneumatic brake *(qv)*, even though many modern brakes were made by the same company. The straight air brake relies on a positive pressure of air in a pipe and cylinders keeping the brakes off. If the air escapes either deliberately or by accident, the brakes apply. It is, therefore, fail-safe. (Compare with Vacuum Brake *(qv)*.)

Wolmar, Christian
Well-known journalist and author on various issues including transport and especially the interface with politics. His titles of particular relevance include *"Broken Rails"* (about the British national rail system) and *"Down the Tube"* (dealing with LUL), both books published by the Aurum Press.